Faith and Praxis in a Postmodern Age

Edited by

Ursula King

Cassell

Wellington House, 125 Strand, London WC2R 0BB
370 Lexington Avenue, New York, NY 10017-6550

www.cassell.co.uk

© The editor and contributors 1998

First published 1998

British Library Cataloguing-in-Publication Data
A catalogue for this book is available from the British Library.

ISBN 0-304-70260-9 (hardback)
      0-304-70261-7 (paperback)

Typeset by BookEns Ltd, Royston, Herts.
Printed and bound in Great Britain by Biddles Ltd, Guildford
and King's Lynn.

Cassell

Cassell
Wellington House, 125 Strand, London WC2R 0BB
370 Lexington Avenue, New York, NY 10017-6550
www.cassell.co.uk

First published 1998

British Library Cataloguing-in-Publication Data
A catalogue for this book is available from the British Library.

ISBN   0-304-70260-9 (hardback)
       0-304-70261-7 (paperback)

Typeset by BookEns Ltd, Royston, Herts.
Printed and bound in Great Britain by Biddles Ltd, Guildford and King's Lynn.

Contents

The contributors

Stephen Batchelor is Director of the Sharpham College of Buddhist Studies and Contemporary Enquiry in South Devon. He is also an associate member of the Centre for Buddhist Studies in the Department of Theology and Religious Studies, University of Bristol. He is the author of *The Faith to Doubt: Glimpses of Buddhist Uncertainty* (Berkeley: Parallax Press, 1990), *The Awakening of the West: The Encounter of Buddhism and Western Culture* (London: Thorsons/Berkeley: Parallax Press, 1994) and *Buddhism Without Beliefs: A Contemporary Guide to Awakening* (London: Bloomsbury, 1997). At present he is working on a translation and study of Nagarjuna's *Mulamadhyamakakarika*.

Dan Cohn-Sherbok is Professor of Judaism at the University of Wales, Lampeter, and Visiting Professor of Interfaith Dialogue at the University of Middlesex. His numerous books include *Modern Judaism* (London: Macmillan, 1996), *Fifty Key Jewish Thinkers* (London: Routledge, 1996), *The Jewish Messiah* (Edinburgh: T. & T. Clark, 1997) and *A Concise Encyclopedia of Judaism* (Oxford: Oneworld Publications, 1998). He is currently working on a new book dealing with interfaith theology.

Gavin D'Costa is Senior Lecturer in the Department of Theology and Religious Studies, University of Bristol. Among his publications are *Theology and Religious Pluralism* (Oxford: Basil Blackwell, 1986) and the two edited volumes *Christian Uniqueness Reconsidered: The Myth of a Pluralistic Theology of Religion* (Maryknoll, NY: Orbis Books, 1990) and *Resurrection Reconsidered* (Oxford: Oneworld Publications, 1997). He is currently working on a book on the Trinity and world religions.

Martin Forward is Academic Dean, Wesley House, Cambridge, and a member of Cambridge University's Faculty of Divinity. He worked for several years as part-time Lecturer in Islamic Studies in the Department of Theology and Religious Studies, University of Bristol. He is the author of *Muhammad: A Short Biography* (Oxford: Oneworld Publications, 1997), and of *A Bag of Needments for the Road: Geoffrey Parrinder's Contribution to the Study of Religion* (Berne: Peter Lang, 1998), and has edited *Ultimate Visions* (Oxford: Oneworld Publications, 1995). He is working on his next book, *Jesus: A Short Biography*, and is carrying out further research on Islamic attitudes towards modernism.

Sean Gill is Senior Lecturer and Head of the Department of Theology and Religious Studies, University of Bristol. His most recent publications include *The Lesbian and Gay Christian Movement: Campaigning for Justice, Truth and Love* (London: Cassell, 1998) and *A History of Women and the Church of England from the Eighteenth Century to the Present* (London: SPCK, 1994), and he is one of the editors of *Religion in Europe: Contemporary Perspectives* (Kampen: Kok Pharos, 1994). He is currently working on his next book, *Sons of Man: Images of Masculinity Within the Western Christian Tradition*.

Ursula King is Professor in the Department of Theology and Religious Studies, University of Bristol, where she directs the departmental Centre for Comparative Studies in Gender and Religion. Her most recent books include the 1996 Bampton Lectures: *Christ in All Things: Exploring Spirituality with Teilhard de Chardin* (London: SCM Press, 1997), *Spirit of Fire: The Life and Vision of Teilhard de Chardin* (Maryknoll, NY: Orbis Books, 1996), and edited volumes on *Religion and Gender* (Oxford: Blackwell, 1995) and on *Feminist Theology from the Third World* (Maryknoll, NY: Orbis Books/London: SPCK, 1994). Her current research is concerned with comparative gender perspectives and spirituality in world religions.

Michael S. Northcott is Senior Lecturer in the Department of Christian Ethics and Practical Theology, University of Edinburgh. He has recently published *The Environment and Christian Ethics* (Cambridge: Cambridge University Press, 1996) and edited *Urban Theology: A Reader* (London: Cassell, 1998). His current research is concerned with the ethics of the global economy.

Anne Primavesi was formerly Research Fellow in Environmental Theology in the Department of Theology and Religious Studies, University of Bristol. She has published numerous articles and a major book, *From Apocalypse to Genesis: Ecology, Feminism and Christianity* (Tunbridge Wells: Burns & Oates, 1991). She is currently working on a new book on environmental theology.

Martin Prozesky is Professor of Religious Studies, University of Natal, Pietermaritzburg, South Africa. His publications include *Religion and Ultimate Well-being: An Explanatory Theory* (London: Macmillan, 1984), *Christianity Amidst Apartheid: Selected Perspectives on the Church in South Africa* (London: Macmillan, 1990) and *Living Faiths in South Africa,* co-edited with John de Gruchy (London: Hurst, 1995).

Rosemary Radford Ruether is Georgia Harkness Professor of Applied Theology, Garrett Theological Seminary and Northwestern University, Evanston, Illinois, USA. During the 1996 Conference on Faith and Praxis in a Postmodern Age she was Benjamin Meaker Visiting Professor in the Department of Theology and Religious Studies at the University of Bristol. She has authored or edited 31 books. Among the most important recent ones are *Sexism and God-Talk: Toward a Feminist Theology* (Boston: Beacon, 1983; 2nd edn, 1993), *Gaia and God: An Ecofeminist Theology of Earth Healing* (San Francisco: HarperSanFrancisco, 1992) and *Women and Redemption: A Theological History* (Minneapolis: Fortress Press, 1998). Her current research is concerned with gender and theological anthropology and changing views of the family in Christian cultural history.

Keith Ward is Regius Professor of Divinity, University of Oxford, and was formerly Professor of History and Philosophy of Religion at King's College, University of London. Some of his recent books are *God, Faith and the New Millenium* (Oxford: Oneworld Publications, 1998), *God, Chance and Necessity* (Oxford: Oneworld Publications, 1996), and a series on 'Comparative Theology' published by Oxford University Press which so far includes *Religion and Revelation* (vol. 1; 1994), *Religion and Creation* (vol. 2; 1996) and *Religion and Human Nature* (vol. 3; 1998).

Introduction

Ursula King

Postmodernism is now a much debated topic, though one with rather fuzzy edges. Associated with so many different cultural phenomena, this fashionable subject seems to lack clear definition to establish precisely what it is. Perhaps it is part of the open-ended, reflexive and deeply doubting nature of the postmodern predicament itself that exact boundaries are difficult, if not impossible, to determine. In Lyotard's influential work, *The Postmodern Condition*, originally published in French in 1979,[1] postmodernism represents a radical break with the recent past, a condition which calls in particular the nature of modern knowledge and its effects on contemporary culture and consciousness into question. The changing status of scientific knowledge, the exponential growth of information, the new means of communication have all led to a dissolution of long-established certainties and thus created a crisis of legitimation and representation.

Yet one may well ask whether postmodernism is primarily a *condition* that affects knowledge and everything else today, or whether it is more a question of us living in a *postmodern world* so utterly changed and fast moving, a world of postmodernity following earlier *modern* and *premodern* ways of life. Or is it even more a question of living in a *postmodern age* rather than in a postmodern world? In other words, is postmodernism primarily related to our spatial situatedness – living in a world with increasingly different, global characteristics, but also marked by many decentred and destabilized features – or is postmodernism, on the contrary, more related to the times we live in, to our sense of history and its discontinuities, our puzzlement with the present and our fear of an ever more uncertain and uncontrollable future?

Whatever it may be, postmodernism invites critical reflection and sustained debate. It is probably a specifically Western, rather than a universal global phenomenon, but its effects can be felt around the whole world. Postmodernism has been described as a process involving the fragmentation of modern Western culture. A highly ingenious *collage*, it is a celebration of the particular, a condition that calls everything into question, a radical challenge that has to be met. However, most writers on postmodernism are primarily concerned with the dominant features of contemporary culture and public life without considering the relationship of postmodernism to religion. But if postmodernism is such a pervasive condition, what can possibly be its meaning for the faith traditions of the world? And what is the place of faith itself in a postmodern age? How is the long-established religious faith of large human communities and innumerable individuals related to practical concerns in a world marked by division, doubt and ever greater uncertainty?

What is the role of faith and praxis in contemporary pluralistic society? Does faith make a difference in politics and economics? Does it affect attitudes to the environment? Does everybody need a faith to live by? What difference is there between a human faith, a religious faith, a critical faith, and a deeply spiritual faith? How far does religious faith still provide an important focus for national, ethnic and cultural identities? And is faith different for women and men, is it linked to specific sexual identities? Can faith heal and make us whole, strengthen our resolve and responsibility, and help us build a human community of greater peace and justice? Have the different religions the resources for the development of a postmodern ethic for both personal and public life, so much needed today?

These are some of the questions addressed in this series of reflective essays wherein writers of diverse backgrounds, faiths and countries engage critically with different perspectives of postmodernism and their influence on philosophical, theological, ethical, spiritual, sexual and political issues. All of these perspectives have an impact on religious faith and practice in the current world which is now soon moving from one millennium to another.

Faith and praxis

None of the following chapters discusses the meaning of faith and praxis in a comprehensive philosophical sense, but each contribution provides a specific example illustrating either explicitly or implicitly the relationship between faith and praxis within a particular context, religion or country. Faith is here understood as religious faith both in a personal sense and also as a cumulative tradition which has shaped the history of particular communities and people. The contributors also do not provide an overarching definition or detailed discussion of the intellectual and political heritage of the notion of praxis in its classical Marxist sense. Praxis is simply referred to in a more general sense as accepted practice arising out of religious faith and linked to the practical experience of living, the concrete context of daily life with which faith is so closely interwoven.

However, the notion of praxis is an important point of departure and key feature of contemporary liberation theology and also of feminist theology, especially in what has traditionally been called the 'Third World', where praxis is linked with a particular method of social transformation.[2] Such an understanding of praxis is greatly influenced by the philosophical formulations of Western Marxism which define praxis as

a) a type of creative practical activity peculiar to human beings whereby they construct their world, an idea basic to Marx's model of human nature; b) an epistemological category describing the practical, object-constituting activity of human subjects as they confront nature ... ; and c) as 'revolutionary praxis', the putative point of fundamental social transition.[3]

Several of the essays in this book show, at least implicitly, how much of such praxis, in the sense of creative and self-creative activity whereby human beings construct and transform their world and themselves, is deeply rooted in and inextricably linked with different religious beliefs and practices. It is the contention of all contributors that postmodern configurations are exercising a profound influence on the ways in which religion is understood and practised today, although the extent to which this is the case may widely vary. But how to capture the meaning of postmodernism itself, a concept of such fluidity and impreciseness? It may be helpful to clarify the understanding of postmodernism as a dynamic, ongoing process which in spite of its singular novelty still appears to be part of a larger continuum moving from the premodern to the modern and postmodern.

Modern and postmodern

At one level one can argue that postmodern simply means something that is *no longer modern* but comes after it. It is not all that long ago that sociologists, anthropologists and philosophers focused much of their work on defining the characteristics of modernity in contrast to tradition with its premodern features of society and consciousness. The word *modern* is said to derive from the Latin word *modo*, meaning 'just now'. Thus, modern implies belonging to the present or to recent times, and the word has been part of the English language since at least 1500. The notions of modern and postmodern constitute a dichotomous pair of concepts which must be interpreted in relation to each other. Thus modernism and postmodernism are often discussed together and contrasted with each other.[4] But whereas modernism is especially seen as an artistic style and intellectual movement of the late nineteenth and early twentieth centuries, the concept of modernity goes back further. Philosophers connect it especially with the characteristics of the eighteenth-century Enlightenment, but theologians and some sociologists tend to place the onset of modernity rather earlier with the Protestant Reformation of the sixteenth century.

The sociologist Peter Berger[5] has been much concerned with understanding modernity and its challenge for religion, which he has described as the necessity, the imperative, to choose. He has said:

> In premodern situations there is a world of religious certainty, occasionally ruptured by heretical deviations. By contrast, the modern situation is a world of religious uncertainty, occasionally staved off by more or less precarious constructions of religious affirmation ... modernity creates a new situation in which picking and choosing becomes an imperative.[6]

But when he wrote these words almost twenty years ago, postmodernism was not on the explicit agenda for either sociologists or theologians, so it finds no mention in Berger's books of that time. It was the debate about tradition and modernity, about secularization and the loss of faith in modern society that mainly attracted attention then. Yet postmodernism was a rising trend in art and architecture and other fields of cultural production. Postmodern theory developed among linguists, philosophers, feminists and anthropologists; it involved a new evaluation of the understanding of language, its structure and symbolism, the role of sign and metaphor, the nature of the symbolic order, the deconstruction of social and sexual hierarchies. But it was also concerned with the deconstruction of grand theories and narratives, of any claims to universality and essentialism. This meant that the nature of rationality and the claims of universal reason came to be seriously questioned and the privileging of foundational texts and logocentric approaches, so dominant since the Enlightenment, was rejected.

Philosophically speaking, postmodernism denotes the limits of reason, especially of instrumental reason so sure of itself in modern science and technology. As a movement of ideas, the postmodern critique is bound up with the decline of the belief in progress and the rejection of scientism as a narrow, one-sided over-rating of the benefits of science to the exclusion of other human experiences. Thus the modern emphasis on subjectivity and rationality is profoundly questioned, and so is the perception and representation of 'the Other' and of other cultures and traditions. But this does not mean that postmodernism rejects all the gains of modernity, such as the significance of the historical method or the insights of social and cultural anthropology, the autonomy of civil society and culture, the importance of secularity, the freedom of the individual, or racial and sexual equality.

This brief discussion shows that postmodernism is really very eclectic. It is also a phenomenon closely associated with advanced modern capitalism, with consumerism and with Western-originated global trends. A dangerous contradiction would be to turn postmodern conclusions now into new foundations and alternative universalist claims. Much of the postmodern mode of consciousness and praxis is extraordinarily limited, even in its most radical critique. While postmodern critical articulations have clearly shown that the West itself does not possess one single universal foundation, one single tradition, but is multi-layered and truly pluralistic in its history and heritage, though this is not always acknowledged, there is also no doubt that, intellectually, postmodernism remains Western-derived and Western-oriented, in spite of all attempts to accord more recognition to the otherness of others. Given the formative, exclusively Western matrix of postmodernism, it cannot be sufficiently well equipped to account for alternative non-Western beliefs and practices. But not all writers on postmodernism are aware of this large question mark that one can set against their postmodern claims.

Postmodernism remains therefore profoundly ambivalent, with positive and negative sides. Most writers will accept some of its features but reject others. Many refer to postmodernism as synonymous with postmodernity, but I find it helpful to distinguish between the two. Postmodernism can be characterized as a *process* which results in a state of affairs or context described as that of *postmodernity*, a different condition, world or time from that which existed before now. This means postmodernism has no fixity or finality about it, but is itself part of the ongoing historical process of change, so that it will eventually be replaced by some other intellectual framework, a new mood in yet another age and different world again. For many, postmodernism is especially associated with a denial of meaning and a nihilistic attitude destructive of the traditional values of faith. It is therefore especially important to reflect on the relationship between postmodernism and religion in order to see the challenges that are posed by the postmodern condition, and the opportunities that have opened up for a renewed appropriation of religious and spiritual values that have themselves become reinterpreted and transformed.

Postmodernism and religion

Writers on religion, ethics, theology and spirituality have come rather late to a serious consideration of the postmodern predicament and its effects on our world. But even a cursory search soon reveals that, since the early and mid-1990s, publications, conferences and journals have been increasingly concerned with the discussion of postmodernism. This is evident from just a small random sample, whether it is Edith Wyschogrod's revisioning of moral philosophy in *Saints and Postmodernism* (1990),[7] or Charlene Spretnak's *States of Grace* (1991),[8] searching for a recovery of meaning in a postmodern age, thought possible through the core teachings and practices of the great spiritual traditions, or Akbar Ahmed's attempt to analyse the specific relationship between post-modernism and Islam (1992).[9] A stimulating set of papers is found in the collection edited by Philippa Berry and Andrew Wernick, *Shadow of Spirit: Postmodernism and Religion* (1992),[10] in the recent issue of *Religion* on 'Religion and postmodernism' edited by Robert Segal and Thomas Ryba (1997),[11] and the conference papers edited by Ann W. Astell, *Divine Representations: Postmodernism and Spirituality* (1994).[12]

While the advent of postmodernism has created much fluidity and decentredness, and also highlighted the disponibility of all culturally created ideas and things, its influence on religion must not be judged only in a negative light, for postmodernism can also be seen positively as a challenging task, an opportunity, even a gift for religion in the modern world. The postmodern view of the self raises fundamental questions about the nature of personal identity and throws light on the process of what Simone Weil has called 'the decreation of the self', so important in the human approach to the Divine. The modern and postmodern world seems haunted by the absence of God, and yet in some curious way this absence can at the same time become transparent for a new kind of presence. In criticizing the individualism and dualism of modernity, postmodernism makes room for a more holistic and organic under-standing of human existence with its personal, communal and ecological dimensions linked to the sacredness of life.

The creative postmodern approach to language also opens up new possibilities in interpreting the ambiguities of our relational language about God, and in articulating different styles of spirituality. Contrary to the modern assumption of the pervasiveness of nihilism, recent studies illuminate 'the striking affinity between the most innovative aspects of postmodern thought and religious or mystical discourse',[13] and thereby open up new religious possibilities. As Donald Mitchell has said in an essay on 'Buddhist and Christian postmodern spiritualities': 'Postmodern theology rejects modernity's pushing God to a transcendent position outside of our world in a manner that has led to the ultimate atheistic denial of God's very existence. That is, it rejects modern secularism for a type of postmodern panentheism.'[14]

These brief quotations hint at the theological and spiritual possibilities revealed by the process of postmodernism which invite careful analysis and discerning interpretation. Examples of detailed reading and weighing up of postmodern texts and contexts are provided by the contributions in this volume which bear on the intellectual genealogy and growth of postmodern ideas, examining their influence on our understanding of self, nature and God, the construction of personal and social identities, the reinterpretation of religious traditions and spiritual practice, the engage-ment with religious pluralism and the otherness of different faiths.

The essays

Most of the essays in this book were originally presented at a conference which celebrated the thirtieth anniversary of the Department of Theology and Religious Studies at the University of Bristol. The papers given on that occasion have been thoroughly revised and also augmented by some additionally commissioned material. All the pieces included here address questions of wider concern and will be of interest to readers from the general public but also to graduate and undergraduate students, academic colleagues, and anyone seriously engaged with the issues and challenges raised by the postmodern debate.

The individual writers have approached their topics from very different perspectives. Their reflections can be read in the sequence in which they appear here, or they can be treated quite independently and be perused or studied in whatever sequence readers may choose. Each contribution is a piece in its own right and can be read on its own. The chapters have grown out of a most enjoyable and stimulating conference, and are part of still ongoing research work and conversations. As such, they reflect the open-ended nature and continuing quest of postmodernism itself. Thus they are truly 'essays' in the original sense of that word, that is to say trials, enquiries, and scrutinies – attempts to wrestle with the articulation of insights and ideas in an ongoing search for explanation and making sense of the world to ourselves.

The collection opens with Keith Ward's succinct and crisp account of the philosophical background of the dominance of reason during the modern era. The Enlightenment account of human reason has failed us, however, and any rational person now recognizes where the limits of reason lie. Modern science has provided us with a grand narrative, and its mechanistic view of nature, together with its proclamation of an autonomous human nature, can be considered as parents of modernity. Yet is science for ever wedded to modernity? In spite of all recent criticism, science remains committed to reason, but the very conclusions of science have now undermined the authority of reason itself. Ward charts the decline and fall of reason from modernity to postmodernity by tracing the philosophical developments of this process while showing at the same time how Christian theology has been implicated in this. With the rise of postmodernity a new theological task is now set which has not yet been met.

Gavin D'Costa's chapter takes up the historical thread to the present, showing how key ideas have shaped essential aspects of the modern and postmodern world view. One of the important influences concerns the conceptualization of difference, the enigmatic relation of the same to the Other. The idea of 'the Other' has been especially brought into prominence through Western colonial discourse that has operated with a notion of difference which is a distortion of the Other. D'Costa engages with influential writers and their critique of these distorted visions of 'the Other'. How far is Otherness perceived as a mirror-opposite? Sameness and Otherness are relational concepts important for the formation of identity, including religious identities. Today, in a global situation of religious encounter, Christian identity cannot be experienced and defined without a response to religious pluralism. D'Costa's chapter includes a detailed discussion of several Christian responses to such religious pluralism, sometimes formulated as a theology of religions. Inspired by a trinitarian model in his approach to world religions. D'Costa explores a promising 'open pluralism', a notion of great heuristic value for interfaith encounter and dialogue.

Anne Primavesi looks at pluralism from quite a different perspective. She is primarily concerned with the responsibility that dealing with diversity entails. Pluralistic diversity is of great importance in human cultures, but Primavesi looks at it from the far wider and more inclusive horizon of biodiversity, which operates at the level of species, at a genetic level, and at the level of a whole ecosystem. She argues that ecologically inspired attitudes favour diversity in human cultures and can help us to perceive the demands of living with difference. She particularly stresses the need for non-violent ethical relations and the importance of developing an ethic of compassion and love. A responsible encounter with and acknowledgement of biodiversity can also inspire us to respond creatively to the challenge of making people more peaceful in today's conflict-torn world. No single ethical code can achieve this on its own; it is only through community and dialogue that we may be able to attain this task together. From the perspective of religion, this means the valuing of diversity within and between different traditions to take on responsibility together for the ethical issues of our world.

After the consideration of philosophical, theological and ethical issues the discussion moves on to gender and sexual differences, seen through the lens of postmodernism. Rosemary Ruether emphasizes the long historical trajectory of gender inequalities, pointing to the premodern roots of modern and postmodern Christian experience. In tracing the main outline of these developments, Ruether shows how both Hebrew and Graeco-Roman ideas helped to shape the foundations of Christian theological teaching. The equality of the sexes was affirmed in the order of redemption, but the subordination of women to men was clearly established in the order of creation, as interpreted through the Genesis stories and by biblical commentators of the nascent church. But Ruether also speaks of an 'eschatological feminism', an anticipation of a transformed, redeemed human community wherein women could assume preaching, prophecy and leadership roles, as among the Shakers in the eighteenth century, the Quakers, and women of the Free Churches during the nineteenth century, who shared such a view. Thus modern feminism with its claim for the equality of the sexes was born through a political reinterpretation of the Christian thesis of equality in the image of God redemptively restored. Ruether unravels the search for a modern inclusive humanness which accepts the full range of human qualities for both women and men and promises personal wholeness for members of both sexes, a claim which in turn transformed social structures. In the postmodern context of today Ruether pleads for 'an open-ended understanding of community in diversity' which requires both dialogue and solidarity between very different social groups and their sexual perspectives.

Sean Gill takes the discussion on sexual difference still further by looking at the crisis in Christian sexual ethics. He examines the different discursive traditions on homosexuality in the history of Christianity which are now called into question by postmodern epistemology and ethics. The feminist deconstruction of gender hierarchies and the additional development of queer theory open up new possibilities for a life of dignity and respect for people of different sexual orientations, for a creative dialogue about sexuality, and for the realization of human wholeness. Taking difference seriously, not only at the level of abstract thought but in relation to our concrete embodiedness, provides a tremendous challenge for Christian men to articulate a newly understood masculinity and help to develop a viable, vibrant and holistic sexual theology within a postmodern framework.

A discussion on faith and praxis must not only openly engage with all the issues raised by sexuality and the multiple readings of the body in contemporary society, but cannot afford to ignore the attendant questions raised by these richly thematized experiences for the understanding of spirituality. In this area much experimentation and rethinking is occurring across different religious traditions and outside religious institutions altogether. New spiritualities are formulated and practised within a secular context, and these challenge the traditional, homogenized and universal understanding of spirituality in established religious traditions. Ursula King's chapter tries to give a sense of multiple meanings of spirituality and argues for a thoroughly pluralistic understanding of spiritual practice in both traditional, modern and postmodern settings. She also emphasizes the need to develop more holistic, integral spiritualities within the new social context of postmodernity.

Following these six chapters on important issues relating to philosophy, theology, ethics, sexuality, and spirituality, the next five chapters deal with whole religious traditions and cultures – with Buddhism, Islam, and Judaism – and with national and religious identities affecting contemporary politics, whether in Israel, South Africa or Britain. Stephen Batchelor convincingly argues that postmodernity seems to fit Buddhism like a glove because of the fluidity of Buddhism itself. He explores the notion of 'the path' which he considers the key metaphor for the Buddhist way to enlightenment. At the same time he points out that Buddhism has been catapulted from premodern into postmodern societies and now tends to move away from its traditional dependence on organized religious institutions towards more individual forms of religious practice in which each person finds his or her own way. This no doubt accounts for Buddhism's recent success and following in the West or, rather, it is through its transplantation to the different social structures and dynamics of the postmodern West that what Batchelor calls 'the radical edge of Buddhism', its agnosticism and stress on emptiness, has come much more sharply to the fore. In that sense Buddhism presents us with an existential confrontation rather than the consolation given by traditional religion. Batchelor's account is a fine example of letting go of Buddhism as 'a grand, totalizing narrative that explains everything' and adopting a pluralistic view of it as 'a postmodern, postpath practice'.

If Buddhism relates so well to postmodern concerns, what about Islam? How far are Muslims engaged in the debate about postmodernism? The relationship between Islam and postmodernity is perhaps more difficult to trace. From the late nineteenth century onwards there first developed a lively debate about Islam's encounter with modernity and, as Martin Forward argues, this has not yet been concluded. Most central to this debate is the status of sacred scripture, of the Qur'an as God's revelation, whose provenance is non-negotiable for Muslims. The presuppositions of the modern and postmodern world run counter to Islam to some extent, but perhaps Islam is only a particularly clear test case of what at heart is at stake for every faith. Forward's chapter illustrates the debate about modernity with an example from Indian Islam and examines the reactions to postmodern developments by discussing Akbar Ahmed's work *Postmodernism and Islam* (1992).[15]

Dan Cohn-Sherbok's chapter illustrates how faith and praxis are interrelated and held in tension in the historical process that led to the creation of the Jewish State of Israel. By looking at some of the outstanding thinkers who shaped the evolution of secular Zionism it is clear that initially, in Judaism too, much of the debate was about meeting the challenges of modernity. A closer reading also shows that the debate about the history and continuity of Judaism, the debate about who is a Jew (rather than a Jewess) has been conducted in entirely patriarchal terms. But in this complex, rich and for some too closed a debate, the notion of 'the Other' has to be remembered, not only 'the Other' as Palestinian or Arab, or any other non-Jew, but also 'the Other' within Judaism itself. This is striking when studying the Orthodox Jewish opposition to the idea of a Jewish state and the critique of Zionism by Jewish Liberals. Cohn-Sherbok speaks of the depth of hatred of secular Zionism among Orthodox Jews. Is the State of Israel therefore a postmodern creation, and does the existence of the political entity of Israel present a substitute for traditional religious belief in God among secular Jews? Such reflections raise fundamental issues about the relationship between religion and the state, and that of faith and politics. How far has the nation-state been the main modernizing agent in recent history? But can such nation-states still meet all the needs of a postmodern world?

Martin Prozesky's chapter on the new South African situation can lead to similar reflections. Looking at recent history in South Africa presents us with a particularly vibrant example of how the power of faith can relate to practical action, and especially to political praxis. Prozesky emphasizes the profound ambiguity of religions and begins with the clear recognition that religion in South Africa has been both harmful and beneficial. He sides with those who hail religion's power of liberation in the postmodern world, its emancipatory moral dynamic and its core of freedom which can lead to truly transformative praxis. While recognizing the fluidity of postmodern approaches, Prozesky's examples from recent South African history clearly demonstrate how postmodernism dismantles established hierarchies. Such radical transformation also implies the need for profound educational transformations. Reflecting on the interdependent dynamics of faith and politics leads Prozesky to a critique of traditional Christianity which, in his view, has had an 'insufficiently humanizing impact on a world with far too much inhumanity', and is more concerned 'with priestly and pietistic power rather than prophetic or political and above all people's power'. Traditional religion has exercised much discrimination and subordination, not least as far as women and lay people in general are concerned.

South Africa's heritage of religious support for apartheid is a heavy burden for Christianity and raises fundamental issues about the ethics of power. But the recent developments in South African politics provide a great historical example of the transformative powers of faith which open us up to visions of a wider, greater, more just world where the exclusivism, domination and discrimination of religious and social power elites have been overthrown and reoriented in a postmodern world of greater pluralism and inclusivism.

The last chapter in this volume looks at questions of the modern nation-state, its power and powerlessness, from the perspective of contemporary Britain. Michael Northcott's perceptive analysis challenges some of the postmodern cynicism about democracy by looking at the religious, moral and cultural resources available for a renewal of democracy and civil society. This includes some interesting reflections on the differences between Catholic and Protestant forms of Christianity and their respective influence in shaping democratic governance. The chapter also discusses the notion of leadership as service, an idea deeply rooted in biblical texts, and argues for a reformed democratic socialism and a radically participative vision of political economy. In doing so, it makes the important point that spiritual freedom and a free society are intimately related.

It would be impossible to provide a comprehensive coverage of different political cultures and their relationship to religion, of different faiths and world views engaged in postmodern debates and developments, in a single volume. This set of essays is itself a celebration of difference and diversity. While highlighting the many-sidedness, eclecticism and segmentation of postmodernism, the chapters demonstrate the multiplicity of possible responses to postmodern challenges that religious faith and praxis can offer. By exploring creative and sometimes highly innovative reflections, the chapters also prove that, in spite of all postmodern calls for deconstruction, postmodernism is not necessarily destructive of all certainties and meanings, but can provide new threads for weaving dynamic patterns of new significance and promise. The postmodern hermeneutic of suspicion, addressed to all foundational texts, to long-established traditions of faith and praxis, to past history and experience and their canonical interpretations, does not necessarily have to turn against itself and be self-destructive, but can instead lead us perhaps to more wisdom and humility, thereby enabling us to build more just human communities and a world of greater peace and wholeness.

Notes

1. Jean-François Lyotard, *The Postmodern Condition: A Report on Knowledge* (Manchester: Manchester University Press, 1984).
2. Elina Vuola, *Limits of Liberation: Praxis as Method in Latin American Liberation Theology and Feminist Theology* (Helsinki: Annales Academiae Scientiarum Fennicae, 1996).
3. Richard Kilminster, 'Praxis' in W. Outhwaite and T. Bottomore (eds), *The Blackwell Dictionary of Twentieth-Century Social Thought* (Oxford: Blackwell, 1993), p. 507.
4. Richard Appignanesi and Chris Garratt, *Postmodernism for Beginners* (Cambridge: Icon Books, 1995); Peter Brooker (ed.), *Modernism/ Postmodernism* (London and New York: Longman, 1992); Stanley J. Grenz, *A Primer on Postmodernism* (Grand Rapids, MI: William B. Eerdmans, 1996); Paul Lakeland, *Postmodernity: Christian Identity in a Fragmented Age* (Minneapolis: Fortress Press, 1997); John Reader, *Beyond All Reason: The Limits of Post-Modern Theology* (Cardiff: Aureus Publishing, 1997).
5. Peter L. Berger, *Facing Up to Modernity: Excursions in Society, Politics, and Religion* (London: Penguin, 1979); Peter L. Berger, *The Heretical Imperative: Contemporary Possibilities of Religious Affirmation* (London: Collins, 1980).
6. Berger, *The Heretical Imperative*, p. 28.
7. Edith Wyschogrod, *Saints and Postmodernism: Revisioning Moral Philosophy* (Chicago: University of Chicago Press, 1990).
8. Charlene Spretnak, *States of Grace: The Recovery of Meaning in the Postmodern Age* (San Francisco: HarperSanFrancisco, 1991).
9. Ahmed S. Akbar, *Postmodernism and Islam: Predicament and Promise* (London and New York: Routledge, 1992).
10. Philippa Berry and Andrew Wernick (eds), *Shadow of Spirit: Postmodernism and Religion* (London and New York: Routledge, 1992).
11. Robert Segal and Thomas Ryba (eds), 'Religion and postmodernism: a review symposium', *Religion: An International Journal*, 27.2 (1997).
12. Ann W. Astell (ed.), *Divine Representations: Postmodernism and Spirituality* (New York and Mahwah, NJ: Paulist Press, 1994).
13. Astell, *Divine Representations*, p. 14.
14. Donald W. Mitchell, 'Buddhist and Christian postmodern spiritualities' in Astell, *Divine Representations*, pp. 129–48; the quotation is on p. 134.
15. Akbar, *Postmodernism and Islam*.

1

The decline and fall of reason

From modernity to postmodernity

Keith Ward

Do we live in a postmodern age? Such an age has been characterized by Lyotard as one in which there are no grand meta-narratives, no total explanations, no overall structures of meaning, no universal foundations of knowledge. As a matter of fact, this age is virtually the first in history in which there is something like a universal foundation of knowledge and a grand narrative which covers the whole of the universe. The foundation is natural science, and it is accepted even by every tribe in New Guinea which watches television. The narrative is the evolutionary history of the universe from the Big Bang to the catastrophic crunch, and the total explanation is the theory of everything, the grand unified theory, which may be just round the corner.

In contrast, it has become much harder to believe in God and in Christian revelation, a narrative which never succeeded in its aim of conquering the world, and has now settled uneasily into partial dominance in a number of more or less clearly demarcated geographical areas. This is for a number of reasons – the growth of critical history and of scientific knowledge about the universe, the relative lack of over-whelming arguments for the existence of a particular God, and a distrust of claims to exclusive and inerrant revelation. There has certainly been a religious fragmentation, as old structures of authority have broken down, and people have become aware of a bewildering number of alternative views on religious matters. Religious faith has to a large extent been privatized and pluralized. That is, in modern Western Europe a person's religious beliefs are very much their own private affair, and they may well be a mixture from a number of oddly assorted traditions, Eastern and Western. Very few would maintain that there is a defensible and widely accepted coherent set of religious doctrines, worthy of acceptance by all rational persons. We are well aware of how flimsy many of our own beliefs on religious topics are, and how disputed all of them seem to be. Even those who do think they possess a coherent and plausible narrative occasionally realize that they are in a tiny minority, which seems a bit strange, if they are right.

But all this is just the obverse side of the development of the grand narrative of evolutionary science, which seems to have undermined classical religion bit by bit over the last three centuries. We might well say that the hypothetico-deductive method of natural science has been triumphantly vindicated as the sure road to knowledge, and as for ancient dreams of liberation, we are on the threshold of taking charge of human nature itself, through genetic control, and directing it towards a more hopeful future, free from disease and suffering.

Science does have its mysteries and puzzles. Perhaps many scientists are now less self-confident about being able to provide an answer to every problem than they were some years ago. But it would, I think, be quite mistaken to think that the scientific narrative is at an end. If science is modernity, then modernity is still very much in cultural control. But a problem has arisen. It is very difficult for the narrative to include an acceptable account of such late arrivals on the evolutionary scene as consciousness, freedom, truth, moral obligation and religious belief.

The hard line to take is that these arrivals are illusory appearances, which can be dispelled by a cold hard scientific stare. Consciousness is a set of brain-states; freedom is lack of constraint by external causes; truth is a matter of the survival value of beliefs that have enabled organisms to adapt to their environment; obligation is programmed social behaviour which has also passed the test of evolutionary fitness; and religion is a projection founded on psychological needs and insecurities, or perhaps (on Richard Dawkins' account)[1] a randomly generated belief-virus which has simply not been eliminated from the meme-pool (the set of culturally inherited beliefs). Human reason itself, on such a scientific account, turns out to be the result of chance mutations which have had some survival value, but its workings are wholly subject to impersonal and non-purposive laws of nature. Science remains committed to reason, and its exponents often show a quasi-moral commitment to the rigour of its methods and the heroic acceptance of its less palatable truths. But the conclusions of science have undermined the authority of reason, by showing it to be a pragmatically useful aid to survival in the unending struggle for life in an arena of scarce resources.

A central fault line appears in the scientific narrative. It presents itself as the only rational basis of knowledge and values, the revealer of the truth about the cosmos and the way to human well-being. Yet what it reveals is that there is no purpose, that human life, like everything else, is driven by blind selection pressures and impersonal natural processes. What we call reason and truth are the appearances of brain processes which are as fragile and contingent, as accidental and transient, as all other complex organic events. It is tempting to say that, once we see through the illusion, we are free to vary the conditions of rationality and truth as we will – that is the postmodern option. There are only belief systems, forms of life, without foundation or justification beyond themselves. Even this, however, is a truth claim. There is no escaping from truth, and there is no living with it either. That is the unhappy consciousness of the hard scientific narrative, as propounded by Richard Rorty, Edward Wilson, and – Rorty claims, however implausibly – Wittgenstein and Heidegger.[2]

Those who take a softer line are faced with the considerable problem of giving an account of human consciousness in terms of the grand narrative of science. One can see the history of European philosophy since the sixteenth century as a series of struggles to produce such an account, to construct a wider narrative which can reconcile the facts of science with the facts of human consciousness. In particular, attempts were made to accommodate some version of the crumbling narrative of Christendom, without appeal to discredited authorities or notions of rationally uncriticizable divine revelation. They form part of what Alasdair MacIntyre has called the 'Enlightenment Project', of seeking a rational secular foundation for belief and action.[3]

Until that time it has been widely accepted within Christian Europe that the universe was created by a wise God, and thus both had some intelligible purpose and were efficiently ordered towards achieving that purpose. That purpose is the creation of free creatures, who in working out their own destiny engender a batter between good and evil powers, a battle in which evil will be inevitably defeated and the good will enter eternal bliss.

In this narrative, creation is intrinsically rational, and humans are created in the divine image, and so share in the rationality, the wisdom, of God. Creation is corrupted by destructive and irrational powers, and that means that human reason may be perverted by egoism and pride. What is required is a return to true rationality, in alignment with the divine wisdom, the original divine order and goal of creation. That in turn requires faith, trust in the power of God, revealed historically in Jesus, to combat egoism and give humans a share in the divine wisdom. On this scheme, faith is not set against reason. It is required to restore true wisdom in the midst of a corrupted and estranged human world. Faith enables one to see the true order and goal of creation, because it puts human wisdom in relation to the divine wisdom, in which this order and goal are rooted.

Something went wrong with this picture of human existence. The causes of its going wrong are complex and varied, and I will only briefly mention two of them. I think one thing that went wrong was a strong neo-Platonic influence, to the extent that it identified divine wisdom with a spiritual archetypal world of pure natures, to be contemplated by pure intellectual intuition. Platonism always had problems with particularity and history, and with the idea that anything new could happen in history, or that it would matter if it did. Moreover, the idea of experimenting on the material world had the feel of the artisan about it, whereas the truly wise would be content with pure theory. This attitude of aristocratic unconcern with the historical and the particular carried on through the Aristotelian retrieval of the thirteenth century. It was compounded by a second factor, the attribution to Aristotle of an authority that would have shocked him considerably, and the identification of that authority with the divinely authorized teaching of the Church. The late medieval view of the order of nature was that of Aristotle's crystalline spheres, and the beatific vision, shared only by a rather restricted number of human beings out of the entire universe, was its goal. The faith which enabled one to perceive this order was acceptance of the authority of the Church in such matters. Thus any criticism of authority was seen as rebellion against God. The growth of empirical science was bound to show that most of Aristotle's views in physics were mistaken, and this was bound to come into conflict with that religious view.

Reason had to be separated from faith, because faith was now seen to require the acceptance of unreliable authorities, like Aristotle, and experimental science required a different approach to reason than that of the ancient Greek academy, which regarded experimentation as sordid. See Plato's classic remark, in *Timaeus*,[4] that astronomers who relied on observations would be reincarnated as birds for being so stupid.

Descartes set himself to provide such an approach. He never seriously doubted that the universe was a rational structure, created by a rational God. His picture is in many ways the traditional Christian one of a cosmic Reason creating an intelligible universe. The debt of the Enlightenment, and of the natural sciences, to Christianity is a large one. Human reason did nothing but discern God's wholly rational thoughts, and that is why reason is able to understand the universe by rigorous mathematical thinking. There is something odd about this concept of reason, however. For Descartes the universe is rational in a rather restricted and peculiar manner, for any idea of a goal or purpose is now excluded from consideration. This is the consequence of separating reason from faith. It is faith which speaks about the purpose of creation, and it is safer for scientists and philosophers to leave that topic to those who think they know about such things, and have the Inquisition to support them. Reason deals only with the mechanics, the processes, of nature, and can safely set aside all questions of ultimate ends.

This separation of faith, as a revealed teaching about the ultimate purpose of creation, from reason, as a neutral investigation of the mechanics of nature, without reference to values or purposes, has been determinative of European intellectual history. Of course, the idea of purpose was not at first entirely abandoned. Nature was seen as a deterministic machine, and machines are precisely built for a purpose. Further, they are products of intelligent design, not a random assembly of parts. But reference to a purpose and to a design both imply a personal reality underlying the machine, and they imply that the person is, not a ghost in the machine, but a disembodied mind outside the machine. Natural science at first ignored this aspect of its presupposed world view, as not lying within its province, but later began to attack it as superfluous to the observed existence of the machine. The universe becomes a self-designing machine without a purpose. The task of reason is now not to discern its ultimate goal or meaning, but to uncover its basically pointless principles of design. Faith is not required at any point, and its assumption of an ultimate purpose is in conflict with reason, understood as the exposure of the ultimately pointless principles which fully explain how the thing works. Moreover, the attempt of faith to communicate with a disembodied person who has been excluded from the universal machine can be depicted as a futile attempt to leap beyond the bounds of human knowledge. The leap of faith becomes a leap beyond reason, so it might equally well land anywhere or nowhere. It has been completely marginalized.

Cartesian reason seeks to be self-validating, without appeal to authority, and without recourse to faith. It has to generate from itself a set of necessary, self-evident principles – what Kant was to call 'synthetic *a priori* truths' – and derive from them, by steps accessible to any rational mind, together with the aid of experimental confirmations, the whole of human knowledge, in systematic order. If this programme can be carried out for all human beliefs, one will have a universal and necessary foundation for knowledge, derived from reason alone, and therefore a basis for universal human agreement and the ending of all ideological wars and disputes.

For the system to work, the universe itself must be modelled on a deductive system, so that what happens in it must be deducible from the laws of its operation and its initial state. The universe is seen as a deterministic machine, ordered in accordance with what came to be called the principle of sufficient reason, which decrees that, for every event, there is a 'sufficient' cause. Such causes necessarily produce specific effects, so that if the nature of the cause is known, all the effects are thereby known as well. If one knows the initial state of the universe, and all the laws of nature, one will be able to predict with absolute certainty everything that will ever happen. The laws are themselves deducible from analytic or self-evident first principles, and the initial state is actually the being of God, the first sufficient cause, from whose necessary nature the whole universe necessarily flows.

The Cartesian universe is one whose necessary structure flows from a necessary being, which cannot be other than it is. That is what securely grounds mathematical/scientific method as the correct way of understanding the universe, and what makes any other approach – faith or acceptance of mere authority – irrational and unacceptable. Reason had become a more secure route to God than religion. But the drawback was that the God whom reason discovered was a purely rational, mathematically calculating, all-determining being who could never do anything other than it did, a self-sustaining calculating machine.

If the Cartesian God was depersonalized, the Cartesian universe was by the same process desacralized. When the material universe was conceived as a realm in which spiritual beings were continually active, then trees, caves and springs were vibrant with spiritual energy and personal meaning. The earth itself was holy – not, indeed, for Christians, with a holiness which inhered in its own existence as such, but with a holiness which was directed to glorifying God and making both the one divine and many angelic presences manifest. All spirits and demons, all direct divine causal influences, all feelings and sacred meanings, were cleared from the cosmic calculating machine by the cold fire of pure reason. Where powers of good and evil had fought, where angels had walked and demons lurked, there now was only the rule of impersonal law. The only mind was the one unseen, remote mathematical Intelligence, which churned out its predeterminate conclusions with dispassionate and impersonal necessity.

The desacralization of nature was important for the rise of science. Without it, no objective experimental approach to the physical world would be possible, since one would always be afraid of infringing on the rights of spirit powers that might be present and vengeful. Yet it also led to the attitude that humans can do whatever they want with the natural world, regarding it as a mere tool for fulfilling human desires, with no intrinsic value of its own. Lynn White, in a rather well-known paper,[5] accused Judaeo-Christian theism of giving rise to the attitude that nature can be used or abused in any way by human beings. He did this largely by appeal to Genesis 1:28: the divine command to humans to 'fill the earth and subdue it; and have dominion ... over every living thing'. This is, however, a very implausible reading of Genesis. To subdue (*kabash*) is to order and bring under one's rule. Thus one might 'subdue' a garden by pulling out weeds and encouraging the growth of beautiful flowers. The command in Genesis clearly makes humans subordinate to the purposes of God in creation, and in effect orders humans to be sharers with God in ordering the world to the divine glory. The Qur'an catches the meaning exactly when it speaks of humans being vice-gerents of God, working to implement the divine plan for creation. Once that meaning is seen, it is not possible to think that humans can use the earth in any way they want, or that they might despoil and destroy it, if they wish. God has created the earth in order to realize its proper goodness, and humans have the task of helping in this divine task. As long as the earth is seen to be the creation of a God who wills goodness, responsibility towards the earth is an essential part of 'dominion'.

Descartes does still see the earth as created by God. He provides a good example of the way in which belief in a God who created the universe through Wisdom, and as an intelligible unitary and interconnected whole, forms a fruitful conceptual background for the birth of the scientific view of the universe as governed by intelligible laws. Nevertheless, his rationalistic view is a much more plausible precursor of that despoiling attitude to the world which Lynn White rightly deplores, than is the Book of Genesis. Whereas for medieval Christianity, the world showed forth the glory of God, and gave continual intimations of the divine presence and action, for Cartesianism the world becomes a machine from which God is effectively excluded, except for being its necessary and sufficient cause. Human reason can explain all the processes of nature without ever referring to God. There are no divine acts which escape the eye of reason. Even animals become part of the machine, insensate and without true consciousness. It is only when the world is seen as a machine, and when a personal God has been excluded from its causal processes, that one can truly tinker with it and modify it in any way one wishes. The mechanistic view of nature and the deductive model of autonomous human reason are the parents of modernity. But this was an unstable marriage from the first.

Mechanistic science freed the world from the arbitrary actions of demons and angels. But it also led to the effective exclusion of a God who could give the universe purpose and objective value. There is a central paradox in the Cartesian view. God, as the ultimately rational principle, is the foundation of the rationality of the universe. Yet God is excluded from playing any part in the strictly law-governed processes of nature. Similarly, it is the free activity of reason, working in accordance with the laws of logic, which discerns the rational structure of the universe. Yet reason must itself be part of the mechanism, and all its activities must therefore be determined and not free. Descartes at the same time made reason the supreme human attribute, and also undermined its authority by subordinating it to the deterministic laws of nature. Descartes' solution to this paradox was the bifurcation of human nature into a mechanistic physical part and a quite different rational, thinking part.

Virtually everyone agrees that this solution cannot work, because there is no obvious way of re-uniting the two parts of human nature which have been thus divided. The Divided Self which Descartes constructed was an attempted union of autonomous reason and deterministic causality. Reason is a conscious, self-critical, reflective capacity, under the epistemic obligation to scrutinize its own processes and apply rigorous criteria to all its natural beliefs and habitual propensities. In being autonomous, it declares its own freedom from all tradition and external influence, having the ability and the right freely to come to its own decisions. In Descartes' system, reason first clears away all preconceptions and then elaborates its own first principles, accepting only clear and distinct conceptions which can survive the most rigorous examination. Reason is free, conscious and self-critical.

What reason discovers, however, is that nature proceeds in accordance with mechanistic laws. Nature is determined, unconscious and ineluctable. The gulf between conscious freedom and unconscious necessity is bridged by making physical laws a set of deductions from necessary first principles, and by making human reasoning into a deductive process which mirrors the process of nature. In human minds, the cosmic mechanism makes a model of itself, which is in fact a model of the original mathematical archetypal system in the mind of God. Yet Descartes, by the very invention of this elegant copying model of cosmic and human reason, also creates the insoluble problem of explaining how the mind could be exhorted to the free, critical activity of reason, while at the same time being part of a deterministic structure of nature. In Descartes the impact of new scientific knowledge encourages a view of human reason as superior to and critical of all received tradition, and a view of the physical universe as governed by mathematical, impersonal laws, not moral or spiritual causes. The clash of those two ideas, of autonomous reason and impersonal physical law, was to bring about the decline and fall of reason in European thought.

The decay can be seen most clearly in the work of Immanuel Kant. In Kant's essays on history, he writes of the hope that education and liberal democracy will prepare the way for a universal ethical commonwealth, and the rule of reason over nature. The ethical commonwealth is the empire of reason, which freely legislates only those principles which can be legislated by all rational persons, and which accepts as knowledge only those beliefs which can be verified by possibly universal observation. All human beings are members of that empire, and the destiny of the world is to move through a temporary phase of conflict (against the reactionary forces of blind tradition or religious fanaticism) to the complete and open rule of reason.

There were deep instabilities in this view which rendered it fragile from the first, and which led to its virtual collapse in twentieth-century European thought. Critical reason is given absolute authority, and yet one cannot be sure that it has any objective foundation in reality. Reason decrees that a perfectly ethical commonwealth will come into historical existence, and yet it cannot guarantee that such a thing will actually occur. Practical reason decrees that one ought to act in accordance with the moral law, and yet it also, in the system of natural determinism, ensures that one cannot act otherwise than one does. Human beings are transcendent over nature, in absolute moral dignity, and yet they are also parts of a necessitarian machine.

One can trace one strand of the collapse by considering Kant's account of the role of reason in moral thinking. For Kant, morality is rational and universal goal-directed action. One discovers what is morally right by asking what general ends of human action could be universally willed by goal-directed beings. In general, the two ends of action thus discovered are the happiness and perfection (the realization of all positive creative and intellectual potentialities) of human beings. Particular moral rules are the universal principles which can be followed by all rational beings in seeking those necessary ends of action.

It has not gone unnoticed that much more disagreement than Kant expected can exist in the application of this method to particular cases. It is not obvious, for example, that an absolute prohibition on lying and suicide would follow from the Kantian method. It is not obvious just how much altruism or personal indulgence would be allowed, or how conflicts between competing duties in particular cases should be resolved. Self-legislated morality leaves many more areas for disagreement than Kant thought, and perhaps makes it possible for many people to follow rules that they would be prepared to legislate universally, but which other people regard as immoral. It is hard to account for this on Kant's system alone, and one can see an incipient individualistic prescriptivism in the method that Kant himself would have been horrified to contemplate.

More serious, however, is the almost entirely hypothetical nature of the Kantian method. One is to do what a perfectly rational being *would* will, in a world where all rational beings will similarly. But, in an unjust world, where all do not will similarly, and where living by universal principles is often unlikely to produce any positive results, is it reasonable to act as if in a rational world? May it not be more reasonable to compromise on absolute rational principles in order to produce good results and to aim mostly at the well-being of those I like, including myself? It is arguable that a person who insists on acting on principles of absolute rationality in a world of organisms engaged in a desperate power struggle for scarce resources is in fact rather crazy. As Aristotle said, the rational person is a person who knows where the limits of reason lie. Kant had already drawn the limits of reason in such a way that reason could give no knowledge of reality as it really is. There is no reason to think the world in itself is rational, only that we have to treat it as though it were. But do we really *have* to? Kant's own arguments for the absolute necessity of Euclidean geometry and Newtonian physics have been undermined by the subsequent progress of the natural sciences. Is this assumption that it is necessary to follow the dictates of reason any more plausible? It may even be irrational, as Peter Geach once suggested, to follow the dictates of absolute reason simply for its own sake.[6] Once it is seriously questioned, it becomes hard just to accept that dutifulness is the only thing good without qualification. It may even be, to use the sociobiologist Michael Ruse's chilling phrase, a 'delusion of biology', a genetically programmed belief, without objective foundation.[7]

It seems clear that there is a world-view underlying Kant's ethical method, without which it would collapse into irrelevance. Beneath the realm of appearances lies the noumenal realm. Reason, as the constructive, legislating power in all knowledge and rational activity, must be conceived as belonging to that realm, and as eventually bringing phenomenal nature wholly under its control. One should obey the voice of reason, just because it is the deepest voice of one's own true nature, the hidden basis of phenomenal reality and its ultimate master.

Unfortunately, human reason cannot bear the weight thus assigned to it. Kant himself recognizes that practical reason has not the power to ensure that the moral goal – the realization of happiness and perfection – will in fact be realized. It has not the power to eliminate evil, nor to bring about justice, nor to ensure the social co-operation necessary for the attainment of such a goal. At that point he lamely, and to virtually no one's satisfaction, introduces God as one who might add some 'unknowable supplement' to our moral efforts, and ensure that we obtain the happiness that virtue deserves.

But the critical philosophy forbids us any knowledge of the noumenal realm. So we cannot properly claim that reason, whether divine or human, is the reality which underlies the phenomenal, or that the postulates of reason have any relevance to what will actually happen in future. Reason has a purely immanent role, within the phenomenal. And if its role there is not strictly necessary – or, in the case of morality, is unable to guarantee the goal it presupposes – it is relegated to being an optional choice. Once one discerns the powerlessness of reason, the denial of its authority is not far behind. Confined to the phenomenal realm, it becomes at best a pragmatically justified instrument of thought.

If humans have evolved through a struggle for dominance which has required kinship preference and aggression against competitors, then rationality has its greatest benefit in devising better means to those ends. There is no survival utility in devising a purely formal set of absolute principles which would obtain in a purely rational universe of co-operating persons. If there is such a thing as a 'sense of obligation', it will be best explained as an evolutionary device for enforcing modes of behaviour which promote the survival of one's kin-group. It is unlikely that those moral intuitions which comprise such a sense of obligation will match the imaginary dictates of pure reason, and it was a doomed *tour de force* on Kant's part to argue that they did. Once one sees this, it becomes apparent that pure reason carries no sense of obligation with it. The once categorical maxims of pure reason are reduced to being guidelines as to what would happen in an ideally rational society, though they will often be quite inappropriate to the world we actually live in.

It is only in the context of belief in an objective rational creator that the morality of universal reason can have binding authority. If the universe is grounded in a universal Intelligence, who intends specific goals for human persons, and provides a way for them to achieve those goals, then the laws of universal reason, ordered to a goal of intrinsic value, will have the force of obligation for any agent who is aware of the real nature of things. When theistic belief is rejected, the very idea of a universal reason loses its hold, and the formal principles of reason can no longer exercise justifiable authority over human desires and objectives. Before long, Kant's austere principle of autonomy, which expressed the universal mastery of pure reason over all natural desires, was to become the principle of maximal individual choice, leaving all individuals free to do what they want as long as they permit others to do the same. The ultimate, self-refuting, application of the principle is that individuals are permitted to accept the principle itself only if they want to. Morality is wholly subordinated to desire or to the will to power. The material world is released from the demands of reason, and the rational restraints of experimental science can be overthrown. Freed at last from the illusions of faith, the fall of reason left the way open for myths of blood and soil to take root in the very heartland of European intellectual culture.

The moral of the story is that the Enlightenment idea of pure reason was always only the fading echo of the voice of God. When it collapses at last into evolutionary naturalism – the recognition that reason is a pragmatically useful device in the struggle for survival – the idea of one universal Reason collapses with it. We may now seem to be in a postmodern world, where many forms of life may co-exist, with many more or less fragmented narratives, and no underlying coherence or agreement, where the will, unconstrained by objective canons of reason, may value whatever it chooses. Yet there is an underlying narrative which enables us to speak of this as a 'postmodern world'. It is the narrative of a form of science which has led to the exclusion of values and purposes from the objective world.

I have suggested that the hard materialist programme impales itself on the fact that it makes an absolute claim to truth and rationality, while undermining the authority of all such claims. Cartesian dualism extols the supremacy of the rational mind, while subordinating it to the blind processes of a deterministic universe, and so making it helpless to act. The Kantian defence of pure reason collapses into pragmatism and the individualistic exercise of arbitrary choice, which sets each individual potentially against every other, and certainly against the omnipotent will of God. The Enlightenment project of making human reason a final authority and effective agent of change has failed.

Christian theology is hardly in a position to rectify the ills of modern culture, having helped to produce many of them. Yet one can see that a way of responding to the failure of the Enlightenment project would be to construct a properly scientific narrative which could yet build purpose and value into objective reality, and see human freedom, and human faith too, in terms of a creative response to particular discernments of objective values, and invitations to realize them in history. The Christian tradition does, in my view, contain the resources for making such an attempt. If I am right, this would be the most important task for theology in this partly modern, partly postmodern age.

Notes

1. Richard Dawkins, *The Selfish Gene* (2nd edn; Oxford: Oxford University Press, 1989).
2. Richard Rorty, *Philosophy and the Mirror of Nature* (Princeton: Princeton University Press, 1980).
3. Alasdair MacIntyre, *After Virtue* (London: Duckworth, 1981).
4. D. Lee (trans.), *Timaeus* (London: Penguin, 1965), p. 12.
5. Lynn White, 'The historical roots of our ecologic crisis', *Science*, 155 (1967) pp. 1203–7.
6. Peter Geach, *The Virtues* (Cambridge: Cambridge University Press, 1977), p. 8.
7. See Michael Ruse, 'Evolution and ethics' in *Evolutionary Naturalism* (London: Routledge, 1996), ch. 8.

2

Trinitarian *différance* and world religions

Postmodernity and the 'Other'

Gavin D'Costa

the idea of truth as a grasp on things must necessarily have a non-metaphorical sense somewhere.[1]

In this chapter I want to suggest that the doctrine of the trinity has the resources to overcome a profound problem located in the writings of some postmodern theorists: that the 'Other' is always in danger of being destroyed and disfigured because of the cultural and intellectual grids within which 'we' place the 'Other'. I want to relate this postmodern problematic to the question of Christianity's relationship to other religions in the modern world. Does our theology of the 'Other' come under a similar critique? I shall explore this question by first briefly surveying the territory exposed by theorists such as Levinas, Derrida, Said and McGrane. I then engage with one of the few postmodernist theologians (Kenneth Surin) who has used such theorists to develop various incisive criticisms of Christian theology of religions. After presenting a critique of Surin, I build upon his constructive insights to suggest how the trinity may offer the resources to break out of a very real impasse within the field of theology of religions precisely because the trinity moves away from the modern concern with the individual self (constructed during the Enlightenment) and gestures loving *différance*.

Recently in a number of disciplines such as anthropology, philosophy, literary and cultural studies there has been close attention to the dynamics involved in the representation of the Other. While there is no single unified thesis emerging, there is an intriguing overlap or family resemblance of opinions that the non-European has been distorted in the Western representations of the Other and that this construal cannot be detached from the colonial and imperial history of Europe.

In anthropology, for example, Bernard McGrane has asked whether the last four centuries of portrayal of the non-European amounts to much more than a distorted and negative mirror image of the European self.[2] In philosophy Emmanuel Levinas and Jacques Derrida, each in quite different ways, responding to Heidegger, have challenged the Western philosophical tradition regarding its totalizing control and occlusion of the Other. Hence, Levinas' challenge that ontology destroys Otherness by assimilating it to Sameness and Derrida's criticisms of European logocentricism which, he writes, is 'nothing but the most original and powerful ethnocentricism, in the process of imposing itself upon the world'.[3] In literary and cultural studies Edward Said's notion of 'colonial discourse', established in his major work *Orientalism*,[4] has generated much debate and research centred on the construction of distorted visions of the Other, the Oriental, within Western colonial discourse. For example, Rani Kabanni's study, tellingly named *Europe's Myth of the Orient*,[5] uncovers the sexual fantasies implicit in Western literary and artistic representations of the Orient. It is an excellent illustration of Said's thesis, although it avoids the theoretical problems raised in Said's analysis which have been taken up and challenged most startlingly by writers such as Gayatri Spivak and Homi Bhabha.[6] It is worth noting that the spectre of Michel Foucault hovers behind both McGrane and Said's work, partly explaining the preoccupation with the preconditions of representation that increasingly run across interdisciplinary lines.[7]

To illustrate some of the issues in slightly more detail, McGrane with rather broad brush strokes, and somewhat derivatively from Tzvetan Todorov,[8] constructs a disturbing excavation showing that the portrayal of the Other, the non-European within European history, says much about the horizon of interpretation employed by the European and the political social relationship of the European to this Other. Obviously, very little about the Other as really Other is produced in this catalogue, but I will return to this in a moment. So for instance, the Renaissance was characterized by the Other interpreted on the horizon of Christianity. It was Christianity which fundamentally came between the European and the non-European other. Within the Christian conception of Otherness anthropology did not exist; there was, rather, demonology. It was in relation to the Fall and to the influence of Sin and Satan that the Other took on his historically specific meaning.[9]

McGrane's characterization of this and other periods is far too generalized and neatly schematized, but he nevertheless makes an important point. After the Enlightenment ignorance and error replace sin. With the slow erosion of religious belief, there developed a 'psychology of error and superstition, an ontology of ignorance, and an epistemology of all the forms of untruth and unenlightenment'.[10] Demonization is replaced by ignorance, by a lack of enlightenment. Defoe's *Robinson Crusoe* (1718) emblematically reflects both these periods and anticipates the next in the representation of Friday: partly fallen, clearly ignorant, and definitely uncivilized.

In the nineteenth century the influence of geology (Lyell), evolutionary theory (Darwin) and anthropology (Tylor) provides the horizon of interpretation, so that the non-European Other is organized in terms of stages of development, 'between the prehistorically fossilized "primitive" and the evolutionary advancement of modern Western science and civilization'. The evolutionary ladder of savage, primitive, civilized is established and different groups positioned along its rungs, with the European at the top.[11] Finally, when McGrane comes to the twentieth century, he fiercely contests the predominant episteme of cultural relativism in which difference becomes cultural difference alone, thereby masking the real challenge that the Other poses. He rehearses the now well-worn arguments against such relativizers and their absolute claim that all is relative must itself be relative, and their hidden imperialism in assuming a non-relative vantage point from which to make this observation about all cultures.[12] He argues that culture becomes the dominant paradigm for interpreting the Other. Cultural relativity becomes the grand text into which difference is encoded; the non-European Other is seen as 'fundamentally and merely, culturally different'.[13] Ironically, in this mode of portrayal, difference is reduced to sameness and inoculated from any real interaction. So while in the sixteenth to nineteenth centuries there was a tendency to portray the Other in metonymic mode, a distorted mirror image of the European in the construction of the Other, in the twentieth century the Other is simply reflection, homogenized by assimilation, culturally relative, made Same, rendered safe, and thereby 'achieves' the respect of secular liberalism. While one excludes Otherness as negative mirror image, the modern includes it by total assimilation. Both thereby distort, but in opposite ways.

So what of the Christian theologian involved in the question of the status and meaning of other religions? I would suggest that we have much to learn from these materials. To remain with McGrane for the moment. First, McGrane's study alerts us to the horizon within which we proffer such portrayals. Second, the history of portrayal says much about the constructors and producers of such knowledge, their horizon of interpretation, and the power relations within which these constructions take place. Third, McGrane is not interested in theology as such, but the construction of the Other has, since the Renaissance, been powerfully influenced by prevailing 'theologies of religion'. Hence this specific and very important element is not given the appropriate attention it deserves. McGrane's work and most of the others I have quoted have not focused specifically on the portrayal of other religions within predominantly Christian and Christian-influenced circles. Such concentration of attention would not of course exclude the significance of the wider aspects of portrayal, but would help raise more sharply some of the theological questions I want to isolate.[14] Fourth, and very germane to my main concern, McGrane's study indicates a tendency in the European history of the portrayal of the Other to veer in one of two directions, but two directions held together by the same centrifugal force, which would be for Levinas: ontology, and for Derrida: logocentrism. The first direction is in terms of hierarchical inferiority, subjugation, power and control (be it in the categories of demonization, unenlightenment or primitive tribe) so that Otherness bears the opposite negative reflection of the image maker and can be subjected to that maker. The second direction is to make Otherness sameness (be it in terms of cultural relativization, liberal humanism's espousal of the universality of values such as justice and equal rights, or whatever) so that while it seems that equality is granted, it is always 'granted', that is, bestowed in terms of the portrayer's system of representation. The centrifugal force holding both these tendencies together is the Western Imperial Self, either destroying the Other, on the one hand, or alternatively homogenizing the Other. Both movements of course collude in different types of destruction and effacement.

Fifth, McGrane like Said fails to really address the question of relation of the Other to the 'real' Other, Orientalism to the Orient, the question of the possibility of the Other being free to be Other, and the possibility of representation without control, knowledge without coercive power. It would of course be impossible to have knowledge without power *per se*, but the real question as to the possibility of non-coercive representation still remains unresolved. When McGrane and Said address this problem, at the end of their respective studies *Beyond Anthropology* and *Orientalism*, McGrane advances an undernourished hybrid mixture of existentialism, insights from Levinas and the notion of Socratic dialogue, extolling ignorance and dialogue;[15] and Said urges an individualist humanism extolling experience and sympathy which curiously runs counter to his implicit presuppositions that individuals are not prior to structures, but rather created by them. Hence, the very real question remains about the conditions within our 'theory' or 'theology' which could facilitate less distorted and non-coercive representation. I now want to focus more sharply on the fourth and fifth of these points: how to transcend the dichotomy of sameness–otherness/assimilation–demonization/total identity–incommensurable difference, and the underlying centrifugal force which in either direction results in distorted vision and the destruction of the Other; and how to formulate a theology which allows for the possibility of non-coercive (self) re-presentation of the Other.

To develop my argument, I will turn to Kenneth Surin, one of the few theologians who takes his cue from McGrane, Todorov, Foucault and like-minded thinkers when analysing the theology of religions.[16] Surin makes two very important points which will help focus my concern. The first is incisive and valid, the second problematic. The first is an argument showing how modern forms of Christian theological pluralism (in the work of John Hick, for example) efface the Other for the sake of homogenization; despite the tolerant liberal rhetoric there is an imperialist occlusion.

He notes that in pluralism:

All the adherents of the major religious traditions are treated 'democratically' in the 'pluralist' monologue *about* 'difference' (which of course is entirely relativized because 'difference' or 'otherness' is for the 'pluralist' always only 'cultural'). In this monologue, the 'pluralist', like McGrane's anthropologist, speaks well of the 'other' but never to the 'other', and indeed cannot do otherwise because there really is no intractable 'other' for the 'pluralist'. Constitutive features of the 'pluralist' position – for instance, its claim that since we 'all' partake of a 'universal soteriological process' (a claim that in itself is not necessarily problematic) *all* claims to particularity must therefore be deemed to be 'mythological'; its ceaseless 'relativizing' of just about everything else; and its making 'complementary' of any surplus that cannot be homogenized by such powerful 'relativizing' strategies – serve effectively to decompose or obscure that radical historical particularity which is constitutive of the truly 'other'. Where a certain Christian barbarism presumes its 'superiority' in order to justify the elimination or the conquest of the non-Christian 'other', this monological 'pluralism' sedately but ruthlessly domesticates and assimilates the 'other' — *any* 'other' – in the name of a 'world ecumenism' and the 'realisation of a limitlessly better possibility' (to use Hick's phraseology from the Gifford Lectures).[17]

Surin devastatingly shows how modern pluralism conforms to McGrane's typology of twentieth-century representation of the non-European Other and skilfully locates this representation in liberal capitalism's global pretensions, in the modernist grand narratives that allegedly acknowledge

heterogeneity and plurality, but this acknowledgement is always fatally compromised by [the] deployment of a homogeneous logic, a logic which irons-out the heterogeneous precisely by subsuming it under the categories of comprehensive and totalizing 'global' and 'world' theologies.[18]

If we see in pluralism the tendency to assimilate the Other, to make Same, we might expect to see the reverse in theological exclusivism; to reject by demonizing the Other in terms of a distorted self-image. And what of the midfield player, the theological inclusivist?

This leads to Surin's second point, which I find more problematic.[19] He argues that the inclusivist and exclusivist positions can all be subsumed under the same category in terms of their common

periodization with certain correlative alignments in a Christian theology of religions: the period of Western imperial expansion and government (associated by them with the 'absoluteness' of Christianity, Christian 'exclusivism', 'non-dialogue' et cetera) versus the period of 'post-colonialism' (aligned by them with the 'non-absoluteness' of Christianity, 'inclusivism' and 'pluralism' and even a 'liberal exclusivism', 'dialogue', et cetera).[20]

The other way in which they conspire together is in the assumption that the *solus Christus* teaching must either be revised, eliminated or upheld, whereas Surin argues that it does not properly apply to the question of other religions 'but is instead intended, heuristically, to guide faithful Christian practice'. Hence it is possible that 'a Christian could have no view on the question of the salvation of "non-Christians" (*qua* non-Christians) and still be an upholder of the *solus Christus*'.[21] Surin also aligns these approaches in their shared and problematic presupposition that 'the difficulties that stand in the way of an adequate understanding of the relationships between the various major religious traditions can be overcome if only we are able to get our theories and doctrines "right"'.[22]

And, finally, Surin notes an important commonality between inclusivism and pluralism. He illustrates his point in regard to Las Casas' defence of the Indians against the Spaniards. Las Casas identified the former as 'lambs' and as 'Christians', the latter as 'moors', 'wolves' and 'ravening wild beasts'. Hence, to quote Surin:

> so strong is Las Casas's commitment to equality that he will not characterise the Indians as 'different'. Good proto-Rahnerian that he is, he is prepared to see them as 'unwitting' Christians, and so, as Todorov points out, Las Casas's postulate of equality involves the assertion of identity'.[23]

It meant that Las Casas ended up knowing neither Indian nor Spaniard, and it is this assertion of identity (the Indians were unwitting Christians whether they knew it or not) that finally makes inclusivism no different to pluralism in Surin's eyes. He never properly locates exclusivism in relation to this question of identity.

Now I want to contest all four parts of Surin's second claim in pursuit of transcending the Other–Same dichotomy, although the fourth part is most significant to me. First, while there may be a common periodization among the three writers Surin quotes (Hick, Kraemer and Rahner), it is difficult to align Kraemer to this periodization, as Surin does by means of allusion and then direct quotation of four words from Kraemer's texts.[24] Kraemer's own writings were partially sparked off by William Hocking's pluralist proposals. Kraemer criticized Hocking for assimilating his theology to culture (agreeing with Surin's criticism!), i.e. a liberal pluralist culture dictating a liberal pluralist theology. It is part of Kraemer's genius that he sought to disassociate theology from this cultural–intellectual matrix (and Kraemer and Surin both acknowledge their debt to Barth) and instead establish the rules of theology's discourse from the Gospel. He was also well aware, as is Rahner, that the periodization of pre-colonial days with respect to other religions is far more complex than Surin's representation of it.[25] It is also the case that Kraemer was very well versed in Islam, both intellectually and practically and, far from smothering Otherness, precisely located points of difference whereupon he sought to challenge Islam and other religions. Regarding exclusivism, it is also the case that in the modern period, certain forms of non-liberal exclusivist theological discourse flourish in a way hardly recognized by Surin, so that his characterizations of post-colonial discourse (the non-absoluteness of Christianity, inclusivism and pluralism and even a liberal exclusivism, dialogue, etc.) are crucially flawed.[26]

The point here is that Surin is in danger of trying to sweep too much into his schematization, in danger of precisely doing what he criticizes Hick and others for doing: not allowing for proper representation; attempting homogenization at the cost of the intractable particularity of various positions. It is one thing to provide a close textual study of Hick and justify his criticism of pluralism as assimilating Otherness to Sameness, but another to try and gesture towards the whole debate and absorb all writings under such wide categories. I do not want to labour this point, but I think it is a warning and perhaps indicates the necessity of an archaeological investigation into the context of Surin's own discourse (as a type, not an individual) to locate the desire to homogenize the theology of religions debate.

The other point I want to make here is to note the lost opportunity for analysing exclusivism in terms of projecting Otherness as negative mirror-opposite, leading to forms of hierarchical inferiority, subjugation, power and control. Exclusivism often works in terms of the logic of its representation by seeing the Other only in terms of lack: lacking grace, Jesus, God, salvation. The Other is defined in terms of negative absence. Otherness is fetishized as mirror-opposite. What of course both pluralism and exclusivism have in common is what I have called the centrifugal force of defining the Other entirely in terms of Self. In pluralism's case as Same, and in exclusivism's sake, as negative Other. But before asking whether inclusivism overcomes this dualistic mode of representation I need to address Surin's two other claims.

Surin claims that the *solus Christus* teaching is misinterpreted with a shift in the modern episteme, so that

> the Kraemers and Rahners of this world believe themselves to be compelled to relate the *solus Christus* to the question of the salvation of 'non-Christians', and, equally, the Cantwell-Smiths and Hicks of this world then find themselves obliged to undo the attempts of the Kraemers and Rahners.[27]

Now this raises a question concerning both the history of doctrine (the way in which other religions were viewed in Church history) as well as the nature of doctrine (as grammatical rules, ontological affirmations, etc.) and I cannot hope to deal fully with either of these points. But let me register disquiet on both fronts. As Francis Sullivan and Louis Capéran have shown in great detail, the question of other religions has concerned the Church throughout its history, although conceived of in very different ways (i.e. initially Judaism and Islam were seen more as heresies than as other religions, and the sixteenth century marks the real entry of the non-European Other into Christian consciousness).[28] The *extra ecclesiam nulla salus* axiom which is the historical Catholic counterpart to *solus Christus* was, as Surin indicates, related not so much to excluding others as to distinguishing those within (from heretics and schismatics). But it nevertheless became a springboard from which to think through the question of other religions in an ever increasingly urgent manner from the nineteenth century onward. While one could quite rightly hold the *solus Christus* without determining the question of the salvation of the Other, it is entirely unconvincing to suggest that if one did reflect on the latter, the *solus Christus* principle is irrelevant. This matter partly rests on whether doctrine is entirely construed as grammar and rule-making or as also construing and being construed by a reality that is Other, that is God. So, I would register disquiet at Surin's evasion of the question of the theology of religions, as when he writes:

> It would, I believe, be more productive for us to stand aside from such sterile controversies and get on instead with the business of

registering, in the manner of a Foucault-type 'genealogy', the historical and political forces which brought about this shift of *episteme* (and of course to characterize the *epistemes* in question as well).[29]

Surin simply robs theology of any task and substitutes genealogical analysis. While I share Surin's concerns to promote such analysis, I question his materialist presuppositions that render theological discourse into analysis of the socio-political unconscious.[30]

Penultimately, a few words on Surin's point about 'getting our theories and doctrines "right"' as being part of the cementing episteme binding the three approaches. It is surely a caricature of contemporary theology of religions, especially when both Rahner and Kraemer are at pains to point out that doctrines are only intelligible from the point of practice, and Lindbeck, whom Surin cites with slightly qualified disapproval (as a modernist), actually occupies a position very close to Surin as to the grammatical rule nature of doctrine.[31] And of course, the main intention of Surin's article is to replace the theology of religions project with right theory that will properly facilitate adequate understanding of the relationships between religions in socio-political terms. Surin's challenge is itself therefore not immune from his own criticism.

But now let me address the main point of my disagreement with Surin which also leads into the theologically constructive part of this chapter. Todorov's comment on Las Casas' rendering of the Other as an 'assertion of identity' is incisive, even if not entirely accurate about Las Casas.[32] Surin's criticism of Rahner's inclusivism as finally and strategically aligned to pluralism's assimilation of the Other raises the question entirely untouched in Surin's paper, between what I shall call a 'closed' and 'open' form of inclusivism. As far as I am aware, this distinction has not been formally introduced into the discussion in theology of religions. Surin's target is rightly a 'closed' form of inclusivism and again there his textual paucity in regard to Rahner leaves unresolved the question as to whether Rahner should be seen as an 'open' or 'closed' inclusivist. What is disturbing is that in making this point Surin fails to distinguish between these two forms of inclusivism. 'Closed' inclusivists could be depicted as saying that in Christ or/and the Christian Church we have the truth of God. We can therefore recognize God in other religions in so much as those others look like us, have our God, teach our doctrines. And in this sense the term 'anonymous Christian', detached from its Rahnerian context and used as a typology of inclusivism, indicates that the Christian knows and recognizes God within the Other, either despite the Other or in keeping with the Other. The 'anonymous' here is related to the self-consciousness of the Other. Now this form of inclusivism does fall foul of making the Other Same, recognizing the Other only in so much as they conform to us. And Surin has a good point in thereby noting the affinity between pluralism and what I would call a closed form of inclusivism.

But Surin fails to attend to 'open' inclusivism. Here a remark by Derrida will indicate the way in which I want to transcend the Same–Other dichotomy by transforming these terms by taking them up into a third term: God, both hidden and revealed. I want to suggest that we replace the Western Imperial Self with an eschatological trinitarian God. My project is certainly not Derridean, but what he says of 'différance' is pertinent:

> The term 'différance' can't be stabilized within a polarization of the same and the different. It's at one and the same time an idea rooted in sameness, and radical otherness ... So I'd say that différance can't be enclosed within the same, or the idea of the radically other, about which nothing could be said. It's an enigmatic relation of the same to the other.[33]

It is this enigmatic relation of the same to the other that an open inclusivism seeks to retain and explore. Hence, open inclusivists like myself can be depicted as saying that in Christ or/and the Christian Church we have the truth of God. *But* this truth is never our possession but, rather, we are possessed by it. Now this is important for as we do not possess it, we cannot control or limit it or even claim to have a vantage point somewhere beyond it, by which we know it in its entirely. Furthermore, this truth is not closed in the sense that revelation is *eschatologically* oriented, so while the Church claims to have encountered God in the self-revelation of the Father in Jesus Christ, through her Spirit, it at the same time confesses an ignorance of this God. While we know God, we do not know everything about God. There is a constant tension between Paul's proclamation that God has given us the gift of himself through his Son by the power of his Spirit and Paul's insistence that for now, we only know through a glass darkly.

This point could be put in the technical form: *while the economic trinity is the immanent trinity, the immanent trinity is not the economic trinity until the eschaton.* (In this respect Rahner's 'vice versa' regarding the immanent and economic trinity is problematic.) The 'economic' trinity indicates the historical manner in which we come to know God and the 'immanent' trinity means that this is the eternal God, God in Godself. Hence, it is in this surplus, this Derridean différance, that we find the possibility of avoiding either total assimilation, or total rejection and mirror-projection, or of course (for the more radical relativist, who remains silent in this chapter) a total incommensurability.[34] It is in this surplus that genuine Otherness can become a question mark to my own Christian self-understanding, a question mark to the location of my questioning, and the question mark that bears the trace of revelation.

In terms of the phrase 'anonymous Christian' the anonymous here does not relate to the self-consciousness of the Other (and Rahner's modern turn to anthropology would inevitably end with such a focus on 'self', as von Balthasar had noted as early as *Spirit in the World*), but to the manner in which the Christian does not possess God or know God without remainder, so that there is a sense in which the anonymous relates neither to the self-consciousness of the Other or the Christian, but rather to the mystery of God, who is known in Christ, yet still hidden. This approach, I believe, allows one to overcome the distorting dichotomy, because the centrifugal force at the centre is not homogenizing, the One, the Same. Rather, it is relational and dynamic, revealed and hidden, known and unknown, unpossessable yet possessing, it is 'the enigmatic relation of the same to the other', the possibility of true communion with the stranger and the reality of our continuously striving towards such communion. This is the significance of proleptic eschatological revelation.

Let me expand these comments a little more to indicate the direction in which I would proceed and point to some of the implications of such an approach. I cannot here develop the eschatological trinitarian theology I have begun to reflect upon elsewhere.[35] First, the reason why I think an *open form of eschatological trinitarian inclusivism* is preferable to alternative approaches, including Surin's, is that it allows us to ask the question of God in our relations with the Other, not excluding genealogical analysis, which would help make such theological speech more rigorously self-conscious about its coercive potential. It allows us to ask the question about God without this being a closed question and without it predefining the other person *a priori* (as is the case with exclusivism, pluralism and closed forms of inclusivism). In fact, when we believe that the God who reveals himself in Jesus Christ as Father, through the Spirit, is also only now known through a glass dimly (1 Cor 13:12) and who sends the Spirit so that we may come to grow in love and understanding of the mystery of God (John 16:12ff.), we are aware of that enigmatic relation between the same and other, between the God we know through our Christian tradition and that 'same' God (as God cannot be contradictory) who can yet be so 'Other', who we do not know and do not recognize, and who ceaselessly surprises us, and whom we may yet come to discover in the self-revealing of the Other as Other. In this respect, the eschatological trinitarianism I defend stipulates that in the name of the Father, Son and Spirit, we have only the parameters within which our encounter with God is guided, the grammatical rules that allow us to encounter real Otherness without rendering it incommensurable, but without rendering it as same (positively or negatively). It leaves the question of God's presence in the world religions entirely open and thereby allows for the possibility of the Other's self-definition as a question for us, not as an answer to confirm our theory. And the genealogical self-consciousness that is rightly enjoined upon us is required to constantly question whether we coerce the Other in even inviting self-disclosure.

Let me give an example. In dialogues between Theravadin Buddhist monks and Roman Catholic Benedictine monks, there has been from the Roman Catholic side a growing sense of the presence of the apophatic possibility of the presence of the Father, but a sense of this presence which deeply challenges the all too anthropomorphic sense of 'Father' so often employed in Christianity.[36] It has called into question many traditional Christologies apart from a radical kenotic Christology, and has served therefore in both the *enhancement* and the *destruction* of particular Christian identities through such conversation. Now the reason for choosing this single example from many others that could be used is to isolate this dialectic between enhancement and destruction, in which the same is radically configured and transfigured through the encounter with the Other and its sameness is thereby rendered both familiar and strange, a commentary perhaps and a question mark.

What is important about this dialectic is that it reflects the tradition of the development of doctrine, the deepening of faith. It finds its narrative roots in the pious young man's question to Jesus: 'Teacher, what good must I do to have eternal life?' (Matt 19:16). The young man is of course devout and serious and follows the law sensitively and honestly as reflected in his reply after Jesus has told him to keep the commandments: 'All these I have observed; what do I still lack?' (Matt 19:20). It is of course his sense of something Other, some as yet unfathomed trace present in his own keeping the law, his sense of some 'lack' which draws him into this further questioning. Jesus' reply is a deepening of understanding of those same commandments, yet is also acts to take him out of his understanding of it, so much so that the same is rendered so dramatically Other that we find that the young man can no longer understand or bear the demands of the invitation to this fresh understanding and practice in which the same is transformed by the Other, into something that is the same, yet different: 'When the young man heard this he went away sorrowful' (Matt 19:22). Hence, in this encounter in dialogue we find the young man incapable of hearing, although he has heard, incapable of the practice required of him, although he has already successfully practised and kept the commandments. It is little wonder that Abraham's acceptance of the security of God's promise led him out of his land, into insecurity, into the desert. And this can be interestingly contrasted with Ulysses' return to Ithaca, a circular movement that returns always to its own starting point.[37]

If the church is really a pilgrim church, it has the curious and disturbing task of seeking with the Other a fuller sense of truth through dialogue, while at the same time being the bearer of the truth of Jesus Christ, but a bearer of a truth which is not fully grasped and plumbed, and therefore never fully understood. (One theological implication of this is that 'religious studies' must always be a moment within 'theology' rather than an autonomous objective discipline.[38]) The purpose of this chapter has been to argue for a theological view of other religions which does not distort them into Sameness or Otherness (as negative Sameness), but abandons the binary logic of identification and control, for a trinitarian logic of relationship, freedom, love and service.

Acknowledgement

I am grateful to Nexus for allowing me to use and revise a text delivered as an 'Occasional Paper' (no. 6) in Birmingham: *Christianity and Distorted Visions of World Religions* (Birmingham: Nexus, 1995). I am also grateful for the feedback from that occasion.

Notes

1. Emmanuel Levinas in Alan Montefiore (ed.), *Philosophy in France Today* (Cambridge: Cambridge University Press, 1983), p. 103.
2. Bernard McGrane, *Beyond Anthropology: Society and the Other* (New York: Columbia University Press, 1989).
3. Emmanuel Levinas, *Totality and Infinity: An Essay on Exteriority* (Pittsburgh: Duquesne University Press, 1969); and see Graham Ward's most helpful article on Levinas, 'The revelation of the holy Other as the wholly Other: between Barth's theology of the word and Levinas' philosophy of saying', *Modern Theology*, 9.2 (1993), pp. 159–80. For Jacques Derrida, see *Of Grammatology* (Baltimore: Johns Hopkins University Press, 1976); the quotation is given on p. 3.
4. Edward Said, *Orientalism: Western Conceptions of the Orient* (London: Routledge & Kegan Paul, 1978). See Said's further comments in 'Orientalism reconsidered', and responses to him in Francis Barker *et al.* (eds), *Europe and Its Others* (2 vols; Colchester: University of Essex, 1985), vol. 1. Said's recent book *Culture and Imperialism* (London: Chatto & Windus, 1993) does not really advance his theoretical position beyond individualist humanism and suffers from over-schematization. See Ernst Gellner's incisive review of its shortcomings in *The Times Literary Supplement* (19 February 1993), pp. 3–4.
5. Rani Kabanni, *Europe's Myth of the Orient* (London: Macmillan, 1986).
6. See Gayatri Chakravorty Spivak, *In Other Worlds: Essays in Cultural Politics* (New York: Methuen, 1987); Homi K. Bhabha in 'The Other question: difference, discrimination and the discourse of colonialism' in Francis Barker *et al.* (eds), *Literature, Politics and Theory* (London: Methuen, 1986), pp. 182–96 and 'Signs and wonders: questions of ambivalence and authority under a tree outside Delhi, May 1817' in Barker *et al. Europe and Its Others*, vol. 1, pp. 89–106; and Spivak's 'The Rani of Sirmur', ibid., pp. 128–51.
7. See Michel Foucault, *Power/Knowledge: Selected Interviews and Other Writings 1972–77* (New York: Pantheon Books, 1980). Said, however, criticizes Foucault's Eurocentrism in 'Foucault and the imagination of power' in David C. Hoy (ed.), *Foucault: A Critical Reader* (Oxford: Blackwell, 1986), pp. 149–55, as does Spivak in *In Other Worlds*, pp. 209f.
8. See Tzvetan Todorov's important study which develops the themes I have been outlining above: *The Conquest of America* (New York: Harper & Row, 1984).
9. McGrane, *Beyond Anthropology*, p. ix. McGrane's use of 'his' ironically adds to the occlusion of the Other!
10. McGrane, *Beyond Anthropology*, p. ix.
11. McGrane, *Beyond Anthropology*, p. x.
12. See for example, Hilary Putnam, *Reason, Truth and History* (Cambridge: Cambridge University Press, 1981); Peter Berger, *A Rumour of Angels* (London: Penguin, 1970); and Ernst Gellner, *Postmodernism, Reason and Religion* (London: Routledge, 1992). While they make similar criticisms of

relativism, they of course defend very different notions of rationality and tradition.

13. McGrane, *Beyond Anthropology*, p. x.
14. For examples of the type of studies I have in mind, see Philip Almond, *The British Discovery of Buddhism* (Cambridge: Cambridge University Press, 1988); W. Montgomery Watt, *Christian–Muslim Relations: Perceptions and Misperceptions* (London: Routledge, 1991); Clinton Bennett, *Victorian Images of Islam* (London: Grey Seal, 1993); Wilhelm Halbfass, *India and Europe: An Essay in Understanding* (New York: State University Press of New York, 1988); Paul Hacker, 'Aspects of neo-Hinduism as contrasted with surviving traditional Hinduism' in the collection of his papers *Kleine Schriften*, ed. Lambert Schmithausen (Wiesbaden: Harrassowitz, 1978), pp. 580–608; see also the interesting way he analyses Schopenhauer's transmission of a distorted tradition (neo-Hinduism) in 'Schopenhauer und die Ethik des Hinduismus', ibid., pp. 531–64. (I am indebted to Dr Dermott Killingley for a translation of the latter.) There is of course the question as to the effect these images have on the imaged. See, for example, Hacker's discussion of neo-Hinduism, ibid., and Richard Gombrich's discussion of 'Protestant Buddhism', an amalgam of Western urban influences upon traditional Sri Lankan Buddhism: *Theravada Buddhism: A Social History from Ancient Benares to Modern Colombo* (London: Routledge & Kegan Paul, 1988), ch. 7.
15. McGrane, *Beyond Anthropology*, pp. 126–28.
16. See Kenneth Surin's main piece, 'A certain "politics of speech": "religious pluralism" in the age of the McDonald hamburger', *Modern Theology*, 7.1 (1990), pp. 67–100, subsequently referred to as *MT* (a shortened version of this appears in G. D'Costa (ed.), *Christian Uniqueness Reconsidered* (Maryknoll, NY: Orbis, 1991), pp. 192–212, and it is interesting to see what has been edited out from the former); and see also Surin's 'Towards a "materialist" critique of religious pluralism. An examination of the discourse of John Hick and Wilfred Cantwell Smith' in Ian Hamnett (ed.), *Religious Pluralism and Unbelief: Studies Critical and Comparative* (London: Routledge, 1990), pp. 114–29; and an earlier raid by Surin into this field: 'Revelation, salvation, the uniqueness of Christ and other religions', *Religious Studies*, 19 (1983), pp. 323–43. His criticism of George Lindbeck in another article of 1988 approaches the theology of religions in a very different manner: 'Many religions and the one true faith: an examination of Lindbeck's chapter 3', *Modern Theology* 4.January (1988), pp. 187–209. D. Lochhead, *The Dialogical Imperative: A Christian Reflection on Interfaith Dialogue* (London: SCM, 1988), and David J. Krieger, *The New Universalism: Foundations for a Global Theology* (Maryknoll, NY: Orbis, 1991) both take these issues seriously but Surin's thesis remains the most radical and searching and certainly raises questions about Krieger's careful pretensions to universal discourse.
17. Surin, *MT*, p. 77, referring to John Hick, *An Interpretation of Religion* (London: Macmillan, 1989). I have suggested a similar reading of Hick's

work in 'Taking other religions seriously: some ironies in the current debate on a Christian theology of religions', *The Thomist*, 54.3 (1990), pp. 519–29, as has Gerard Loughlin (to whom I am indebted), 'Prefacing pluralism: John Hick and the mastery of religion', *Modern Theology*, 7.1 (1990), pp. 29–57. Hick responds to Loughlin in the same issue, pp. 57–67. I use the terms pluralism, exclusivism and inclusivism as defined in G. D'Costa, *Theology and Religious Pluralism* (Oxford: Basil Blackwell, 1986).

18. Surin, *MT*, p. 92. I have replaced 'him' with 'the' in the citation.
19. Again, it is interesting to note what Surin has omitted in the *MT* piece as reduced for D'Costa (ed.), *Christian Uniqueness Reconsidered*.
20. Surin, *MT*, p. 70.
21. Surin, *MT*, p. 91.
22. Surin, *MT*, p. 80.
23. Surin, *MT*, p. 77.
24. Surin, *MT*, p. 69, citing Kraemer, *Why Christianity of All Religions?* (Philadelphia: Westminster Press, 1962), p. 22. He cites another text by Kraemer in note 8: *World Cultures and World Religions: The Coming Dialogue* (Philadelphia: Westminster Press, 1960), p. 15, although this does not substantiate his point, but rather indicates Kraemer's sensitivity to ethnocentricism.
25. For the background to Kraemer with respect to this point see O. Jathanna, *The Decisiveness of the Christ Event and the Universality of Christianity in a World of Religious Plurality* (Berne: P. Lang, 1981). Kraemer is far too aware of the disruptive and changing situation in the modern world to be fitted into Surin's characterization of him. After noting that there is an interpenetration of economic, political and social culture, between East and West, he summarizes thus: 'The two situations can be summed up in a single phrase which sounds harmless but is full of explosive and auspicious possibilities: Orient and Occident are both in a process of re-evaluation of themselves and of one another': *World Cultures*, p. 15; see also Kraemer's *The Christian Message in a Non-Christian World* (Edinburgh: Edinburgh House Press, 1938), ch. 1 and his shrewd cultural and political analysis of India, China, Japan, North Africa, Egypt, Turkey and Persia (pp. 229–84, 336–403) and his later review of the changes in these countries, in *World Cultures*, chs 5–10. His views on the Christian Church in the 'developing world' equally run counter to Surin's categorization. See *The Christian Message*, pp. 415–43. There is more truth in Surin's comments about the early Rahner, who himself later admits his being raised in the context of nineteenth-century liberal individualism, but coming to realize that this background was not adequate. Metz played a significant part in helping Rahner see this. See Rahner, *I Remember* (London: SCM, 1985), pp. 76–80, 91–3; 'Basic communities', *Theological Investigations*, vol. 19 (London: Darton, Longman & Todd [as all volumes of *Theological Investigations*], 1984), pp. 159–66; 'Aspects of European theology', *Theological Investigations*, vol. 21 (1988), pp. 78–98; and 'Justification and world development from a Catholic viewpoint', *Theological Investigations*, vol. 18 (1984), pp. 259–74.

26. See for example Carl Braaeten, *No Other Gospel: Christianity Among the World Religions* (Minneapolis: Fortress, 1992); D. Clark, D. Melvin *et al.* (eds), *Proceedings of the Wheaton Theological Conference: The Challenge of Religious Pluralism, An Evangelical Analysis and Response* (Wheaton: Wheaton Theology Conference, vol. 1, Spring 1992).

27. Surin, *MT*, p. 91.

28. See Francis A. Sullivan, *Salvation Outside the Church? Tracing the History of the Catholic Response* (London: Geoffrey Chapman, 1992); Louis Capéran, *Le Problème du salut des infidèles, Essai historique* (2 vols; Toulouse: Grand Séminaire, 1934).

29. Surin, *MT*, p. 91.

30. Surin seems to recognize his implicit pretension towards a master discourse when he says 'This is not to say that there is no place for such theological formulation': *MT*, p. 80. However, it is not clear what this would amount to.

31. See George A. Lindbeck, *The Nature of Doctrine: Religion and Theology in a Postliberal Age* (London: SPCK, 1984), especially pp. 32–46, 74–84, 104–11. Rahner's transcendental anthropology is centred on the existential translation of all doctrinal statements. In this sense it is far from theory as opposed to practice, although Surin is right in saying that it is perhaps not so sensitive to the political implications of doctrine. See P. Mann, 'The transcendental or the political kingdom', *New Blackfriars*, 50 (1968/69), pp. 805–12. For Kraemer, see *The Christian Message*, pp. 61–100, where Kraemer actually criticizes theology which is divorced from practice.

32. Las Casas did not see the Indians as 'different' as far as their humanity was concerned, but he certainly saw them in a different stage in the cultural process from barbarian to civilized, pagan to Christian. See Anthony Pagden, *European Encounters with the New World* (New Haven and London: Yale University Press, 1993), especially pp. 51–89.

33. In Raoul Mortley, *French Philosophers in Conversation* (London: Routledge, 1991), p. 99.

34. I have not included this position in my analysis because of its internal lack of intelligibility! See Paul Griffiths, *An Apology for Apologetics* (Maryknoll, NY: Orbis, 1991), pp. 31–6, where he rightly argues that this position is incoherent and unsustainable.

35. See G. D'Costa, 'Revelation and revelations: discerning God in other religions. Beyond a static valuation', *Modern Theology*, 10.2 (1994), pp. 165–84; 'Christ, the trinity and religious plurality' in G. D'Costa (ed.), *Christian Uniqueness Reconsidered*, pp. 16–29; 'Towards a trinitarian theology of religions' in Catherine Cornille and Valeer Neckbrouck (eds), *A Universal Faith? Peoples, Cultures, Religions, and the Christ* (Louvain: Peeters Press/Grand Rapids, MI: Eerdmans, 1990), pp. 139–55.

36. See Benedictine–Buddhist dialogues; and also R. Panikkar, *The Silence of God: The Answer of the Buddha* (Maryknoll, NY: Orbis, 1989); D. Tracy, *Dialogue with the Other: The Interreligious Dialogue* (Louvain: Peeters Press/Grand Rapids, MI: Eerdmans, 1990), ch. 4.

37. Levinas writes: 'To the myth of Ulysses returning to Ithaca, we would like to

oppose the story of Abraham leaving his homeland forever for a still unknown land and even forbidding his son to be brought back to its point of departure': *En découvrant l'existence avec Husserl et Heidegger* (3rd edn; Paris: Vrin, 1974), p. 191; as translated and quoted by S. Critchley, *The Ethics of Deconstruction: Derrida and Levinas* (Oxford, Basil Blackwell, 1992), p. 109.

38. This claim has serious implications for the suspect claim made by *some* forms of 'Religious studies' to offer neutral methods of retrieval and representation. See G. D'Costa, 'The end of theology and religious studies', *Theology* XCIX.791 (1996), pp. 338–51.

3

Biodiversity and responsibility

A basis for a non-violent environmental ethic

Anne Primavesi

The critical theorist Zygmunt Bauman has said that the postmodern approach to morality is all too often a celebration of the 'demise of the ethical'. Ethics itself is 'denigrated or derided as one of the typically modern constraints now broken and destined for the dustbin of history'. Some of the fragments are marked 'duties', 'absolute obligations', 'the idea of self-sacrifice'.[1]

Against this bleak background I want to ask: 'What are these fragments of? What was the cohesive power which once held them together?' Bauman suggests that it was a traditional way of life, a life lived as if validated by powers no human will or whim could challenge; a life seen as a product of divine creation, monitored by divine providence. Free will meant freedom to choose wrong over right – that is, to break commandments, to deny obligations, to disobey those who administered God's way for the world. Being in the right, on the other hand, was not a matter of choice: it meant, rather, *avoiding* choice, being obedient, following the customary way of life.[2]

Postmodern theologies, feminist, political and practical, have shown that presupposed in this way of life and this self-perception lay a particular theology of sin, one focused on the destructive elements in the human desire for self-realization and freedom. Pride, *the* sin, was equated with the desire for autonomy; was taken as evidence of corrupted will.[3] The fault lines (in every sense of the analogy) in this view of human conduct, in which choice was equated with wrong-doing, contributed to its fragmentation.

An allied fragmentation occurred in the validation of the traditional view of life as one monitored by divine providence. Can we speak in the same way of obedience, of free will, of moral law or of the word 'God' after Auschwitz, after the Gulag, after Cambodia or what we have seen happen in the former Yugoslavia?[4] The denial of obligation by those involved forces us to what Hans Jonas describes as the 'imperative of responsibility'. He says that the tacit interconnected premises of all previous ethics presupposed that the human condition, determined by the nature of the human being and the nature of things, was given once for all; that the range of human action and therefore responsibility was narrowly circumscribed. These premises, he said, no longer hold. Modern technology has introduced actions of such novel scale and consequences that the framework of former ethics can no longer contain them. To honour the laws of the land is no longer enough, and the gods whose venerable right could check the headlong rush of human action are long gone.[5]

Instead, we share a way of life today characterized by choosing one action rather than another, by the presupposition that the good life is the product of good/right choices made by us rather than for us by divine laws. The ability to make choices is the basis of the 'free' market economy, in which the 'freedom' of students, travellers, consumers or surfers on the Internet means that we are constantly coerced or cajoled into choosing one product or option over another. In a postmodern world we are continually asked to choose between actions, between commands on computer displays, between therapies, between manufactured desires and real needs, between long-term solutions and short-term gains, between being indifferent to and being responsible for our own well-being or that of others.

This perceived freedom is, of course, limited by the fact that it is confined, almost exclusively, to those of a certain income, education and status. The Brazilian theologian Ivone Gebara, who has lived in a poor neighbourhood in north-east Brazil, says she has learnt how hard it is to speak about 'choice', that most often poor women in particular have no choice, and the liberal understanding of freedom is far from their reality. They are forced to live in poverty, to eat whatever they can obtain, to work at whatever they can find. When you live daily only to survive, she says, you do not think of yourself as a citizen in a position to choose, especially in relation to political and economic issues.[6]

All of us, no matter where we live, are subject to personal and social as well as economic restraints. Furthermore, there is a growing awareness, which can act as another restraint, that the freedoms offered to us in the consumerist culture are bought at the price of economic and social captivity for others. Nevertheless, even within these limitations, we are constantly presented with the need to make choices: about lifestyle; about relationships; about education; about resources and their use. In order to make responsible choices, we need to be able to assess, compare and evaluate a diversity of options. To find a basis for assessment and evaluation, I shall look at the concept of diversity itself. Why do we have so many choices to make? Then I shall look at our responses to this diversity. Do we feel threatened by having to choose between different options, do we respond to this defensively, or with apathy and indifference? Or offensively, with rage and violence?

I shall take the scientific concept of biodiversity as one which gives diversity a positive value, and explore some of the implications of this for an ethical framework. Our interdependence with the dynamism of the natural world is taken as related to the dynamism of our ability to experience and to apprehend that world. Both are then seen as part of the contemporary theological agenda (the praxis and faith to be reflected upon), which aims to bring action and reflection together in functional as well as intellectual coherence.[7]

Then I shall look at some of the implications of Emmanuel Levinas's presentation of philosophy as ethics, at his description of the ethical relation between people as the only place where God passes, as the only place where we find not the presence, nor the evidence, but only the trace of God's passing. He calls the ethical relation between persons 'the singular epiphany' of God. The mode of this relation is for him necessarily non-violent. His acknowledgement that to restrict responsibility for others to *certain* others only would have the effect of subduing the otherness of the Other in advance does not prevent him, as we shall see, from confining the ethical relation to person-to-person relationships. For me, however, this would have the effect of subduing the other-directedness which is implicit in ethical relationships. I shall therefore expand our ethical relationships (in line with Jonas's imperative and the self-understanding inherent in biodiversity) to include those we have with the non-human world.[8] This will, I hope, offer a framework for a non-violent environmental ethic.

Biodiversity, a term coined by the scientist Elliott Norse, simply means the diversity of life. It is the key to the maintenance of the world as we know it. It holds the world steady.[9] It enhances the potential for survival, the chances of new modes of life, the richness of forms. It should be interpreted in the sense of the ability to co-exist, to co-evolve and co-operate in complex relationships. Ecologically inspired attitudes favour, therefore, diversity in human ways of living, in cultures, in occupations, in economies.[10]

Norse envisions this diversity at three levels which have become standard in environmental discourse: the species level, the genetic level and the ecosystem level. *Species diversity* is the diversity of species within a particular area or within a taxonomic group of organisms: for example, the number of species within the cat family, or the orchid family: the number of species in the Cheddar Gorge or in the state of British Columbia.

Genetic diversity within species, within populations and within populations of a given species is the diversity created by variations in the genetic inheritance of a species which may evolve over a long period of time or may result as an immediate response to some outside force, such as radiation.

Ecosystem diversity is the diversity of communities of organisms in their physical setting. This kind of diversity derives from and is affected by the nature of the ecosystems themselves. The co-evolution of organisms and their environment gives us marine, urban, tropical, low-technology, wild or cultivated ecosystems.[11]

All three levels of biodiversity are essential for the functioning of the physical and living systems of the earth, their interactions with each other and with the well-being of humankind. The emphasis in environmental programmes has shifted from species diversity to ecosystem diversity. Numerical abundance as such, that is, multiplication of similar entities, does not count as diversity here. Biological diversity includes *complexity* (a quality of organisms and their co-evolution and co-operation with the environment) and *symbiosis* (their co-operation and life together).[12]

I want to say at the outset that biodiversity is a fact of life, not primarily a logical, scientific or philosophical construct, a tool of gender analysis or a theory which attempts to deal either with the shortcomings of egalitarianism and/or the demands of pluralism, although it does play a part in all of these postmodern concerns. The concept of diversity may help us to articulate problems arising from the perceived demands, within postmodernism, of living with difference, however experienced. It may encourage us to name our experience of God differently, or give us another perspective on our self-differentiation as a species. But our primary experience of diversity is as the matrix which sustains our capacity for life within the world we inhabit. It is a given, like the orbit of the earth around the sun. Named or not named by us, remembered or not remembered by us, taken into account or not, it sustains every life form on the planet.

Part of its potential for us, however, is that in learning to understand its geophysiological function, its role in maintaining the ability of the whole planet to regulate significant variables such as temperature and chemical composition, we find ways of understanding, thinking and talking about pluralities, commonalities and creative differences in our relationships with others and, I would say, with God. But part of the shift in self-perception which results from taking biodiversity seriously is the realization that what we as a species think or say about it is secondary to its significance within the geophysiological environment of communities of living organisms which constitute our planetary ecosystem.[13]

The second presupposition of this chapter follows from this. Talking or thinking about biodiversity is no substitute for personal experience of it, reflection on that experience and action based on that experience and reflection. We need to dwell with diversity before we translate it into useful categories for communication, for understanding or for choosing our lifestyle. Dwelling with it, in the way I mean, opens us up directly to its mystery and to its reality. It moves us beyond satisfaction with intellectual coherence into commitment to functional coherence. The ultimate test of a world view is its verification through functional viability.[14]

The global scientific assessment of biodiversity has been expressed in political and scientific programmes for safeguarding it, for preserving it from violence and destruction. A theological commitment at the very least raises questions about religious traditions which legitimate thought and actions destructive to the ecological integrity of our earth community. Positively, it encourages us, indeed requires us, to look to other religious disciplines and cultures for ways of preserving the matrix of biodiversity from violence and destruction. If anything at all on earth is sacred, it must be this enthralling vitality and diversity that characterize life on this planet. 'The sacred is not so much a building or an institution as an event, something that happens.'[15] If anywhere, here is the brooding Spirit of God. We have inherited landscapes in which, after several billion years of creative toil which had nothing to do with satisfying human desires, several million species of teeming life emerged and co-evolved until we, a late-coming species, also emerged. To think that the world is nothing but a human resource is, as God pointed out to Job, above all a theological error. Its diverse inhabitants do not belong to us, either as persons or as nations, but to themselves and to God. Noah was not told to save those species that are of 'aesthetic, ecological, educational, historical, recreational and scientific value' to people. He was commanded to save them *all* when they were threatened by human corruption.[16]

The shift of emphasis to the ecosystem, accompanied by the acceptance that the individual or the species can only survive within a viable ecosystem, parallels the shift from an emphasis on ethics in the abstract, as a set of ideas or reflexive, second-order activity to an emphasis on ethical relationships within the ecosystem. In a discussion of the genealogy of Christian ethics, Wayne Meeks reminds us of a central insight from Aristotle: individuals do not become moral agents except in the relationships, the transactions, the habits and reinforcements, the special uses of language and gesture that constitute life in community.[17] The complexity of communities, of life support systems, is such that no single ethical code can apply universally. Rather, the *quality* of ethical relationships becomes paramount.[18]

The key quality I want to stress in ethical relationships is responsibility, responsibility as a particular kind of responding to biodiversity in my species and in my ecosystem. My response is, consciously or not, shaped by my belonging there in a state of 'inter-esse' (Levinas), interbeing (Thich Nhat Hanh), in which my inter-ests, my interbeing are contingent on the reality of being sustained in an ecosystem I share not only with those of my own species but with myriads of others.[19] Only some of them are known to me, only some are visible and tangible, only some have faces I recognize. How do I exercise responsibility when I am part of so many different wholes? In what spirit do I respond?

The short answer is non-violent response in the spirit of compassion. Response to the Other in this way constitutes the ethical relationship required by biodiversity. Anything else has the potential not only to destroy the object of violence, but ultimately, myself. This destruction occurs at many levels: the personal, the interpersonal, the transpersonal and the communal, the individual and the systemic. All of these levels denote relationships which can be characterized as feedback loops, expressed by scientists as non-linear equations which embody the non-linear reality which is most of our world. These equations address the 'many-body' problem which arises when, in complex systems, we have to add terms to the ideal, two-body system. One type of feedback regulates and the other amplifies the interactions. The perception that the smallest perturbation can be magnified through feedback recognizes an essential tension between order and chaos which, if we take account of it, gives our responsibility for a non-violent ethic further dimensions. The physicist David Peat writes that it is now recognized that the two basic kinds of feedback are everywhere: at all levels of living systems, in the evolution of the ecology, in the moment-by-moment psychology of our social interaction, and in the mathematical terms of the non-linear equations.[20]

The responsibility for the quality of our interactions is given a religious formulation by Levinas. He sees his life's work in proclaiming the primacy of ethics as saying:

The law of God is revelation because it proclaims: You shall not kill. All the rest is perhaps an effort to think that thing – an indeed necessary staging of the scene, a culture where that thing can be understood. It is that which I try to say. 'You shall not kill' means of course 'You shall do everything so that the other lives'.[21]

The image of 'the face' stands in Levinas for what one cannot kill, or at least it is that whose meaning consists in saying 'thou shalt not kill'. Murder, it is true, is a fact. One *can* kill the Other. The prohibition against killing does not render murder impossible. It renders it evil. One can kill, but it is universally acknowledged that it is 'better' not to kill.[22] The moral law still holds, because the face of the sufferer remains, calling us to responsibility. This resonates with Gandhi's advice:

Whenever you are in doubt, apply the following test: recall the face of the poorest and the weakest person you may have seen, and ask yourself if the step you contemplate is going to be of any use to that person.

The face of the sufferer, for Levinas and for theology after Auschwitz, expresses the fact that in the Holocaust the moral law was not destroyed but violated. The moral law stands because the evidence of its violation is still there within the face of the sufferer.

Then, says Levinas, God must be in the moral law. Either God is there, or God is nowhere. God must be conceived strictly in ethical terms because this is the only way to think of God, through the face of the sufferer whose suffering is beyond all theodicy. The trace of God, says Levinas, is the face's commandment to be responsible for and to love the Other. He insists that only because there is still this commandment after the Holocaust is there still God after the Holocaust.[23]

The painful weight of Levinas's thought leads to an expanded reading of an established environmental classic, Aldo Leopold's *A Sand County Almanac*. First published in 1949, a year after his death, it is a record of his conviction that conservation was getting nowhere because it is incompatible with our concept of land. We abuse land, he said, because we regard it as a commodity belonging to us. Were we to see land as a community to which we belong, we might, he said hopefully, begin to use it with love and respect. That land is a community is the basic concept of ecology, but that land is to be loved and respected is an extension of ethics.

In a famous passage he presents us with the reality of our responsibility for the destruction of biodiversity as it is understood today. He describes a wolf howl as 'an outburst of wild defiant sorrow and of contempt for all the adversities of the world'. His interpretation stemmed from his experience of seeing a wolf die. He and some companions were eating lunch on a high rimrock, at the foot of which a turbulent river elbowed its way. They saw what they thought was a doe fording the torrent. When she climbed the bank towards them and shook out her tail, they realized it was a wolf. A half-dozen others, evidently grown pups, sprang from the willows and all joined in a welcoming *mêlée* of wagging tails and playful maulings.

> In a second we were pumping lead into the pack, but with more excitement than accuracy. When our rifles were empty, the old wolf was down, and a pup was dragging a leg into impassable slide-rocks. We reached the old wolf in time to watch a fierce green fire dying in her eyes. I realized then, and have known ever since, that there was something new to me in those eyes – something known only to her and to the mountain. I was young then, and full of trigger itch. I thought that because fewer wolves meant more deer, that no wolves would mean hunters' paradise. But after seeing the green fire die, I sensed that neither the wolf nor the mountain agreed with me.[24]

Leopold goes on to say that the extension of ethics to include other species is actually a process in ecological evolution which has its origin in the tendency of interdependent individuals or groups to evolve modes of co-operation. This is symbiosis – the complex co-operative mechanisms which evolve between organisms and their environments. There is as yet, he said in 1948, no ethic dealing with man's relation to the land and to the animals and plants which grow upon it. The land-relation is still strictly economic, entailing privileges but not obligations. The extension of ethics to this third dimension is, he said, an evolutionary possibility and an ecological necessity. All ethics so far evolved rest upon a single premise: that the individual is a member of a community of interdependent parts. The land ethic simply enlarges the boundaries of the community to include soils, waters, plants and animals – the diversity of life in all its manifestations.[25]

Levinas's concept of interessence, a 'being-linked' of all entities whose interrelations are determined by each being's endeavour to maintain and expend its own existence, infers that if the non-violent ethical relation between humans is the trace of God, and that trace is 'the proximity of God in the face of the other', then the quality of that relation must inform all our interbeing. So when he writes that 'the expression the face introduces into the world does not defy the feebleness of my powers, but my ability for power', isn't this the 'wild, defiant sorrow' Leopold heard in the cry of the wolf? When Levinas writes 'The infinite paralyses power by its infinite resistance to murder, which, firm and insurmountable, gleams in the face of the Other, in the total nudity of his defenceless eyes', isn't this the fierce green fire seen by Leopold?[26] To use Levinas's language, isn't God the one who commands us to be responsible for and to love the cosmos? Doesn't 'you shall do everything so that the other lives' extend to the wolf, the lamb and the child?[27]

The trace left on Leopold's memory by the face of the dying wolf was a revelation to him of the part played by the wolf within its ecosystem. It is one of the sombre facts about biodiversity that its loss, rather than its presence, has revealed its value to us. In this rather negative way we have come to appreciate what the loss of any level of biodiversity might mean for our material and non-material well-being. World-wide response to the loss of biodiversity has been slow, even after the signing of the Convention on Biological Diversity. It calls for responsibility that goes beyond what I do to the attitudes which inform all my relationships. From the perspective of an environmental ethic, it embraces how I live, the kind of choices I make about lifestyle and my approach to consumerism. It involves asking myself certain questions when making these choices: Who benefits? Who loses? What do I contribute? What do I sacrifice? Is my spirituality other-directed? Do those others include not only human beings but all living creatures as the site of transcendence? Is the God of my theology the Exodus God whom we know by accepting responsibility for all others in exodus and wandering: all with whom we share the earth, that is, the other, the neighbour and resident alien, and not only, notice, the friend?[28] Nor is my responsibility limited to those whose faces I can see. The complexity of our interbeing within an ecosystem is such that we cannot limit our responsibility to those nearest us. World-wide webs of trade, pollution and resources connect us to others we never see or meet.

A particularly theological response would be the valuing of diversity within and between religious traditions. This would mean far more than peaceful discussion at conferences. It would mean facing the hostility and wars between religions as a contributory factor in the destruction of biodiversity. The landscape in the former Yugoslavia is broken up into enclaves which correspond all too closely to the religious ones. The land is ploughed by tanks, sown with landmines. The poisoning of the ecumenical substratum in Sarajevo has ensured destruction of its multifaith diversity.

Religion is a major factor in peace and war. The challenge for religions today is to make human beings more peaceful.[29] This peace, says Levinas, cannot be identified with the end of combats that cease for want of combatants, by the defeat of some and the victory of others, that is, with cemeteries or future universal empires. Peace must be my peace, in a relation that starts from an I and goes to the Other in desire and goodness. It starts from an I assured of the convergence of morality and reality.[30]

Notes

1. Zygmunt Bauman, *Postmodern Ethics* (Oxford: Basil Blackwell, 1993), p. 2.
2. Zygmunt Bauman, *Postmodern Ethics*, p. 4.
3. See, for example, Valerie Saiving, 'The human situation: a feminine view' in Carol P. Christ and Judith Plaskow (eds), *Womanspirit Rising* (New York: Harper and Row, 1979), pp. 25–43; Dorothee Soelle, *Thinking About God* (London: SCM, 1990), pp. 56f.
4. Robert Manning writes of Levinas that he conceives the Holocaust as the great overthrow of theology, the end of God conceived as the greatest of all

beings. The Holocaust is that supreme event of suffering that shows once and for all that suffering exceeds any and every attempt to make it bearable and meaningful. Levinas does not mean that the Holocaust is the *only* event that destroys theodicy and the traditional conception of God on which theodicy is based; rather, he says that the Holocaust is paradigmatic of the catastrophic events in this century, such as the Gulag and Cambodia, which also mean the end of theodicy: Robert Manning, *Interpreting Otherwise than Heidegger* (Pittsburgh: Duquesne University Press, 1993), p. 151.

5. Hans Jonas, *The Imperative of Responsibility: In Search of an Ethics for the Technological Age* (Chicago: University of Chicago Press, 1984), pp. 1–8.

6. Ivone Gebara, 'The abortion debate in Brazil', *Journal of Feminist Studies in Religion*, 2.2 (1995), p. 130. The particular plight of women, children, the poor and indigenous peoples is recognized in Agenda 21 of the 1992 United Nations Conference on Environment and Development.

7. See Laurent Leduc, 'Environmental studies and religion: an ecotheological perspective', paper presented to the Environmental Studies Association of Canada Conference, Brock University, St Catherine's, Ontario, 2–5 June 1996.

8. Bernard Waldenfels, 'Response and responsibility' in Adrian Peperzak (ed.), *Ethics as First Philosophy: The Significance of Emmanuel Levinas for Philosophy, Literature and Religion* (London: Routledge, 1995), p. 49.

9. Edward Wilson, *The Diversity of Life* (Cambridge, MA: Belknap Press of Harvard University Press, 1992), p. 15. See also p. 393: biodiversity is 'the variety of organisms considered at all levels, from genetic variants belonging to the same species through arrays of species to arrays of genera, families, and still higher taxonomic levels; includes the variety of ecosystems, which comprise both the communities of organisms within particular habitats and the physical conditions under which they live'.

10. Arne Naess, 'Deep ecology' in Carolyn Merchant (ed.), *Ecology: Key Concepts in Critical Theory* (Atlantic Highlands, NJ: Humanities Press, 1994), p. 121.

11. Transcript of Elliott Norse's testimony before the Supreme Court of British Columbia, Vancouver, 10 February 1994, at the trial of eight Greenpeace defendants arrested at Clayoquot Sound, British Columbia. Norse's categorization has been accepted as normative in the United Nations Environment Programme and its Global Biodiversity Assessment, and in discussions of its implications. See, for example, V. H. Heywood (ed.), *Global Biodiversity Assessment* (Cambridge: Cambridge University Press, 1995). For an overview of the importance of biodiversity and the change in world-view and self-perception needed to preserve and restore it, see Lawrence S. Hamilton (ed.), *Ethics, Religion and Biodiversity* (Cambridge: White Horse Press, 1993), especially pp. 183–214.

12. Arne Naess, *Ecology, Community and Lifestyle* (Cambridge: Cambridge University Press, 1989), p. 22f.

13. See James Lovelock, 'A numerical model for biodiversity', *Philosophical Transactions*, Royal Society, B.338 (1992), pp. 383–91.

14. Leduc, 'Environmental studies and religion'.
15. Dorothee Soelle, *The Window of Vulnerability* (Philadelphia: Fortress Press, 1990), p. 24.
16. Holmes Rolston III, 'God and endangered species' in Hamilton (ed.), *Ethics, Religion and Biodiversity*, pp. 44, 60f.
17. Wayne Meeks, *The Origins of Christian Morality* (New Haven and London: Yale University Press, 1993), pp. 7–13.
18. The rights model, for instance, has served those well who have been able to pursue their rights in court. But what of those who cannot? And what of the fact that human rights as presently formulated and legislated for do not coincide with human needs? So in the Universal Declaration on Human Rights everyone (supposedly) has the right to life, liberty and security of person. But what of clean air, water, sleep, shelter, clothes, sex, protection from climate, from diseases, from heavy, degrading and boring work? These have been classified by Johan Galtung as survival needs – preservation from violence; well-being needs – preservation from misery; identity needs – preservation from alienation; freedom needs – preservation from repression: see Johan Galtung, *Human Rights in Another Key* (Cambridge: Polity Press, 1994), pp. 70–107.
19. On Levinas's use of the term 'interesse' see Peperzak, *Ethics as First Philosophy*, p. 189. See Thich Nhat Hanh, *The Heart of Understanding* (Berkeley, CA: Parallax Press, 1988), pp. 3–5.
20. See John Briggs and David Peat, *Turbulent Mirror: An Illustrated Guide to Chaos Theory and the Science of Wholeness* (New York: Harper and Row, 1989), pp. 24–9.
21. Emmanuel Levinas, *Transcendance et Intelligibilité* (Geneva: Editions Labor et Fides, 1984), p. 41.
22. Emmanuel Levinas, *Ethics and Infinity* (Pittsburgh: Duquesne University Press, 1985), pp. 10, 86.
23. Manning, *Interpreting Otherwise than Heidegger*, pp. 153f.
24. Aldo Leopold, *A Sand County Almanac* (New York: Ballantine Books, 1991), pp. 137–9.
25. Leopold, *A Sand County Almanac*, pp. 238–9.
26. Emmanuel Levinas, *Totality and Infinity* (Pittsburgh: Duquesne University Press, 1969), pp. 196–9.
27. This undoubtedly goes beyond Levinas's own intent. See Peperzak, *Ethics as First Philosophy*, pp. 189, 156f. For a sympathetic view of why, in the light of his own history, he refused to extend his ethics to the non-human world, on the grounds that the being of a human being is absolutely different from anything else, see Manning, *Interpreting Otherwise than Heidegger*, pp. 155–7. Like Manning, however, I see no reason why Levinas's logic and terminology should not be extended to consider other 'traces' of God than the ethical relationship between persons. See also John Llewelyn's detailed discussion of the area of agreement between Levinas and Kant on the human face as the only one in which there is a trace of any being to which we can be directly beholden: John Llewelyn, *The Middle Voice of Ecological Conscience: A*

Chiasmic Reading of Responsibility in the Neighbourhood of Levinas, Heidegger and Others (London: Macmillan, 1991), pp. 49–67.
28. David Tracy, 'Response to Adrian Peperzak on transcendence' in Peperzak, *Ethics as First Philosophy*, pp. 194f.
29. See Johan Galtung, 'The challenge of religion' in Alan Race and Roger Williamson (eds), *True to This Earth: Global Challenges and Transforming Faith* (Oxford: Oneworld, 1995), pp. 63–75. See also my systematization of non-violent theological communication in 'Accepting diversity: healing a violent world' in Michael Cordner (ed.), *Pastoral Theology's and Pastoral Psychology's Contributions to Helping Heal a Violent World* (Surakarta, Indonesia: Dabara Publishers, 1996), pp. 11–20.
30. Levinas, *Totality and Infinity*, p. 306.

4

Gender equity and Christianity

Premodern roots, modern and postmodern perspectives

Rosemary Radford Ruether

Before one can speak about modern and postmodern perspectives on gender equity in Christianity it is necessary first to define this question in its premodern context and world view which to a large extent still continue in traditional Christianity today. Thus, one must first understand this premodern world view of gender and how this shaped and limited the distinctive insights of the Christian message of redemption in Christ.[1]

Christianity was shaped by a pervasively patriarchal world in both a Hebrew and a Graeco-Roman form. Patriarchy means 'the rule of the patriarch' or male head of family. Family in the Hebrew and Graeco-Roman context did not mean the nuclear privatized family of modern industrialism, but an extended multi-generational kin network situated in a slave-owning household that was the basic productive unit of society. In Roman law the term *familia* included wife and children, slaves, animals and land. *Familia* meant all those people and things over which the *paterfamilias* ruled as lord.[2]

In Roman law all of these persons and things were property at the disposal of the patriarch over which he held sovereign power. He could beat, imprison, kill or sell these persons, although this was limited by other social constraints in the case of his legal wife and children. Females in this system of patriarchal rule were defined in relation to him, as his wife, his daughters or his female slaves. All were defined in different ways, by their sexual, reproductive, work or household management roles and limited to the household by these roles.

The power roles in public life, political, military, cultural and religious, were reserved for men of the ruling class. Women were excluded from higher education, educated professions, and political and military leadership. In the Graeco-Roman world, women might have cultic roles, but these pertained primarily to their female sphere. In pre-70 CE Judaism the temple priesthood was reserved for men. Women were marginalized by purity laws from the inner precincts of the temple.

Study to prepare for the rabbinate also came to exclude women, although there was dispute about this in the first century. There is evidence from Philo and rabbinic tradition of women who studied Torah, and inscriptions show that wealthy women were patrons of synagogues.[3] Gender roles were in some flux in first-century Judaism, and this flux is reflected in early Christianity. Openness to women's leadership as teachers, prophets and patrons of churches in early Christianity should be seen, not as a departure from a monolithically patriarchal Judaism, but rather as an expression of diversity within Judaism of the time.[4]

The early Jesus movement was shaped by a combination of sapiential and apocalyptic Judaisms. It nourished both a vivid expectation that the Kingdom of God was about to dawn and that its crucified teacher would return as the Messianic Son of Man and a belief that God's saving power was already present. The risen Christ whose future advent was expected was also the Word and wisdom of God through whom the world was created in the beginning. Christians reborn through Christ's resurrection and the outpoured Spirit already communed with God in a spiritually restored cosmos.

This fusion of horizons of an eschatological future and a restored creation was expressed in a belief that the social divisions of pure and impure, male and female, Jew and gentile, slave and free had already dissolved. The diseased and broken are healed, the poor lifted up and the mighty put down from their thrones. The power of the demonic has been broken, although the full manifestation of its victory is yet to come. Yet here and now redemption can be tasted in healing miracles and spiritual gifts and in celebratory meals where all share as equals across the former lines of division.[5]

These experiences of inclusive community that broke down the former divisions were expressed in a baptismal theology that pointed both back to origins and forward to fulfilled messianism. The notions that gender divisions were overcome, that women could prophesy and heal, travel on itinerant missionary journeys and take leadership roles in local communities was an early but also contested expression of this notion of equality in Christ. How the other terms for this equality, Jew and gentile, slave and free, were interpreted so they lost a prophetic meaning in a consolidated Christian society could also be the subject of extensive studies, but in this chapter I will focus on the fate of the gender pair in the baptismal formula, that 'In Christ there is no more male and female'.

The world of early Christianity was structured not only socially but ideologically by patriarchy. Social hierarchies were presumed to reflect the cosmic order created by God. God rules the world much as the patriarch rules the family and the emperor the state. The laws of society follow the laws of the cosmos given by God. The modern notion that these social structures are human constructions, not divinely ordained necessities, was unthinkable.

Yet there were also critical thinkers among Graeco-Roman philosophers who questioned whether women, slaves and barbarians were intrinsically inferior and 'naturally' under subjection. The conquered peoples of the Near East, Jews, Greeks, Egyptians and others, were restive under Roman imperialism and disinclined to believe that its rule reflected the mandate of heaven. The fusion of Jewish prophetic-apocalyptic thought with Hellenistic Jewish mystical philosophy offered several ways of imagining a new world order where given gender hierarchies were transcended.

One way of thinking about this came from Philonic philosophy. Philo taught that the human was first created in a spiritually unitary form as image of the divine Logos. Only when the masculine intellect failed to rule over the feminine affective part of the soul, but was seduced by it, did gender division arise. The female was separated out from the male as an expression of the fall into sin. Only then did sex, sin and death appear. The unitary image of God is the primary expression of the human, while male and female is a later devolution.[6] Philo believed that through celibacy the human, male or female, could be restored to this original spiritual unity and saw this expressed in the Therapeutae, a Jewish monastic community of celibate men and women.[7]

The baptismal formula of Galatians 3:28 was probably shaped originally by some version of this Philonic view of creation in which redemption meant transcending the fallen stage of creation when man became 'male and female', and being restored to original unity.[8] A more radical way of explaining this two-stage creation was to attribute it to two different cosmic powers, a higher divine power which is spiritual, uniting male and female in a spiritually androgynous form, and then a fall in which lower demonic powers appeared who created the present oppressive cosmic system sunk in ignorance and death. Sparks of the higher spiritual world have been trapped in bodies, sex and death, but the higher powers have sent down a Redeemer who is awakening them from their ignorance and forgetfulness of their true nature and showing them the way to escape back to their true heavenly nature and home. The enlightened ones or Gnostics have thrown off ignorance and are already communing in their restored spiritually androgynous nature in which there is no more male and female.[9]

Christians of more traditional Jewish background would vehemently reject these speculations of a dualistic creation that severed the Creator of the cosmos from the God of Heaven and put aside gender division, marriage and procreation. For them the physical world and the division of humans into male and female for marriage and procreation is the order that God created from the beginning. Disobedience to divinely given gender relations is the problem. Redemption means return to proper obedience to God which is also obedience to the patriarchal order. Yet they also accepted the belief that women had souls equally capable of receiving redemption in baptism, and in the world to come there will be 'no more marrying and giving in marriage'.[10]

The struggle over gender in New Testament and second-century Christianity was fought out in the terms of these competing world views. All accepted that gender hierarchy was the cosmic order. The question was about the status of this cosmic order; whether it was of God and had to be acceded to as long as God's created order lasts, although this will be transcended in a heavenly world to come, or whether it is due to a fall of the soul away from God or even a fallen power that broke away from God and created a fallen cosmos and so can be transcended here and now through spiritual transformation.

The mainstream of Christian orthodoxy would be defined by those who took the first line, together with modified elements of Philonic thought, while the second, more radical, options were marginalized and rejected, although reappearing again and again in new forms on the margins of Christianity.

Augustine in the late fourth and early fifth centuries defined the view that would be passed down as orthodoxy through the Middle Ages and largely continued in magisterial Protestantism. In his early commentaries on Genesis Augustine played with a more Platonic view similar to that of Philo.[11] But he rejected this in his later work for a view that Adam and Eve were created in the beginning in real physical and sexually differentiated bodies. Sexual intercourse and physical offspring were part of God's original design, and not just features that appeared after sin and as a remedy for mortality.

Yet Augustine held on to the Platonic view that God created the Idea of the Human on the first day. This is the spiritual essence of Humanity, the image of God, that all humans, male and female, possess apart from their sexual differentiation. Yet in the actual production of the human being, the male was created first and then the female from his side, to indicate the relation of superiority and subordination by which the genders are to relate in their biological and social roles. For Augustine, gender hierarchy is not a fruit of sin, but an integral part of God's original plan for creation-society, in respect to the relation of men and women in sex, childbearing and social order,[12] although it will have no place in heaven when these roles will have disappeared.

Augustine believed that originally Adam and Eve would not have died and would have reproduced physically but without orgasm or concupiscence. But with the Fall these privileges have disappeared. The Fall plunges humanity into both sin and death, the loss of original immortality and the free will to obey God. Humans are now bound to sinful pride, unable to obey God as a free act of the will, and their sexual relations are corrupted by sinful lust through which the legacy of sin is transmitted from parents to offspring. Women's subordination which women would have accepted in the original creation is now worsened to servitude, to be coercively enforced due to sinful resistance to the obedience that woman owes man as her head.[13] This has not changed for virginal women, even though they anticipate the heavenly state when these social roles will have disappeared. But, as long as earthly life persists, even virginal women must submit to male authority and have no public leadership roles. Indeed virginal women manifest their converted minds by willingly submitting to male authority and having no will of their own.

This Augustinian view was continued through the Middle Ages. Aquinas worsens Augustine's view of female 'natural' subordination by adopting an Aristotelian socio-biology which taught that women were biologically defective, lacking the fullness of humanness mentally, morally and physically and therefore being naturally under male domination and unable to exercise public leadership in either church or society. Yet, Aquinas inconsistently maintains the Augustinian view that women are spiritually equal to men as image of God, and have been equally redeemed in Christ. In heaven, when all social roles related to biological sex and reproduction will have disappeared, they will be equal according to spiritual merits without regard to gender.[14]

In the sixteenth century Luther and Calvin discard Aristotelian socio-biology and the Augustinian view that humans were created first as essential idea prior to physical creation. They teach that Adam and Eve were created equal in the image of God in their interior nature, but in their maleness and femaleness, ordained from the beginning for marriage and procreation, they are unequal. As gendered body, Luther believes that Adam was from the beginning superior to Eve in 'glory and prestige', although each was perfect in their distinct masculine and feminine natures. Calvin has a juridical view of this distinction between equality in the image of God and the subjugation of women according to gender. Although equal in soul before God, the male as male was given dominion over all created things, with woman included among those things over which he rules.[15]

For both Luther and Calvin this original 'natural' subordination has been worsened by sin into female servitude to the male. For Luther the male sphere has been widened to include coercive political and military power unnecessary in paradise, while the female is now severely restricted to the home as punishment for her greater culpability in sin.[16] Both also believe that sex has now been corrupted by lust, but for them this means that marriage is necessary to provide the legal outlet for a lust which otherwise would run rampant in immorality.[17] The Reformation insistence that gender subordination reflects both God's 'orders of creation' in original creation and Eve's punishment for sin would continue to be taught as Protestant orthodoxy up to the present day.

Despite the prevalence of Augustinian anthropology in Western Christianity, alternative forms of eschatological feminism did not disappear. Apocalyptic and mystical groups continued to arise in medieval Catholicism and left-wing Protestantism. Such groups believed that the original equality of soul, prior to the fall into sex, sin and death, is being restored here and now through an outpouring of the Holy Spirit. Eschatological restoration of original equality is already present for those who have been transformed.

This transformation continued to be expressed by the practice of celibacy. Through celibacy humans transcend sexual division and recapture their spiritual oneness. Transformed women can then act as equals in the redemptive community, preaching, prophesying and taking leadership roles. But this equality is not projected outward as a mission to change society, but rather entails a withdrawal into the sectarian community which has departed from the fallen world and anticipates the heavenly order still to come.

Perhaps the most developed expression of this premodern eschatological feminism is found in the Shakers who arose in England in the late eighteenth century and then flourished in America in the nineteenth century. Shaker theology is rooted in mystical and millennialist forms of Christianity from the medieval period which were continued in left-wing Protestant mystics, such as Jacob Boehme.[18] The Shakers believed that God is androgynous, both Father and Mother, and humanity made in the image of God reflects this maleness and femaleness. But this maleness and femaleness would have originally been spiritual in form. Only with sin did humanity fall into sex, sin and death.

Christ came to redeem humanity according to the male aspect of God, but redemption is incomplete until there is the revelation of the female or Wisdom aspect of God. This completed revelation of God and redemption of humanity took place in Ann Lee, the foundress of the Shakers, or the Millennial Church of Christ's Second Appearing. Celibacy restores humans to their original spiritual nature and anticipates the Heavenly World. This means that women are fully the spiritual equals of men, but in a way in which spiritual maleness and femaleness parallel and complement each other as revelations of the male and female sides of God. Thus Shakers organized their communities in parallel orders of brothers and sisters, led by Elders and Elderesses.[19]

Gender equity: from premodern to modern and postmodern paradigms

I have thus far argued that the original Christian idea of gender equity in the image of God restored in Christ was fundamentally truncated by the assumption that gender hierarchy was the order of creation which inseparably tied sexual functions in marriage, and procreation. Both orthodox and mystical-millennialist forms of Christianity shared this same assumption, but held different views about the God-given status of this order of creation and whether the holy could transcend it here and now. A changed view of gender equity in human society was possible only when this fundamental link between creation and gender hierarchy was re-evaluated.

This re-evaluation began to take place among some pro-woman humanists and left-wing Christians, especially the Quakers, in the sixteenth and seventeenth centuries. The Catholic humanist, Cornelius Agrippa von Nettesheim, in his 1509 treatise on the 'Nobility and Superiority of Woman', argued that women were created equally with man in the image of God in the beginning, but in those matters having to do with her specific femaleness, the woman is superior to the male, more attuned to life and virtue. He denounced male domination of women as simply unjust tyranny and in no way an expression of reason, nature or the will of God. Christ came to restore women to their equality and gave them equal leadership in the church, but men have refused to accept this. Churchmen even misread the message of Christ in order to justify continuing unjust laws that prevent women from taking their rightful place in culture and political life.[20]

The Quakers in the seventeenth century took the view that men and women were created equally in the image of God as full human persons, not as neutral souls distinguished from gendered bodies. Male domination, and other forms of usurpation of power by some over others, appeared in the Fall and are themselves the primary expression of sin. But God continued to empower women equally with men to speak as prophets, even 'under the Law'. In Christ all such usurpation of power has been overcome. Women were mandated by Christ to announce the good news of the resurrection. Only those who have not been transformed in the Spirit, who have not 'seen the light', continue to try to silence women. By so doing they show that they still belong to the 'seed of the Serpent' and not the 'seed of the woman' who is Christ.[21]

These Quakers and humanists began a paradigm shift in the interpretation of original and restored equality, but this idea did not become a mandate for change of church and social institutions until the nineteenth century, when such reinterpretations of Christianity were joined to democratic theory flowing from the Enlightenment. Democratic theorists reinterpreted the Christian doctrines of creation and sin. For them all human beings possess the same essential human nature. This human nature is characterized essentially by reason and moral conscience.

Human rights are based on this common humanity. But unjust human societies have arisen in which some have usurped unjust power over others, turning rights into class privileges for an aristocratic class, and depriving others of their basic necessities. The democratic revolution means political redemption whereby these unjust class structures are overthrown and a new political order constituted in which the common humanity given by God to all is translated into equal rights before the law. This new doctrine of egalitarian original nature was expressed in the American Declaration of Independence of 1776 in the ringing phrase: 'We hold these truths to be self-evident, that all men are created equal.'

Yet the writers of this Declaration did not imagine that women were included in these rights of man, nor men in servitude, such as Indians or Blacks. The definition of equal rights was confined in practice to the white propertied male. In the 1830s the contradiction between this view of universal human rights and the continuation of slavery under the American Constitution began to be challenged by the abolitionist movement. Within abolitionism there arose the first American feminists. Sarah and Angelina Grimke, Lucretia Mott and Susan B. Anthony were all Quakers in background, while Elizabeth Cady Stanton rejected her original Presbyterian upbringing for humanism.

Nineteenth-century feminist leaders took their stand on the assertion that 'all men and women were created equal',[22] that women possess the same essential human nature as men. Male domination was unjust usurpation of power that is contrary to God's original intention whereby God created woman and man to be side by side, not one over the other. As Sarah Grimke put it in her 1836 *Letters on the Equality of the Sexes*, 'All I ask of our brethren is that they will take their feet from off our necks and permit us to stand upright on that ground which God has designed for us to occupy'.[23] To make women fully equal to man in education, economics and politics means overcoming a system of sinful injustice and remaking society based on God's original intentions. Some nineteenth-century feminists included ordained ministry in the church in this agenda, while others, like Elizabeth Cady Stanton, asked whether Christianity was hopelessly patriarchal.[24]

Thus, modern feminism was born in a political reinterpretation of the Christian thesis of equality in the image of God redemptively restored. This assumes that there is some essential human nature which all human beings share as members of a common species that is the subject for equal rights. The early feminists, such as Susan B. Anthony, who emerged from the abolitionist movement were strong universalists, insisting on equal human rights for women and men, across all race and class divisions, reaching out to Blacks, Indians and working-class people.[25]

But, towards the end of the nineteenth century, this universalism became truncated in the women's movement, tacitly accepting discrimination against 'the uneducated', Blacks and Catholic immigrants.[26] The notion of a common human nature gave way to an increasing stress on an anthropology of complementarity in which women are seen as morally superior, 'naturally' altruistic and caring, while men are egoistic and aggressive. This dualistic anthropology of feminine and masculine 'natures' of men and women lent itself to a spectrum of political expressions, ranging from conservative to reform to radical.

Conservative men and women argued that women's feminine nature necessitated that they stay in the private sphere of family and not venture out into the rough world of public life. This view became the basis of the new argument of conservative churchmen against women taking public roles in professions and politics.[27] But feminist social reformers argued that women's superior moral nature demanded that they gain political rights and education so they could enter the public sphere to clean it up and elevate it from its moral degradation by drunkenness, dirt, sexual immorality, poverty and war.[28] A few radicals concluded that women should separate from degraded men altogether and create separate female societies where they could cultivate the more refined community of which only women are capable.[29]

All of these options would return in the renewed feminism that arose in the 1970s. Feminist theory continues to be torn between a one-nature and a two-nature anthropology.[30] Both are inadequate. The one-nature view is tied to androcentrism. The common human nature that all share has been defined in terms of male norms of reason, moral will and the detached ego, and women allowed to be 'equal' only in those areas where they can operate 'like a man'. Many feminists have argued that it is necessary to recognize women's difference.[31] Yet the prevailing view of male and female difference is tied to a split of altruism and egoism, nurture and aggression. Such a view of women's nature not only precludes women's capacity to 'compete' with men in the 'male world', but it is also implicitly classist and sexist, moulded by the ideology of the white leisure-class women who do not have to 'work'.[32]

Feminists in the 1970s and 1980s searched for a way to go beyond the one-nature/two-nature debate and to sketch an inclusive humanness which included for both men and women the full range of human qualities from which each had been excluded by assigning some to men and some to women. Men needed to become whole by becoming sensitive and caring of others, and women needed to incorporate rationality and autonomy without losing their culture of relationality. This enlarged humanness would demand journeys into personal wholeness for men and women, each starting from their different histories, and also transformed social structures that would allow for this enlarged wholeness.[33]

Yet even as this discussion of what an enlarged wholeness in relation would mean for transformed humans, male and female, in transformed society, the postmodern debates began to question the whole concept of universals, not only essential maleness and femaleness, but also essential humanness. All such notions of an essential self and universal human values or nature are social constructions, feminist postmodernists argued. We have to recognize infinite particularity. Every effort to define the essential and universal human is always a projection of the Western dominant male who makes himself the norm of the human and excludes everyone else who does not fit this definition. By the same token, any effort of women to define some universal experience of being woman, as a basis of feminist critique, is inevitably based on a racist, classist affluent woman who does not recognize how her notions of 'women's experience' are only those of her limited class and cultural context. Feminism must give up any notions of an essential self that posits a universal human nature, and simply recognize infinite particularity.[34]

I agree that we need to go beyond both an androcentric reduction of the human to qualities traditionally associated with the male and notions of femininity associated with leisure-class females. But the postmodern insistence on infinite particularity, its view that all definitions of self and group identity are 'mere' social constructions, can easily lead, not to a more inclusive justice for poor women of colour and non-Western culture, but, rather, new ways of justifying women's subjugation in societies which are not postmodern but still premodern. As Korean feminist theologian Chung Hyun Kyung has put it, 'It is dangerous to argue for post-modernity in cultures which are still premodern toward women'.[35]

What this means is that, in international meetings in which standards of human rights are expanded to include women's rights as human rights, such as have taken place under United Nations auspices in Cairo and Beijing in recent years, one increasingly finds the postmodern argument of the rights of cultural difference used to deny the applicability of ideas of women's rights to women in traditional societies. Our cultural differences must be respected, men from Arab, African and Asian societies insist (oddly and selectively supported by the Vatican). There can be no critique of customs, especially when justified by religion, such as daughters receiving only half of the inheritance of sons, genital mutilation, denial of education, employment and political participation, and forced veiling and segregation of women.[36]

At the very moment when the movement for women's rights is becoming global, when women from many cultures around the world are seeking to include themselves in what the United Nations has defined as women's rights as universal human rights,[37] the ground for the very idea of human rights is being cut out from under those women struggling on behalf of the poorest and most oppressed women of the world.

What is needed is not a biased essentialism that excludes cultural diversity, but also not such a fragmentized nominalism that there is finally no basis for solidarity between women and men across classes and cultures. Rather, we need an open-ended understanding of commonality in diversity, one that can embrace all life-enhancing forms of diversity, while questioning those cultural patterns that confine some groups of people to poverty, servitude and violence on the basis of gender, race or class difference.

This means that we have to have some notions of what 'good humanness' means as norm and goal of personal development and social reform. While any definition of good humanness will always be a cultural construction, this does not mean a purely arbitrary social construction based on nothing. There are some criteria for what makes for humans living together in well-being and what does not, and these are not unknown to us across our many cultures and diverse contexts.[38]

The goals of religions and of social, economic and political systems need to be guided and called to account by some norms of human well-being that are inclusive of people of every culture, both women and men. This cannot be defined from one perspective. It demands a 'hearing into speech' of women (and men) in many social contexts, who construct an understanding of what human flourishing means for them. There can be dialogue and solidarity between groups only when each can articulate its own perspective and be heard by the others with full respect. This is the revolution into which we are called in order really to move beyond a modernity defined by Western male dominance.

Notes

1. The term 'premodern' could mean both the many indigenous cultures of tribal societies and the various 'classical' cultures that arose with the development of early empires. In the context of this chapter, it refers specifically to the synthesis of Hebrew and Graeco-Roman classical cultures created by Patristic Christianity in the second to fifth centuries CE and passed down as traditional Christianity, beginning to be challenged by the 'modern' paradigm of the Enlightenment in the late eighteenth and nineteenth centuries.

2. D. Herlihy, 'The household in classical antiquity' in *Medieval Households* (Cambridge, MA: Harvard University Press, 1985), pp. 1–28.

3. Philo, 'The Therapeutae' in Nathan Glatzer, *The Essential Philo* (New York: Schocken, 1971), pp. 311–30. The Rabbinic writings preserve the tradition of Bruria, a woman who was trained and taught as a rabbi: see Judith Hauptman, 'Images of women in the Talmud' in Rosemary R. Ruether (ed.), *Religion and Sexism: Images of Women in the Jewish and Christian Traditions* (New York: Simon and Schuster, 1974), pp. 203–4. For Jewish women as elders and patrons of synagogues, see Ross S. Kraemer, *Maenads, Martyrs, Matrons and Monastics: A Source Book on Women's Religions in the Greco-Roman World* (Philadelphia: Fortress, 1988), pp. 218–21.

4. See Bernadette Brooten, *Women Leaders in the Ancient Synagogue* (Brown Judaic Studies 36; Chico, CA: Scholars Press, 1982).

5. Dominic Crossan, *The Historical Jesus: The Life of a Mediterranean Jewish Peasant* (San Francisco: HarperSanFrancisco, 1991).

6. Philo, 'On the creation of the world' in Glatzer, *The Essential Philo*, pp. 28–34.

7. Glatzer, *The Essential Philo*, pp. 311–30.

8. See Ronald MacDonald, *There Is No More Male and Female* (Philadelphia: Fortress, 1987), pp. 26–30.

9. See B. Layton (ed.), *The Rediscovery of Gnosticism*, vol. 1: *The School of Valentinus* (Leiden: Brill, 1980).

10. On Tertullian and Origen in relation to Montanism, see Christine Trevett, *Montanism: Gender, Authority and the New Prophecy* (Cambridge: Cambridge University Press, 1996), pp. 66–76, 174–5.

11. Augustine, *Genesis against the Manichees*, I. 19, 30: in Roland J. Teske (ed.), *The Fathers of the Church*, vol. 84 (Washington, DC: Catholic University Press of America, 1991), pp. 76–8.

12. Augustine, *Genesis ad Litteram*, ed. J. H. Taylor, *Ancient Christian Writers*, vol. 41 (New York: Newman Press, 1982), *passim*.

13. For Augustine's understanding of gender in sin and the Fall, see Kari Børresen, *Subordination and Equivalence: The Nature and Role of Woman in Augustine and Thomas Aquinas* (Kampen: Kok Pharos, 1995), pp. 71–2.

14. Børresen, *Subordination*, pp. 147–225.

15. Martin Luther, 'Lectures on Genesis' in James Atkinson (ed.), *Luther's Works* (Philadelphia: Fortress Press, 1966), vol. 1; John Calvin, *Commentaries on the*

Book of Genesis, ed. John King (Edinburgh: Calvin Translation Society, 1847), vol. 1, *passim*.

16. Luther, 'Commentary on I Timothy' in *Luther's Works*, vol. 28, pp. 202–3.
17. See Luther's 'Sermon on the estate of marriage' in *Luther's Works*, vol. 44, pp. 9–10; Calvin, *Institutes of the Christian Religion*, ed. John T. McNeil (Philadelphia: Westminster Press, 1960), p. 146.
18. See Clarke Garrett, *Spirit Possession and Popular Religion from the Camisards to the Shakers* (Baltimore: Johns Hopkins Press, 1987).
19. For Shaker theology, see Kathleen Deignan, *ChristSpirit: The Eschatology of Shaker Christianity* (Metuchen, NJ: Scarecrow Press, 1992), pp. 65–156.
20. Heinrich Cornelius Agrippa von Nettesheim, *Female Preeminence or the Dignity and Excellency of that Sex Above the Male* (London, 1670); for a recent analysis of Agrippa's treatise, see Barbara Newman, 'Renaissance feminism and esoteric theology' in her *From Virile Woman to WomanChrist: Studies in Medieval Religion and Literature* (Philadelphia: University of Pennsylvania Press, 1995).
21. Margaret Fell, in Christine Trevett (ed.), *Women's Speaking Justified and Other Seventeenth Century Quaker Writings about Women* (London: Quaker Home Service, 1989), pp. 5–16.
22. 'Declaration of sentiments and resolutions: Seneca Falls, July 19, 1848' in M. Schneir (ed.), *Feminism: The Essential Historical Writings* (New York: Vintage, 1972), pp. 76–82.
23. Sarah Grimke, *Letters on the Equality of the Sexes and the Condition of Women* in *The Public Years of Sarah and Angelina Grimke: Selected Writings, 1835–39* (New York: Columbia University Press, 1989), p. 208.
24. For Elizabeth Cady Stanton's thought on Christianity, see Mary Pellauer, *Toward a Tradition of Feminist Theology: The Religious Social Thought of Elizabeth Cady Stanton, Susan B. Anthony and Anna Howard Shaw* (New York: Carlson, 1991), pp. 105–52.
25. On Susan B. Anthony's universalism, see Kathleen Barry, *Susan B. Anthony: A Biography of a Singular Feminist* (New York: Ballantine, 1988), especially pp. 126–45.
26. Barry, *Susan B. Anthony*, pp. 195–224; also Eileen Kraditor, *The Ideas of the Women's Suffrage Movement, 1880–1920* (New York: Norton, 1980).
27. See Horace Bushnell, *Women's Suffrage: The Reform Against Nature* (New York: Scribners, 1869).
28. For Victorian feminist reformism, see Carolyn S. Gifford in Rosemary S. Keller and Rosemary R. Ruether (eds), *Women and Religion in America: The Nineteenth Century* (San Francisco: Harper and Row, 1981), pp. 294–340.
29. Late Victorian separatism is represented by Charlotte Perkins Gilman's novel *Herland* (New York: Pantheon, 1979).
30. See Rosemary R. Ruether, *Sexism and God-talk: Toward a Feminist Theology* (Boston: Beacon, 1983), pp. 99–109.
31. French feminism has been particularly influential in a renewed emphasis on women's difference: see Luce Irigaray, *Ethics of Sexual Difference* (Ithaca, NY: Cornell University Press, 1993).

32. See Rosemary R. Ruether, 'The cult of true womanhood and industrial society' in Eugene C. Bianchi and Rosemary R. Ruether (eds), *From Machismo to Mutuality: Woman–Man Liberation* (New York: Paulist Press, 1976), pp. 39–53; and Rosemary R. Ruether, 'Between the sons of white and sons of blackness: racism and sexism in America' in *New Woman, New Earth: Sexist Ideologies and Human Liberation* (Boston: Beacon Press, 1995), pp. 115–30.
33. See Ruether, *Sexism and God-Talk*, pp. 109–15; also Mary Grey, *Redeeming the Dream: Feminism, Redemption and Christian Tradition* (London: SPCK, 1989), pp. 61–83.
34. See Marianne A. Marchant and Jane L. Purpart, *Feminism/PostModernism/Development* (London: Routledge, 1995).
35. This concern was shared by Chung Hyun Kyung in a personal conversation during the Fourth World Conference on Women, in Beijing, China, 7 September 1995.
36. See Rosemary Ruether, 'Culture and women's rights', *Conscience*, 16.4 (Winter 1995/96), pp. 13–15.
37. See the Final Document of the United Nations Fourth World Conference on Women, Beijing, China, 4–15 September 1995.
38. See Hans Küng and Karl-Josef Kuschel (eds), *A Global Ethic: The Declaration of the Parliament of the World's Religions* (New York: Continuum, 1993).

5

From dualism to difference

Christian theologies of human sexuality and the quest for wholeness in a postmodern age

Sean Gill

The crisis in contemporary Christian sexual ethics

Dorothy Sayers, the Anglican playwright, novelist and theologian, once remarked with understandable exasperation that 'the Church is uncommonly vocal about the subject of bedrooms and so singularly silent on the subject of board-rooms'.[1] This is a view with which many of us will no doubt sympathize, living as we do in what Anthony Giddens has called a sexually addicted civilization.[2] Yet while I do not want to suggest that in the contemporary world the most serious ethical dilemmas facing Christians are necessarily related to issues of human sexuality, in no other area has the impact of postmodernism been so visible and so contentious. Postmodernism is itself, of course, a much controverted term. For this reason, it may be helpful at the outset to distinguish between its use as a descriptive label, on the one hand, which draws attention to the way in which economic and social change, and the impact of global communications, have combined to bring about a juxtaposition of lifestyles and a relativization of moral values in Western societies and, on the other, its adoption by sections of the intelligentsia as an intellectual credo which denies the existence of universal and trans-historical standards of truth and morality. These phenomena are, however, closely related, and their combined impact upon Christian thinking in the field of sexual ethics has been the promotion of acrimonious disagreement and uncertainty.

Considered as a cultural process, the effects of postmodernism upon Western sexual mores are evident all around us, and one illustration may suffice. Recently I spent a month travelling in Italy. Unlike many other parts of Europe, anyone seeking admittance to a major basilica still has to negotiate the arcane regulations associated with propriety of dress – are a man's shorts long enough and a woman's shoulders sufficiently covered to allow access to sacred space? Here no doubt – so the Church's critics would claim – are to be found the last atavistic vestiges of a long Christian tradition of denial of the goodness of the body and of a morbid distaste of human sexuality. Yet on nearby news-stands, quite openly displayed, one can buy pornographic magazines in which the cold objectification of sex and of the human body are hardly life-affirming. Other conundrums present themselves to the perplexed observer. On some beaches naked sunbathing and swimming are common, on others they are taboo – likely to be met with angry admonitions to think of the children present. Italian society still in fact retains a strong sense of family values and of reticence in sexual matters; nevertheless in every town of any size, and on most major trunk roads, prostitution flourishes openly and the women employed in this way, usually poor and of African origin, have difficulty keeping up with demand. What is striking about this situation is not that conflicting moral norms co-exist – historically there have always been sexual sub-cultures – but that now they all inescapably form part of everyone's daily experience. To judge from the Italian press, publicly aired debate over issues such as abortion, contraception, divorce, and gay and lesbian rights further exacerbate the sense of moral vertigo which many people feel.

Reactions to this situation in Western societies are sharply polarized. Nor is this surprising, for as the anthropologist Mary Douglas has suggested, there is an intimate connection between the way in which we perceive the physical and the social body, making sexuality the vector for many wider fears about the proper ordering of society.[3] Thus in the realm of sexual politics and ethics we are often presented with starkly contrasting images of the postmodern condition: on the one hand, a nightmare scenario of an amoral society threatened by promiscuity, AIDS, family breakdown and the sexual exploitation of children and women; on the other, a celebration of difference and diversity in a society freed from the oppressive authoritarianisms of the past, and in which once demonized sexual minorities can find human dignity and self-fulfilment.[4]

The intellectual implications of adopting a postmodern epistemology have been equally divisive. Here a traditional view of Christian sexual ethics, which has attempted to ground morality upon a foundation of either biblical authority or natural law impervious to historical and cultural change, has been challenged by a postmodern assertion of the humanly constructed nature and hence relativity of all ethical systems. Though these purport to embody timeless truths, they have in reality, it is claimed, been constructed from an androcentric and heterosexual perspective which has disadvantaged both women and sexual minorities.[5] This fundamental difference of approach is well illustrated by comparing the text of the Vatican's 1975 *Declaration on Certain Questions Concerning Sexual Ethics* with the 1977 study *Human Sexuality: New Directions in Catholic Thought*, which was commissioned by the Catholic Theological Society of America. The former sets out to refute the view that 'so-called norms of the natural law or precepts of Sacred Scripture are to be regarded only as given expressions of a form of particular culture of a certain movement of history', and concludes that all genital sexual acts outside of marriage are morally impermissible.[6] The latter rejects the appeal to traditional natural law theory as the basis for asserting the objective and unchanging nature of Christian sexual ethics on the grounds that 'the argument fails to acknowledge sufficiently the pre-reflexive, historical embodiedness of every thinker and every moralizing human community'.[7] In the case of the Catholic Church's teaching about sexuality, the authors list as instances of such limitations 'inadequate knowledge of biology, as well as religious taboos, the tradition of subhuman treatment of women, and a dualistic philosophy of human nature'.[8] In formulating a Christian sexual ethic, the report argues for the acceptance of a norm of creative growth and integration of the human person which would rule out exploitative and self-destructive sexual behaviour, but which would not necessarily be incompatible with a range of sexual practices, including heterosexual sex outside of marriage or homosexual sex within committed relationships.

For those who welcome what they see as the creative and liberating effects of postmodern perspectives for human sexual relations, the oppressive and life-denying rigidities of the traditional ethic are all too evident. *Per contra*, those who reject the postmodern turn in ethics do so because they find there only a morass of relativism, the outcome of which, they fear, will be a nihilistic rejection of all sexual norms. In the rest of this chapter I want to explore these issues in more detail by focusing primarily upon the question of homosexuality and Christian sexual ethics. In doing so my aim is not to engage with the many kinds of argument advanced for and against a change in the Christian Church's traditional stance in this area (though my advocacy of such change will become clear enough), but rather to explore how the whole debate can illuminate what is at stake in the controversy over postmodernism and sexual ethics. Since it is the problematizing of tradition which lies at the heart of the contemporary crisis of values, I shall begin by considering two traditions of discourse about homosexuality, or to adapt Jean-François Lyotard's formulation, two meta-narratives concerning human sexuality in the light of postmodern critiques of their validity.[9] These might be described as the Judaeo-Christian tradition of sexual ethics, and the post-Enlightenment tradition of sexual science – traditions whose founding fathers include St Paul, St Augustine and St Aquinas, on the one hand, and Krafft-Ebing, Havelock Ellis and Freud, on the other. I then want to explore the implications of the collapse of the unquestioned authority of these traditions not only for gay liberation movements in particular, but for the construction of a meaningful theology of human sexuality in general.

Homosexuality and the Judaeo-Christian tradition

Christianity inherited from Judaism a sexual ethic strongly committed to the defence of procreation and family life, and any other form of sexual activity was regarded as an abomination.[10] No references to homosexual behaviour are found in the four Gospels and few elsewhere, of which the most important are in the Epistle to the Romans, where Paul denounces such conduct as a feature of pagan society,[11] and the First Epistle to the Corinthians where he warns that such activity – listed along with adultery, theft and drunkenness – is a bar to entering the Kingdom of God.[12] In recent years much discussion of these passages has centred upon the question of their relevance for contemporary ethics, given that the New Testament world knew nothing of the modern understanding of sexual orientation.[13] Nevertheless, Paul's repudiation of homosexual behaviour is in keeping with his Jewish inheritance and with his insistence that sexual activity be limited to monogamous, permanent marriage. Augustine's few references to homosexuality are strongly influenced by the traditional but false exegesis of the story of Sodom as evidence of God's divine punishment of behaviour which he regards as a form of perverted lust.[14] As with the writings of St Paul, James Boswell has argued against seeing in Augustine's use of the word unnatural in this context a blanket condemnation of homosexuality *per se*, but rather of those heterosexuals who indulged in activity which went against their natural sexual inclination.[15] However, given the strong emphasis found elsewhere in Augustine's writings upon procreation within marriage as the whole permissible locus for sexual activity, this seems unconvincing. While it may be true, as Boswell argues, that Aquinas's condemnation of homosexual acts as contrary to natural law may represent a very different and more sophisticated understanding of the concept of the natural than any known to Paul or Augustine, it represents a development and not a new departure in a tradition consistently hostile to any expression of homosexual genital activity. The force of this prohibition is lost by treating Christian attitudes to homosexuality in isolation from the wider sexual ethic of marriage and procreation which the early and medieval Church espoused and which Protestantism, with its hostile re-evaluation of celibacy, did little to alter.

It is the authority of this tradition as a whole which postmodernism now calls into question. Divinely ordained sexual norms apprehended by the use of human reason properly deployed have been transmuted into Foucaultian discourses of power, whose appeal to notions of the natural disguises their all too human origins and their attempts to marginalize dissident voices. Exercises in what Foucault has aptly called the archaeology of knowledge have undermined the authority of the dominant Judaeo-Christian sexual ethic in a number of significant respects.[16] For example, before we accept Augustine's rejection of homosexual behaviour as a form of perverted lust we ought to consider how alien his understanding of human sexuality as a whole is from our own, based as it is upon a dualistic philosophy deeply suspicious of human sexual activity as a threat to the higher faculties of mind and will. For Augustine, all forms of sexual intercourse – including those within marriage – are to be regarded as a consequence of the Fall, as occasions for the transmission of original sin, and therefore in a very real sense as lustful.[17] Similarly, in appraising Aquinas's arguments we ought to be aware of the extent to which he relies upon a now discredited Aristotelian biology in which only the father is the active generative force in conception.[18] Protestant theologians, who are more likely to appeal to the

Bible alone as the source of authoritative teaching in the realm of sexual relations, have also been made aware of the extent to which the ethics of the New Testament are coloured by what to us are unacceptable notions of ritual purity and of women as a form of sexual property within a patriarchal society.[19] More generally, it has been the growth of a powerful feminist critique of Christian teaching about sex as instrumental in the subordination of women and in the maintenance of gender hierarchies which has done most to undermine the authority of the tradition.[20] The feminist deconstruction of gender hierarchies as socially constructed rather than immutable truths fallen from heaven has also had a direct bearing upon arguments about male homosexuality. As has been recognized, one powerful impulse behind the high levels of homophobia within Western society has been the fear of homosexual behaviour as in some senses inappropriately passive and therefore feminine – a revealing insight into the sexism which lies at the heart of our culturally constructed discourse of polarized gender identities.[21]

In trying to assess the impact of this tradition on the lives of gay men we must proceed with some caution. For much of the history of Western society the concept of homosexuality as a distinct identity was unknown, and the Church condemned particular sexual acts, most notably sodomy. There was also a wide gap between what the Church proscribed and people's actual behaviour. Nor was the severity of ecclesiastical and secular punishment constant. European society in the eleventh and twelfth centuries became harsher in its attitude towards homosexuality than it had been previously as part of the development of what R. I. Moore has called a persecuting society in which the fear of minority groups such as religious heretics, Jews and lepers tells us more about the insecurities of the majority in a period of economic and social change than it does about any actual threat which such groups posed to the dominant social order.[22] Perhaps as a result of concerns over the population crisis occasioned by the Black Death after 1348, denunciations of sexual deviancy as a grave threat to society became shriller and legal penalties harsher – often including burning alive, though this was usually reserved for cases involving rape. Even so, most men convicted of sodomy faced fines, public whipping, exile, the confiscation of their property and the denial of their right to make a will.[23] Even more than the Jews, they also lived in a society in which demonization by the Church made the threat of violence an ever present one, and the possibility of developing any kind of cultural identity non-existent. As the popular Franciscan preacher St Bernardino of Siena put it, homosexuals were the Devil's creatures and 'as refuse is taken out of the houses ... so wicked men should be removed from human commerce by prison and death'.[24] Notwithstanding the development of more liberal Christian attitudes, homophobia of this kind still characterizes the tradition as is evident in right-wing Protestant fundamentalist attempts to re-criminalize homosexual activity in Britain,[25] and in the Vatican's opposition to the granting of equal rights to gay and lesbian people in employment and in military recruitment in America.[26] Both of these campaigns continue to employ the language of demonization and contagion that has characterized the tradition from its outset. For homosexuals, the postmodern rejection of the authority of traditional Christian moral discourse spells not anomie and bewilderment, but the first real possibility of a life of dignity and self-respect.

This necessarily brief historical excursus bears directly upon contemporary debates over the implications of postmodernism for our society in a number of ways. It has become fashionable to bewail the loss of what, it is claimed, was once a coherent moral order. We live, in Alasdair MacIntyre's phrase, after virtue.[27] Yet such language is in reality no more than a form of conservative nostalgic rhetoric of dubious historical accuracy. The moral consensus implied by labels such as 'Christendom' and 'the age of faith' turns out on closer inspection to conceal a series of conflicting world views and social practices.[28] In so far as an attempt was made to sustain a dominant moral discourse, its results were literally murderous for groups whose lifestyles and beliefs were perceived as threatening it. Talk by its critics of the failure of the Enlightenment project to safeguard toleration and human rights on the basis of an appeal to human reason may involve no more than the claim that Enlightenment values have insufficient epistemological grounding to command universal assent. This is unexceptional in the sense that it is not clear that any ethical system ever has had or could claim to have this authority. Yet often such language seems to imply that over the past two centuries such values have been tried and found wanting. Nothing could be further from the truth. Western society has not been characterized in the twentieth century by the predominance of a liberal social order, but by repeated attempts to impose totalitarian political systems upon peoples – attempts which have sought legitimation in religious, political or ethnic world views. The pervasiveness of these attempts, whatever their ideological underpinnings, points to a deep-seated need in human beings to transcend the inevitably fragmentary and transitory nature of existence. As the

Czech novelist Milan Kundera suggests in his satirical excoriation of the evils of Communism, *The Book of Laughter and Forgetting*, its supporters were not moved by a crude desire for power alone but by a utopian vision or idyll which he described in this way:

> I emphasise: *idyll* and *for all*, because all human beings have always aspired to an idyll, to that garden where nightingales sing, to that realm of harmony where the world does not rise up as a stranger against man and man against other men, but rather where the world and all men are shaped from one and the same matter.[29]

The danger posed by fundamentalist religious traditions is that they seek to realize that dream whatever the cost in human suffering. It is for this reason that the postmodern project, which begins with Nietzsche, is profoundly moral in its intent, however unsettling its implications, and it is for this reason, too, that Christianity badly needs to seize the opportunity which postmodernism affords for the creative re-evaluation of its theology of sexuality.

Sexual science and the demise of sexology

This is not, however, to imply that the incredulity towards the possibility of meta-narratives, which Lyotard claims lies at the heart of the crisis of legitimation in modern society, is any less serious for the tradition of post-Enlightenment reason and empirical science than for the meta-physical world view which it set out to replace. If the Judaeo-Christian tradition of theorizing about sexuality is in disarray in a postmodern age, then the same can be said of its putative successor, the tradition of scientific discourse which dominated the nineteenth century and much of the twentieth. In many ways this was almost the archetypal Enlightenment project, seeking to replace outworn religious prejudice and custom through the application of reason to human sexuality as to other areas of existence. Taboo secrecy and sin were to be replaced by openness, objective classification and understanding. One of the key texts in the creation of the new science was Richard von Krafft-Ebing's *Psychopathia Sexualis*, which appeared in 1886. According to its author, who was Professor of Psychiatry and Neurology at the University of Vienna, scientific study alone could disperse the miasma of erroneous opinions upon which unjust legal sentences had been promulgated in this area.[30] The English pioneer Havelock Ellis, who began his six-volume *Studies in the Psychology of Sex* in 1899, was similarly confident in the power of science to transcend the traditional approach of the theologians whose competency in this area Ellis now regarded as altogether superseded.[31]

Yet although the preconceptions of the founders of sexology were very different from those of the Judaeo-Christian tradition, they now seem no less questionable. Thus in his discussion of the differences between men and women Krafft-Ebing could claim that:

> Undoubtedly man has a much more intense sexual appetite than woman. As a result of a powerful natural instinct, at a certain age, a man is drawn toward a woman ... With a woman it is quite otherwise. If she is normally developed mentally, and well bred, her sexual desire is small. If this were not so the whole world would become a brothel and marriage and a family impossible. It is certain that the man that avoids women and the woman that seeks men are abnormal.[32]

The androcentrism of the first generation of male sexual researchers has, not surprisingly, attracted feminist criticism,[33] while its implications for homosexuals are equally clear: a traditional model of the sinfulness of sexual acts has given way to an 'objective' classification of abnormality in which biologically determined male-initiated heterosexual coitus is the norm.[34] In Ellis's initial formulation, 'Sexual inversion is caused by inborn constitutional abnormality towards persons of the same sex'.[35] His conclusion was that it was 'an aberration from the usual course of nature' and one which, while it was not the province of the criminal law to punish, 'bears for the most part its penalty in the structure of its own organism'.[36]

Freud's most significant contribution in this area lay in the distinction which he drew between the sexual instinct and its object, and in what he saw as the 'polymorphously perverse' nature of infantile sexuality. This had the effect of problematizing all forms of sexual orientation including heterosexuality:

> Psycho-analytic research is most decidedly opposed to any attempt at separating off homosexuals from the rest of mankind as a group of a special character ... On the contrary, psycho-analysis considers

that a choice of an object independently of its sex – freedom to range equally over male and female objects – as it is found in childhood, in primitive states of society and early periods of history, is the original basis from which, as a result of restriction in one direction or the other, both the normal and the inverted types develop. Thus from the point of view of psycho-analysis the exclusive sexual interest felt by men for women is also a problem that needs elucidating and is not a self-evident fact based upon an attraction that is ultimately of a chemical nature.[37]

But although Freud was strongly opposed to the imposition of criminal sanctions upon homosexuals, his stance was nevertheless ambiguous in terms of the development of any widespread acceptance of gay men in society. The radicalness of his insights into the fluidity of sexual orientation was still tempered by his belief that although less natural and more difficult to attain than had previously been assumed, heterosexuality remained the normative ideal towards which socialization should endeavour to lead the individual. This meant that what Freud called 'any established aberration from normal sexuality' could be seen as 'an instance of developmental inhibition and infantilism'.[38] It was the complexity of Freud's views which allowed his successors to argue that a homosexual orientation should be regarded as a psychiatric illness amenable in varying degrees to treatment – a view that was not to be repudiated by the American Psychiatric Association until 1973, and only then by a small majority.[39]

Viewed from our own day, the tradition of objective scientific study of homosexuality was part of a much wider concern with the classification and regulation of sexuality which was in many respects a secularized version of the theological view which had preceded it. Like its predecessor, it was formed upon presuppositions which were anything but objective. What purported to be a tradition of detached scientific enquiry was deeply influenced by the cultural assumptions and social anxieties of the age. The androcentrism so evident in Freud's theory of sexual differentiation, which problematizes female rather than male development, was part of a much wider late nineteenth-century white middle-class crisis of identity. For example, many of the pioneers of sexual research were also fearful of the effects of unrestrained breeding by the lower classes and espoused eugenic programmes as a remedy for what they saw as the potential eclipse of the productive middle classes by the offspring of the undeserving poor.[40] Nor do their scientific strictures against the evils of masturbation as a source of both physical and mental decay seem so great an advance upon Aquinas's condemnation of the practice for its waste of potentially procreative semen. The medicalization of homosexuality was ultimately no more emancipatory for gay men than the tradition it sought to replace.

The possibility of postmodern Christian sexual ethics

What I have tried to do by examining two traditions of discourse about human sexuality and their implications for gay men is to highlight the potentially emancipatory effects of the postmodern rejection of their authority. Yet at this point we need to be aware of some of the more troubling and paradoxical implications of the current situation which, since they apply to all movements of social and theological liberation, can be well illustrated by reference to current debates about postmodernism and ethics within feminism. As Lisa Cahill poses the problem, 'many feminist deconstructions of moral foundations create a normative vacuum which cripples their political critique' while 'they allow values like autonomy and freedom, traced to Enlightenment roots, to slide in as tacit universals, operative without intercultural nuancing or explicit defense'.[41] If we fully accept the force of the postmodern claim that we have no God-given nor humanly constructed vantage point beyond history and culture which we can access either through Scripture and the magisterium, or by appealing to some version of Kantian moral universalism, does it not follow that the provisionality and relativism of our moral judgements seriously weaken their force as instruments of transformation and liberation for women's lives?[42] How, for example, when we seek to combat what we perceive to be the oppression of women in a variety of cultural contexts do we steer between the Scylla of ethnocentricism dressed up as an appeal to universal human rights, on the one hand, and the Charybdis of an ethically and politically paralysing moral relativism, on the other?

Gay liberation movements have faced the same dilemmas, rejecting not only traditional Christian sexual ethics, but also liberal appeals to universal frameworks of human rights, on the grounds that the latter grant toleration to lesbian and gay minorities without challenging the notions of polarized and immutable gender and sexual hierarchies which have helped to create discrimination and exclusion in the first place, and which downplay crucial differences of class, race and culture in the creation of injustice.[43] Yet the advent of queer theory – which seeks to dissolve all traditional categories of gender and sexuality – also threatens by its celebration of exuberant diversity to undermine any appeal to a common set of moral values upon which claims for legal, social and theological change could be based. To put it crudely, between the Christian fundamentalist homophobe and the gay Christian liberationist, who is to judge? Do we in fact have a sufficiently coherent notion of a Christian sexual ethic upon which to ground a project of gay Christian liberation at all?[44]

One way of approaching these issues is to be clear that any Christian sexual ethic must reject as inadequate the most prevalent secular approach which is well exemplified by Steven Seidman in his book *Embattled Eros: Sexual Politics and Ethics in Contemporary America*. Advocating what he calls a pragmatic sexual ethic which renounces the task of making global judgements, he attempts to steer a middle course between traditional and libertarian accounts of sexual ethics concluding that 'from my post-modern pragmatic standpoint particular sex acts and intimate arrangements carry no intrinsic moral significance'. Yet this stance is immediately contradicted by his insistence that freedom of choice and consent are foundational moral values to be applied in this area.[45] From a Christian perspective the call to love God and our neighbours as ourselves implies that relationality, of which our sexuality is a profound part, is at the heart of our being, and that its use or misuse has social implications which the individualism of much contemporary thinking about sexual ethics tends to ignore. Grounding a Christian sexual ethic upon the primacy of love will not, as in Seidman's view, void particular sexual acts of their intrinsic moral significance, but it may lead to a re-evaluation of that significance in ways which are far more able to embrace difference and diversity. If, for example, we cease to judge sexual acts primarily in terms of their potential for procreation but rather in terms of their capacity to promote loving relationality and human growth, then homosexual relationships can be evaluated very differently from the ways they were in the past. This is evident from a section in the Anglican Church's report *Issues in Human Sexuality* where heterosexual and homosexual relationships are judged by the same moral criteria:

> Among both there are the shallow, the immature, the inconstant, the selfish and the cruel. There are the promiscuous, those interested

only in physical satisfaction, and those seemingly incapable of commitment and loyalty at any level of the personality. But equally among both there are those who grow steadily in fidelity and in mutual caring, understanding and support, whose partnerships are a blessing to the world around them, and who achieve great, even heroic sacrifice and devotion.[46]

As this passage indicates, if in a postmodern world we are to take Augustine's injunction to love and do as you will as the basis for formulating a viable Christian sexual ethic, this need not mean that we succumb to an anything goes form of moral relativism – rather, that the demands made upon us in terms of ethical discernment may well be as great if not greater than they once were. If we are to meet them successfully, we must not shy away from the creative challenges involved in taking difference seriously.

Postmodern Christian sexual ethics and the challenge of difference

In her discussion of the implications of postmodernism for making ethical judgements, Laurie Shrage has argued that the cultural pluralism and relativism which such a perspective implies need not, as its critics have claimed, result in a kind of subjectivism which argues simply on the basis of what is right for one's own particular group or sub-culture. Thoroughgoing pluralism, she claims, 'provides greater familiarity with the great arc of human possibilities in order to educate our perceptions'. But this process of ethical growth can only occur if we are prepared to genuinely confront the challenge posed by the other on its own terms and thereby to become more aware and more self-critical of our own presuppositions and their limitations. What then might this mean for Christian sexual ethics and the issues posed by homosexuality?

Consider for example the case of heterosexual men confronted by the otherness of homosexuality and who are prepared to go beyond the kind of homophobic stereotypes which make such a genuine encounter impossible. Here what might be gained ethically would include some insight into the injustices of a sexual apartheid of which they are a part. It might also allow them to explore the implications of seeing masculinity not as a uniform hegemonic biological given but as a far more diverse and fluid socio-biological construct. Deconstructing the myth of modern masculinity, which forces men to fear and reject both the feminine and homosexual aspects of their own natures, not only promotes a more just social order, it also frees men from a model of masculine behaviour which is increasingly being seen as profoundly pathological and damaging to men themselves, and which traditional Christianity has done much to foster.[47] The example of gay relationships might also contribute to healing rather than – as conservative critics claim – deepening the wounds in contemporary family life. The crisis facing the family, which is only too evident in spiralling rates of divorce across the Western world, stems in part from its manifest and repeated failure to meet the emotional and spiritual needs of its members. Gay and lesbian people have long and ever richer experiences of forming loving relationships, not on the basis of legal contract and social pressures to conform, but on the strength of the mutuality and self-giving love which they bring to them. Moreover, such relationships are often far more open to the formation of communal networks of support and friendship than is the case with the beleaguered nuclear family.[48]

The challenge of difference in such an encounter cannot, however, be a one-way process if it is to be a genuine and ethically transformative one. Thus, to regard all heterosexual men as somehow in thrall to a model of macho masculinity which denies the importance of feeling, vulnerability and mutuality in human relationships, is merely to substitute one kind of stereotype for another. It is most obviously to ignore the important connections between male sexuality and nurturing involved in parenthood. Moreover, in so far as there is some truth in this critique of contemporary masculinity, gay men are hardly immune from its force, very frequently duplicating in their own lifestyles and relationships traditional patterns of inequality and the avoidance of deep emotional commitment. In considering the problems facing the family gay men need also, as feminist and lesbian critics have pointed out, to become self-critical of their position within not simply a heterosexual but also a heteropatriarchal social order in which they may be oppressors as well as victims. This becomes even more the case when issues of Western gay liberation are seen in the wider context of racial and global economic inequality and injustice. The commercialization of sex and the power of the pink pound and dollar have been significant factors in the emergence of a liberated, and predominantly white, Western gay male identity. They also reveal the extent to which gay men have become part of the dominant global capitalist order. As Robert Goss has argued, gay and lesbian

Christians cannot exclude other oppressed groups from their own practices of liberation, otherwise 'their resistance from the margins is doomed to replicate the social strategies, structures, and value systems of their oppressors'.[49]

As will be apparent from these very brief observations on the implications of taking difference seriously, my aim has not been to engage in moral debate over particular questions, but rather to try and see what consequences postmodernism might have for the way in which we go about doing so, taking one particular issue in contemporary Christian sexual ethics as a test case. What conclusions can we draw? First, postmodern Christian ethics in the area of human sexuality do not have the power to resolve incommensurable differences of theological method and first premises. The debate between Christian fundamentalist and more liberal attitudes to homosexuality makes this abundantly clear. Nevertheless, the increasing impact of an ever more widely disseminated pluralism of values and lifestyles does make it increasingly difficult to avoid the conceptual challenge of difference by resort to defence mechanisms which seek to denigrate and stereotype otherness. Second, a postmodern Christian sexual ethic based upon the imperative of love and relationality need not succumb to a vacuous tolerance or paralysing relativism. Many forms of sexual behaviour in our society are to be rejected from a Christian standpoint as selfish, manipulative, exploitative, irresponsible and shallow. Third, and most importantly, even if it is the case that we can have no unmediated access to an absolute and unquestioned ethical standpoint outside of history or culture, in making moral judgements, we can still go beyond the mere assertion of our own values based only on our own experience or that of the sub-culture to which we belong. Taking difference seriously in the field of human sexuality can result in a mutually self-critical and enriching dialogue capable of bringing about a much needed re-envisioning of our sexual theology as a whole. None of this is easy, nor has it ever been. The Christian Church, whatever its past and present failings, has always attempted to take seriously the profound challenges and opportunities posed by the delights and the dilemmas of our sexual embodiedness. Postmodern culture need not signal the end of that tradition but rather its continuation and enrichment.

Notes

1. B. Reynolds, *Dorothy Sayers: Her Life and Soul* (London: Hodder and Stoughton, 1993), p. 337.
2. A. Giddens, *The Transformation of Intimacy: Sexuality, Love and Eroticism in Modern Societies* (Cambridge: Polity Press, 1992), p. 203.
3. M. Douglas, *Natural Symbols* (London: Cresset Press, 1970), p. 65.
4. A representatively pessimistic assessment of our postmodern sexual condition is A. Storkey, 'The rise and fall of "sex"' in J. Davies and G. Loughlin (eds), *Sex These Days* (Sheffield: Sheffield Academic Press, 1997), pp. 79–97. For a much more positive evaluation which urges us to welcome the fact of erotic flux and to 'go with the flood' see J. Weeks, *Sexuality* (London: Routledge, 1986), pp. 118–20. It may be of course that there are substantial elements of truth in both analyses and that in both approaches the complexities of the situation have been smoothed over rhetorically in the interests of a larger agenda. In Storkey's case this is the claim that our society is on the point of a moral collapse from which only a revival of traditional Christianity can save us; for Weeks it is the belief that the acceptance of sexual pluralism may be a significant step towards the creation of a genuinely democratic and non-exploitative society. Neither hope now seems likely to be realized.
5. L. Cahill, *Sex, Gender and Christian Ethics* (Cambridge: Cambridge University Press, 1996), pp. 1–13.
6. A. Kosnick *et al.* (eds), *Human Sexuality: New Directions in Catholic Thought* (London: Search Press, 1977), pp. 302–5.
7. Kosnick *et al.*, *Human Sexuality*, p. 54.
8. Kosnick *et al.*, *Human Sexuality*, p. 1.
9. J. Lyotard, *The Postmodern Condition: A Report on Knowledge* (Manchester: Manchester University Press, 1984).
10. P. Coleman, *Gay Christians: A Moral Dilemma* (Philadelphia: Trinity Press International, 1989), pp. 54–5.
11. Romans 1:26–7.
12. 1 Corinthians 6:9–10.
13. See for example J. Boswell, *Christianity, Social Tolerance, and Homosexuality* (Chicago: Chicago University Press, 1980), p. 109; G. Coleman, *Homosexuality: Catholic Teaching and Pastoral Practice* (New York: Paulist Press, 1995), pp. 56–72; J. Siker (ed.), *Homosexuality in the Church: Both Sides of the Debate* (Louisville: Westminster John Knox Press, 1994), pp. 3–35; M. Vasey, *Strangers and Friends: A New Exploration of Homosexuality and the Bible* (London: Hodder and Stoughton, 1995), pp. 113–40.
14. A. Oulter (ed.), *Augustine: Confessions and Enchiridion* (London: SCM Press, 1955), pp. 70–1. See too *City of God*, XVI, 30 for the same point.
15. Boswell, *Christianity*, pp. 150–1.
16. M. Foucault, *The Archaeology of Knowledge* (London: Tavistock Publications, 1972).
17. Augustine, 'On marriage and concupiscence' in P. Schaff (ed.), *A Select*

Library of the Nicene and Post-Nicene Fathers of the Christian Church, 5 (Grand Rapids, MI: Eerdmans, 1978), pp. 266–7.

18. For a detailed discussion of this topic see K. Børresen, *Subordination and Equivalence: The Nature and Role of Woman in Augustine and Thomas Aquinas* (Kampen: Kok Pharos, 1995).
19. W. Countryman, *Dirt, Greed and Sex: Sexual Ethics in the New Testament and Their Implications for Today* (London: SCM Press, 1989), p 237
20. For this subject in general see C. Mackinnon, *Feminism Unmodified: Discourses on Life and Law* (Cambridge, MA: Harvard University Press, 1987), pp. 1–17; and from a specifically Christian theological perspective, B. Harrison and C. Heyward, 'Pain and pleasure: avoiding the confusions of Christian tradition in feminist theory' in J. Nelson and S. Longfellow (eds), *Sexuality and the Sacred: Sources for Theological Reflection* (Louisville: Westminster John Knox Press/London: Mowbray, 1994), pp. 131–48; and R. Ruether (ed.), *Religion and Sexism: Images of Women in the Jewish and Christian Tradition* (New York: Simon & Schuster, 1974).
21. For a more extended treatment of this theme see S. L. Bem, *The Lenses of Gender* (New Haven: Yale University Press, 1993), pp. 165–7. As Grace Jantzen has observed of Hildegard of Bingen's typical abhorrence of homosexual acts in the medieval period, its basis lay in a rejection of the possibility that men might adopt the role of women and as a consequence 'change their virile strength into perverse weakness': quoted in G. Jantzen, *Power, Gender and Christian Mysticism* (Cambridge: Cambridge University Press, 1995), p. 234.
22. R. Moore, *The Formation of a Persecuting Society* (Oxford: Blackwell, 1987).
23. J. Brundage, *Law, Sex and Christian Society in Medieval Europe* (Chicago: Chicago University Press, 1987), pp. 533–5.
24. J. Richards, *Sex Dissidence and Damnation: Minority Groups in the Middle Ages* (London: Routledge, 1991), pp. 146–7.
25. M. Durham, *Sex and Politics: The Family and Morality in the Thatcher Years* (London: Macmillan, 1991), pp. 124–6.
26. R. Peddicord, *Gay and Lesbian Rights. A Question: Sexual Ethics or Social Justice?* (Kansas City, MO: Sheed & Ward, 1996), pp. 123–9.
27. A. MacIntyre, *After Virtue: A Study in Moral Theory* (London: Duckworth, 1985).
28. For medieval Europe see the recent collection of essays, S. Waugh and P. Diehl (eds), *Christendom and Its Discontents: Exclusion, Persecution and Rebellion 1000–1500* (Cambridge: Cambridge University Press, 1996). This emphasizes the diversity of beliefs and values which co-existed during the period and seeks to go beyond a simple dialectical model of repression and rebellion to examine the ways in which different marginalized groups negotiated and in some cases succeeded in redefining the boundaries of orthodoxy. For a more extended critique of what he calls MacIntyre's narrative of decline and fall see J. Stout, *Ethics After Babel* (Cambridge: James Clark & Co., 1988), pp. 200–19.
29. M. Kundera, *The Book of Laughter and Forgetting* (London: Faber and Faber, 1996), p. 11.

30. R. Krafft-Ebing, *Psychopathia Sexualis, with Special Reference to Contrary Sexual Instinct: A Medico-Legal Study* (London: F. J. Rebman, 1894), p. iv. This was an English translation of the enlarged and revised German 7th edition.
31. H. Ellis, *Studies in the Psychology of Sex* (New York: Random House, 1936), vol. 1, p. xxix.
32. Krafft-Ebing, *Psychopathia*, p. 13.
33. M. Jackson, *The Real Facts of Life: Feminism and the Politics of Sexuality c. 1850–1940* (London: Taylor and Francis, 1994).
34. For the development of a scientific model of homosexuality and its implications see G. Hawkes, *A Sociology of Sex and Sexuality* (Buckingham: Open University Press, 1996), pp. 56–71; J. Weeks, *Sexuality and Its Discontents: Meanings, Myths and Modern Sexualities* (London: Routledge, 1985), pp. 64–79.
35. Ellis, *Studies*, p. 1.
36. Ellis, *Studies*, p. 356. Like Krafft-Ebing, Ellis distinguishes between what he regarded as congenital and acquired inversion, or 'pseudohomosexuality', the latter the result of individual weakness or faulty social institutions such as single-sex schools and capable of treatment by 'sound social hygiene'.
37. S. Freud, *Three Essays on the Theory of Sexuality* (London: Imago Publishing Company, 1949), pp. 23–4.
38. Freud, *Three Essays*, p. 108.
39. For Freud's views and their impact in this area see H. Abelove, 'Freud, male homosexuality, and the Americans' in H. Abelove, M. Barale and D. Halperin (eds), *The Lesbian and Gay Studies Reader* (London: Routledge, 1993), pp. 381–93.
40. J. Weeks, *Sex, Politics and Society: The Regulation of Sexuality Since 1800* (London: Longman, 1989), pp. 128–38.
41. Cahill, *Sex, Gender and Christian Ethics*, p. 2.
42. For two outstanding discussions of these issues from a feminist perspective see S. Benhabib, *Situating the Self: Gender, Community and Postmodernism in Contemporary Ethics* (Cambridge: Polity Press, 1992); and L. Shrage, *Moral Dilemmas of Feminism* (London: Routledge, 1994).
43. I have discussed this point and its implications for a Christian sexual theology in S. Gill, 'Odd but not queer: English Liberal Protestant theologies and the gay paradigm', *Theology and Sexuality*, 3 (September 1995), pp. 48–57.
44. These questions are discussed from a secular gay liberation perspective by J. Weeks, 'Values in an age of uncertainty' in D. Standon (ed.), *Discourses of Sexuality: From Aristotle to Aids* (Ann Arbor: The University of Michigan Press, 1992), pp. 389–411.
45. S. Seidman, *Embattled Eros: Sexual Politics and Ethics in Contemporary America* (New York: Routledge, 1992), p. 201.
46. Church of England, *Issues in Human Sexuality: A Statement by the House of Bishops of the General Synod of the Church of England* (London: Church House Publishing, 1991). The report's failure to draw the logical implications from this insight and to accept a fully inclusive Church, and its reliance upon

notions of the primacy of procreation and of gender complementarity, are examples of its confused attempt to harmonize both pre- and postmodern perspectives.

47. Two helpful theological explorations of the connections between masculine identity, sexism and homophobia are J. Nelson, *The Intimate Connection: Male Sexuality, Masculine Spirituality* (London: SPCK, 1992), pp. 59–64; and M. Pryce, *Finding a Voice: Men, Women and the Community of the Church* (London: SCM Press, 1996), pp. 75–94.

48. This theme is explored by E. Stuart, *Just Good Friends: Towards a Lesbian and Gay Theology of Relationships* (London: Mowbray, 1995), pp. 102–17.

49. R. Goss, *Jesus Acted Up: A Gay and Lesbian Manifesto* (San Francisco: HarperCollins, 1993), p. 174.

6

Spirituality in a postmodern age

Faith and praxis in new contexts

Ursula King

Has spirituality still a place in an age of postmodernity? References to spirituality are so frequent and occur in so many different contexts now that it seems imperative to reflect on the meaning and significance of spirituality within the new contexts of our increasingly more interconnected world. Spirituality, like postmodernism, defies exhaustive description and unequivocal definition. Neither term is essentialist in its signification, and both concepts invite multiple strategies of interpretation to make their meaning more transparent.

To comment on postmodernism first, it certainly involves the celebration of diversity and recognizes that ambiguity and complexity are present in all intellectual, political and cultural positions. A much discussed concept, postmodernism has been in vogue since the 1970s. Most closely associated with the creative arts and literature, it is also much found in current philosophical and theological debates. While post-enlightenment modernity privileged certain kinds of knowledge, especially instrumental knowledge closely associated with scientific theory and praxis, postmodernism denotes the limits of an instrumental reason too sure of itself and questions the central modern emphasis on subjectivity and rationality.

There is much that is ambiguous and contradictory in postmodernism, but it is important to recognize that its intellectual stances invite us to re-examine all previous approaches to knowledge, power, art and religion. The postmodern critique is particularly addressed to what has been called 'the transcendental pretence of modernity', a position which has exalted and universalized thinking itself and assumed that the workings of one's own mind and one's own culture – and that has mainly meant Western culture – reflect what is universally rational and human. Moving away from such an objectivist and positivist position to a constructionist outlook where the certainty of knowledge is replaced by an ongoing process of interpretation also implies that postmodernism cannot claim a new position for itself, but has to be understood as a dynamic, ongoing process which must in turn be open to further experimentation and revision. It has been pointed out that the postmodern challenge requires unflinching honesty and scrupulous self-reflection, that any position is provisional and open to further critique and revision. As Morny Joy has written:

> postmodernism can be construed as providing a system of know-ledge that acknowledges the complexities and contradictions that result when, in trying to free oneself from ... absolutist and elitist posturings, one ineluctably tends to repeat the same configurations. A conscious postmodern position would be one that, realising the unavoidable nature of this conundrum, still endeavours to change the given formations without becoming cynical, and without indulging in reverse discrimination. At the same time a critical awareness needs to be maintained of the extent to which every new position is inextricably related to the forms and structures that are being contested.[1]

Postmodernism has brought with it much experimentation which has produced both painful fragmentation as well as a rightful recognition of the particular and local. At the same time there exists the desire for greater unity and convergence, for a wholeness of individual and society, and a clearer recognition of our global interdependence. There is also the acknowledgement of the urgent need for profound personal and social transformation. The rise of postmodernism thus provides new oppor-tunities to elucidate the relationship between praxis and action and thereby creates new openings and challenges for theological and religious reflection.

Postmodernism, spirituality and contemporary culture

Besides fragmentation and experimentation, postmodernism is accompanied by multiple processes of transformation, by the heightening of difference and the recognition of the other. Innovative experiments are taking place not only in contemporary art, philosophy, politics and literature, but also in contemporary spirituality. In fact, it seems that the increasing growth of interest in spirituality is very much a hallmark of postmodern consciousness and culture which provide a new context for both faith and spirituality.

The kind of experimentation currently taking place in spirituality within and across religious traditions, inside religious communities and outside religions altogether, is only possible in an open, secular society in search of meaning and integration, of greater coherence and new identity. Historically and etymologically, the word 'spirituality' is linked to the history of Christian theology and praxis,[2] but today the concept is used generically as transcending the assumptions of specific religious traditions. It has become a general code word for the search of direction, purpose, and meaning related to the deepest dimension of human existence. Spirituality is thus no longer exclusively based on an *a priori* theological standpoint, but is rooted in a search, in experimentation, questioning and exploring.

The diversity and plurality celebrated by postmodernism are also a characteristic of spirituality. Historically and comparatively speaking, one can only refer to spirituality in the plural, to the rich and sometimes contradictory diversity of *spiritualities*, linked to particular times, places and cultures. There exist many different spiritualities in the faiths of the world, in both the past and the present.[3] Each of the religious traditions knows of different schools of spirituality which represent specific cultural expressions of particular religious ideals. But one can say that there is also spirituality in the singular, a lofty ideal, an idea about perfection, wholeness, transcendence which is difficult to embody and concretize except through the individual and particular. But this idea, however represented and expressed in actual life, is part of the history of the human spirit and its being called beyond history. Human history is always also a history of spirituality, a history resonant with longings for the permanent, everlasting and eternal, for wholeness, peace, joy and bliss which have haunted human beings through the ages, and for which many people are still yearning today.

From a historical and anthropological point of view, different spiritualities can be seen as different cultural forms or expression of different religious ideals within diverse religious traditions. From the point of view of a person of faith and the life of religious praxis, spirituality forms part of the history of the breakthrough of the spirit into history and a piercing beyond history. Spirituality, not as an idea or concept but as praxis, is a perennial human concern which entails encounter with self-transcendence. Yet the way in which this concern is expressed today is closely linked with the development of contemporary culture and its postmodern expressions. In the past, religious faiths have been the traditional bearers of the spirit and taught particular spiritual paths and disciplines, whereas today spirituality also occurs in a non-religious and secular context so that one has to enquire whether spirituality is ultimately possible without religion.[4] Tom Boyd has claimed 'that the current attempt to split spirituality away from religion is an expression of postmodern thinking', yet he contends that 'spirituality and religion, while distinguishable, cannot be separated'.[5]

Our current global socio-political situation is one of terrifying, but also hopeful, complexity where we can reflect on the transformative potential of spirituality. Perhaps we are in the early stages of forming a new world society which will be as different from today's society as the post-industrial revolution was from life in the preceding millennia. We are at a decisive stage in the history of human consciousness and culture. Numerous new opportunities exist for shaping a new understanding and new attitudes to the world as a whole, and by this I mean our natural, social and cultural worlds as well as the worlds of our imagination, creativity and spirituality. What is most urgently needed is the attainment of wisdom which must ground and feed the will to action and transformation. Such wisdom must be developed through the inner development of each individual and the transformation of our communities. Throughout history, religions have attempted to foster such wisdom, but so far with few outward signs of success. While the religious traditions of the world possess great stores of spiritual resources, a simple return or revival to past forms of spirituality is not enough to meet contemporary spiritual needs.

Since first writing this essay I have come across a set of papers edited by Ann W. Astell (1994) under the title *Divine Representations: Postmodernism and Spirituality*,[6] which raise many questions germane to my own reflections. One of the contributors to this volume, Elena Lugo, poignantly asks: 'Is it possible for spirituality in its secular, even religious, context to respond to the *skepticism, fragmentation* and *aimlessness* that afflict postmodern philosophy?' Together with her I would argue that spirituality can so respond, although we might differ as to the most appropriate way in which this can be done. But it is helpful to quote her description of spirituality here:

> We mean by *spirituality* a fundamental vital source and point of reference for our mind, will and heart, a basis of orientation or conscious direction of human activity and inquiry. Spirituality is the pursuit of meaning, of an intimation of purpose and sense of vital connection to one's ultimate environment – the dimension of depth in all of life's endeavours and institutions. In short, a spirituality functions as a principle of enlightenment, integration and finality without which our self-reflection, self-realization and self-surrender would become superficial, chaotic and aimless.[7]

This wide-ranging description helps us to see why spirituality acquires a new significance within the context and debates of postmodernism. It may first be helpful, however, to reflect on some of the many meanings associated with spirituality.

Multiple meanings of spirituality

Spirituality has become a fashionable word used in widely different contexts today, but it is often unclear what is meant by this term. The concept is used in both religious and secular contexts, in debates about religious education in schools, in debates among theologians outside the Western world, in discussions among feminists, ecologists and peace workers, among people of different faiths and of none. Reflecting on 'the extraordinary popularity of the idea of spirituality and the proliferation of its use in courses, conferences, discussions, journals and books', a British scholar of religious studies recently commented on

> the widespread and radical differences that exist over the use of the term, its possible meanings and significance. For some it represents the move of phenomenological studies of religion into a new key, stressing subjectivities and experience as over against dispassionate objectivity, the soul rather than the form of religion. To others it

signifies an escape from the unnecessary confines of religion into the more inclusive realm of our common humanity, rendering any necessary reference to the transcendent obsolete. To yet others its obscurities and ambiguities render it an empty and misleading slogan.[8]

Many feel indeed uneasy with references to spirituality or the spiritual, because they interpret it in a dualistic way where the spiritual is conceived of in contrast to the material, the physical, the body and the world. Yet the concept of the spiritual is not always shunned; sometimes it is preferred to the concept of the religious, because it is less clearly linked to specific religious institutions and thus possesses a more diffuse meaning. From yet another perspective, the spiritual is not so much seen as diffuse than as more centred, as the very heart and depth dimension of religion, especially realized through religious and mystical experience.

The widespread interest in spirituality today is linked to the modern emphasis placed on the subject, on the discovery of the self and a more differentiated understanding of human psychology. Although many religions do not possess a precise word for 'spirituality', this term is now applied across different religious traditions; inside and outside particular religions as well as in many interfaith and secular contexts. In contemporary secular society spirituality – whatever its meaning – is being rediscovered as a lost or at least hidden dimension in a largely materialistic world. This process is both facilitated and heightened by the exploration of numerous traditional writings on spirituality, now made widely available through new translations and helpful commentaries.

Compared with the Christian Middle Ages, the onset of modernity brought a loss of spiritual life and substance in the West. But this began long before the Reformation. The gradual separation of spirituality from theology occurred gradually throughout the Middle Ages and led to a division between affectivity and conceptual knowledge. Spiritual life, previously so central to a whole culture and so taken for granted, moved increasingly to a marginal position within society as a whole, but also within Christian theology itself. Thus modern spirituality developed into a highly private mode of religious expression. This had perhaps already begun in the fourteenth and fifteenth centuries with the movement of the so-called *devotio moderna*, a modern form of devotion linked to progressive interiorization and the methodical structuring of Christian prayer into a series of inner exercises. This development was highly influential in post-Reformation spirituality, not least the spirituality of the Jesuits with their foundational text, *The Spiritual Exercises*. Over the following centuries a mystical, ascetical and spiritual theology developed which was based on highly abstract, systematic texts on the interior life. It is only in the present century that this spiritual theology has been replaced by a new emphasis on religious experience, leading to a more dynamic and inclusive understanding of spirituality among Christians.

In a traditional Christian context spirituality – *spiritualitas* – was closely connected with the celebration of the Christian mysteries, particularly the eucharist; it was linked with Christian ideals of holiness and perfection preached by the gospel. The word spirituality eventually found its way into different European languages, and from 1500 onwards spirituality could mean the quality or condition of being spiritual, and regard for things of the spirit as opposed to material or worldly interests. This understanding indicates the presence of a strong polarity, often developed into a sharp and mutually exclusive dualism whereby the spiritual was seen as distinct from, and frequently opposed to, the material, bodily, and temporal. In Christianity as in other religions, spiritual ideals were often expressed and embodied by groups of ascetics, monastics and renouncers who had a strong tradition of denying the value of the body and the world.

In an attempt to get away from a dualistic and falsely idealized understanding of spirituality, several attempts have been made to provide a more integral and inclusive definition. In recent works spirituality has been described as an attempt to grow in sensitivity, to self, to others, to non-human creation and to God, or as an exploration into what is involved in becoming human.[9] In this sense, spirituality is related to the quest for full humanity. Sandra Schneiders has described spirituality as

> that dimension of the human subject in virtue of which the person is capable of self-transcending integration in relation to the Ultimate, whatever this Ultimate is for the person in question. In this sense, every human being has a capacity for spirituality or is a spiritual being.[10]

Here the term spirituality is applied to a dimension of all human beings, to the actualization of that capacity, and also to the study of that dimension. The question has been raised whether it is really possible to be spiritual without being religious. In a contemporary context this is certainly so – this is also an aspect of our postmodernity. But there can be no doubt that education towards greater awareness is needed for all people to discover this spiritual dimension and capacity within themselves in order to actualize this potential. As Sandra Schneiders rightly says: 'very, very few people will become accomplished in the spiritual life without studying it in some way, whether theoretical or practical'.[11]

In the past, such education for spirituality was always given in the context of one particular faith, within the definite social and institutional setting of a particular religious tradition. Spirituality was lived experience, it was a praxis which became formulated in particular teachings, as spiritual disciplines and counsels of perfection, which could guide others in turn on the path to holiness. But this holiness was not always *wholeness*, in the sense in which we understand it today as the integral development of the whole human person in balanced relationship with others, embedded in community. It often was very one-sided, anti-social and especially anti-woman.

Much spirituality in the past was developed by a social, cultural and intellectual élite that was exclusively *male*. A comparative study of the counsels of holiness and perfection in different religions reveals that the spiritual search of men was often related to their contempt of the body and the world. Frequently this included a specific contempt for women. Yet in spite of the most difficult conditions and obstacles women have struggled throughout the ages to follow their own spiritual quest. Yet the world history of renunciation and asceticism, which remains to be written, is certainly responsible for a great deal of misogyny. Much spirituality of the past can be seen as deeply dualistic in dividing men from women, men from each other and from the world, and in separating too sharply the experience of the body, work and matter from that of the spirit. Much of spirituality was entirely *unwholesome*.

So how are we to assess the current interest in spirituality, the availability of 'spiritual classics' or the 'wisdom texts' of different religions for the general reader, and the efforts to promote the spiritual development of pupils in British schools? Much critical thinking and debate are needed here, for a simple revival of past spiritualities is not enough. It could even be harmful. The old agendas of spirituality were too prescriptive, too much embedded in an ascetic and mystical flight from the world, too much centred on self-denial, which could be self-destructive rather than a path to real growth and fuller being. They were also too much tied to particular institutional settings and prescriptive, normative teachings, too much wedded to particular theological doctrines, to external authorities, dependence and heteronomy. A merely *historical approach* to studying different forms of spiritual life in the past, or a *theological approach* where the teaching of spirituality is tied to particular doctrines, is not sufficient for the development of the spirituality our society needs today. The contemporary *anthropological approach* to spirituality emphasizes that spirituality is intrinsic to the human subject as such. It is an approach which facilitates the resurgence and renewal of spirituality within a secular context. But one must ask then whether such an inclusive, universalizing understanding of spirituality gives at present enough attention to the social and political dimension of the human being in its definition of the human.

Christianity has always had a strong emphasis on the communal dimension, whether understood as the worshipping community, or the institution of the church, or the communion of saints, the body of Christ, or the Kingdom of God. Yet much of traditional spirituality has nevertheless been very individualistic in stressing the search of the soul for God and the salvation, sanctification or liberation of the individual. In medieval times the predominant locus of sanctification where the spiritual ideal could be lived to the full was the monastery, the convent, the cloister. These institutions represented a parallel community separated from mainstream society. With the rise of Protestantism the place of sanctification shifted from the cloister to ordinary life in society with its day-to-day relationships and responsibilities. Thus at the beginning of the modern period a new '*spirituality-of-being-in-the-world*' developed, which was not without earlier parallels, but could now flower in new forms. Soon the tension, and even conflict, between religion and science, developed. Contemporary sensibility still wrestles with this important issue – the challenge posed by the modern knowledge and world view of the sciences, the tension between our knowledge of the external world and that of our inner world of mind, consciousness and personal experience.

Today our approach to human beings is primarily pragmatic. But such an approach denies the need for self-transcendence, for a deeper, more reflective and contemplative awareness, for the discovery and exploration of a spiritual dimension which a perspective of faith sees as integral to all human beings. How far are our whole cultural ethos and our education able to make us into true human beings? How far are we not *under-humanized* or *de-humanized* in modern society rather than encouraged to develop our human potential to the fullest, a question which the French scientist and mystic Pierre Teilhard de Chardin asked with great poignancy?

In an earlier age when Christian religious ideals still informed the entire culture of the West, the human being was primarily understood in relation to the divine, to God. The naturalistic-scientific approach of modernity tends to relate the human being primarily to the animal and life worlds of the biosphere. These different approaches – to the world of our natural environment, to the depth dimension within ourselves, to the fullness of the Spirit, to the life of God – need to be combined and linked with each other in a way that is new and culturally transformative and creative. How can we develop a wholesome, truly world-affirming and culture-transforming spirituality? Perhaps it is the very questions and problems raised by modernity, and the new possibilities opening up with new, postmodern perspectives, that will also provide us with the opportunities to develop a truly holistic and transformative spirituality.

Contemporary spirituality is at the crossroads. The knowledge and presence of eastern religions in the West, the rise of new religious movements, the development of atheistic and agnostic humanisms have all contributed to the questioning of traditional spiritualities in their specifically religious contexts. To achieve a new religious breakthrough, a genuine transformation of both consciousness and society, it is no longer enough to return to the past and revive ancient spiritual ideals and instructions. The increasing process of globalization affects the interchange of spiritual ideals as much as anything else and makes us conscious that humanity possesses a religious and spiritual heritage whose riches are indispensable for the creation of a much needed global religious consciousness.

Will the rise of such a consciousness lead to a new flowering of spirituality in an age of postmodernity? This is a difficult question to answer but one can speculate about it. I would argue that it will. There are numerous current signs of a growing interest in spirituality, not only at the level of practice, in the growth of retreat houses, the increasing number of spiritual counsellors and spiritual writings, but also at the theoretical level of critical debate and new understanding. That the topic of spirituality attracts so much attention is part of the postmodern configuration where the previous trust in certainty, rationality and objectivity has broken down and the modern dominance of the rationalist–mechanistic thought patterns governing a positivistic science and technology has come under heavy criticism. The frequently mentioned paradigm shifts which are so characteristic of postmodern thinking are also important in spirituality, for in contemporary society spirituality is reflected upon and practised in a new context.

The importance of spirituality in a new social context

By now we have seen the proliferation of all kinds of personal, mystical spirituality which have developed relatively independently, without an impact on the whole of society. Today the public domain of politics and economics is marked by the *absence* of spirituality, rather than its presence. But in strong contrast to this absence there are also many signs of a hunger and thirst for 'things of the spirit', often expressed in very different and contrary ways. Postmodernism has dislodged the autonomous subject, but following Ricoeur in distinguishing between a naïve, a critical, and a reflexive subject, it is above all the critical–reflexive subject in process of transformation who is especially important in contemporary explorations and experiments of spirituality. But I first want to mention some important changes affecting the understanding of spirituality today.

Of all historical cultures, that of modernity is perhaps the most one-dimensional and the least open to transcendence. It is marked by great spiritual poverty and alienation where many people are deeply spiritually wounded or atrophied. The sociologist Peter Berger has referred to our modern world as a culture with no windows on the wonders of life. For many people there is no sense of a transcendent horizon, of the depth dimension and degrees of interiority to which human consciousness can have access. While modern psychoanalysis is exploring ever further the recesses of our conscious and unconscious mind, we seem to have lost a sense of the soul, a sense of the spiritual nature and destiny of the human being.

With regard to Christian spirituality, one can say that while it certainly enjoys a continuity with the past, it too has undergone some fundamental changes since the coming of modernity. It has been argued that 'the spiritual life has a history of its own which admits of epochal distinctions' and that there are some specific 'religious characteristics which distinguish spiritual life in the modern age from that of an earlier period'.[12] One significant difference is that postmodern society lives more under 'the shadow of spirit', to quote a book title,[13] than in the blazing light of full spiritual presence and power.

A full discussion of the new social and political contexts would require an analysis of the major characteristics of postmodern society with its complex global developments. I cannot undertake such a large task within the limits of this chapter, but I want to single out the democratization of human aspirations and the fundamental role of education in both its formal and informal sense, as a life-long process of learning and growth, as greatly significant for the transformation of our world.

Surprisingly perhaps, spirituality has now become an academic discipline, especially in the United States where a growing number of university courses on spirituality have come into existence.[14] But spirituality can be studied in Britain too. There exists an MA in Christian Spirituality at Heythrop College, University of London, whilst the University of Wales at Lampeter has introduced an MA in Comparative Spirituality. This is concerned with studying the spiritual traditions of China, India, the Middle East and Christian West. The Jesuit journal *The Way Supplement* has devoted one of its numbers to the topic 'Teaching spirituality' (1995),[15] which raises the question of whether spirituality can not only be studied, but also be taught. The new *Companion Encyclopedia of Theology* published by Routledge[16] includes a substantial section on 'Spirituality' and so does the *New Handbook of Living Religions*, published by Blackwell and Penguin.[17]

The most impressive scholarly achievement is probably the 25-volume cross-cultural series on *World Spirituality* where each volume concentrates on a particular faith.[18] Its general editor, the American Ewert Cousins, has stated in the Preface that the publication of this series is forging a new discipline in the field of religion, namely the discipline of spirituality which has its own central focus, categories and concepts, and its own distinct methodology. He writes:

> The transmission of spiritual wisdom may be the oldest discipline in human history. Yet this ancient discipline needs to be accorded its own place in academic studies; at the same time it must integrate the findings of other disciplines such as psychology, sociology, and critical historical research ... there is emerging a new discipline: global spirituality. Such a discipline would study spirituality not merely in one tradition or one era but in a comprehensive geographic and historical context. And it would take into account this vast body of data not in isolation but in interrelationship. In this sense, the present series is attempting not merely to retrieve an

ancient discipline in a modern academic mode but to lift it into a global context.[19]

This quotation highlights the importance of spirituality as a topic of study and research in contemporary academic circles. Sandra Schneiders, in her article 'Spirituality in the academy',[20] has described this newly emerging discipline of studies as interdisciplinary, descriptive-critical rather than prescriptive-normative, ecumenical, interreligious, and cross-cultural, as well as a holistic discipline

> in that its inquiry into human spiritual experience is not limited to explorations of the explicitly religious, i.e. the so-called *interior life*. The psychological, bodily, historical, social, political, aesthetic, intellectual, and other dimensions of the human subject of spiritual experience are integral to that experience insofar as it is the subject matter of the discipline of spirituality.[21]

Schneiders recognizes three different phases in the shaping of the study of spirituality as a new field. The first is 'essentially descriptive' and consists of 'historical, textual, and comparative studies', whereas the second phase is 'essentially analytical and critical, leading to an explanation and evaluation of the subject'. This is followed by a third phase which is 'synthetic and/or constructive, and leads to appropriation' in a Ricoeurian sense of 'the transformational actualization of meaning'. All these phases are connected to what she calls a 'triple finality' of spirituality as an academic discipline, which is first of all aimed 'at the production of cumulative knowledge', but is 'also intended by most students to assist them in their own spiritual lives and to enable them to foster the spiritual lives of others'. She concedes that

> While this triple finality contrasts with the traditional understanding of an academic discipline, it is actually not much different from the objective of the study of psychology or art. And increasingly even speculative theologians are realizing that good theology is not an exercise in abstract thought but reflection on the lived experience of the church community which should affect that life.[22]

The understanding of the study of spirituality in an open-ended, general human sense in the academy relates directly to the debates about spirituality within education,[23] especially in schools. In Britain, more than anything else it is the requirements of the 1988 Education Reform Act that schools must foster not only the intellectual, but also the *spiritual* and moral development of children which have stimulated debates about spirituality. How can spiritual development be promoted among children in schools, and what is to be understood by this? Moreover, what criteria should be applied in evaluating such development?

Much work among teachers and their mentors is currently devoted to these questions. Leading the field is perhaps the Templeton Project, a two-year research initiative undertaken by the Christian Education Movement and sponsored by the John Templeton Foundation. This research has tried to find out what spiritual development is, how it can be fostered and measured. It has involved the development of appropriate curriculum materials, now available in the form of a student resource book and a teacher's handbook, both entitled *Looking Inwards – Looking Outwards: Exploring Life's Possibilities*.[24] To foster spiritual development across the school curriculum means that teachers have to be adequately trained for this task, and the need for such training has considerable implications for further and higher education.

What does spirituality mean, especially in the context of education? The Templeton Project uses a broad, inclusive interpretation of spiritual development, a potential open to everyone and not confined to the development of religious beliefs or conversion to a particular faith. Thus, education towards spiritual development is not about religious nurture into a particular faith, but it is the development of an openness, of the capacity for deeper awareness and reflection, of empathy and sensitivity, imagination and creativity. In other words, it is the education of the human spirit which occurs through the arts and the sciences, through the senses, the emotions, the intellect and the will, but also through an appreciation of the specifically religious, and thus may include religious experience.

The lively current debates about the teaching of spirituality in schools and the study of spirituality in the academy highlight the importance of spirituality, its nature and significance, as a contemporary topic of growing and urgent concern. Although now approached in exciting new ways, it is not a new topic. Already in the late 1930s the French thinker Pierre Teilhard de Chardin pointed out the need for a systematic, critical study of spirituality and repeatedly emphasized the indispensable necessity for the human community to pay as close attention to its spiritual energy resources as to its material ones. He wrote that the phenomenon of spirit

> has rightly attracted human attention more than any other. We are coincidental with it. We feel it from within. It is the very thread of which the other phenomena are woven for us. It is the thing we know best in the world since we are itself, and it is for us everything.[25]

This passage expresses well the dialectic between the spirit within us and the spirit beyond us. Our self-reflective, centred, not diffuse consciousness must be the point where we can encounter and touch the reality of the living spirit through deepened awareness and inner perception. Several religions know of the 'inner eyes' of faith through which we can perceive the world and ourselves within a transformative spiritual vision. For Teilhard de Chardin the evolution of the entire cosmos, and of consciousness, was linked to the central phenomenon of spirit and spirituality. For him the hypothesis of a cosmos in spiritual transformation best explained the features of the world around and within us. Spirituality was understood by him within an overall evolutionary approach whereby consciousness is endowed with a dynamic, process-like nature, so that the era of the spiritual expresses itself as a process of growing spiritualization, a process at work in both individuals and society, leading towards personal and social transformation.[26]

In today's postmodern society new ideas about transformation and integration, about embodiment, inclusiveness of language and praxis, about the re-imaging and renaming of Ultimate Reality abound. And so does a growing sense of the interdependence and sacredness of all life, and of our special human relationship to the whole earth and the cosmos. To develop a *holistic, integral spirituality* which can respond to our new situation demands creative and critical rethinking of our traditions. Too often spirituality has been understood like a solid, reassuring fortress, clearly demarcated by the boundaries of tradition, narrowly defined and unchanging. But it is much more helpful to approach spirituality through the image of the journey, as something to be explored and ventured, as a process of growth and transformation. This process has assumed new meanings in our contemporary context.

There is much we can relate to in the spiritualities of the past. They can awaken and inspire us, but they also need to be reformed and reformulated. Faced with the choice of so many different spiritualities, what can the traditional and the new spiritualities offer us today? What is most distinctive about each of the spiritual traditions?

These questions can only be answered by looking at particular spiritualities in specific contexts, a task I cannot attempt here. But I do want to underline the general point that while we recognize more clearly than ever before the multiple kinds of spirituality existing in both past and present, there is also the growing awareness of the necessity for an appropriately developed spirituality responding to the needs of today. Spirituality will not be effective as a means of personal and social transformation if it remains merely a luxury for the few, accessible only to an educated élite and privileged class. It has to be understood not as a luxury, but as a necessity for all, a source of empowerment most needed in our broken postmodern world.

The Indian theologian Samuel Rayan distinguishes three different models of spirituality which provide a helpful clarification in this context.[27] He speaks first of *distributive spirituality* where some persons in society follow a spiritual life while others do not. Then there is an *alternating model of spirituality* where the same persons alternate their activities between spiritual practices and other engagements, and finally, he speaks of an *interpenetrative model of spirituality* where we all are spiritually engaged in all our actions, so that action and contemplation are integrally connected. This last model is most suitable for our society, so that the depth and integrity of a spiritual attitude are interconnected with social action, with 'response-ability' in the sense of being able to respond to all situations in the struggle of life for wholeness. In other words, in our postmodern context it is not so important what spirituality *is* but what it *does*. What it does to us as human beings.

The transformative potential of spirituality can be seen in the diverse explorations of spirituality within different contexts of the present world. Spirituality is of considerable importance within religious pluralism and interfaith dialogue where the spiritual significance of the other is a central issue. Spirituality is central to many debates of the women's movement, to those of Third World theologians and to ecological concerns. It is particularly among the women of the Third World that spirituality is understood as a struggle for life and wholeness. What is sought is a spirituality 'which constructs and nurtures what makes for a fuller life, for finer humanity, for a new earth'.[28] Others speak of an ecological revisioning of spirituality, of a balancing and right attitude to both our outer and inner environment.

The dialectic of the spirit as an immanent presence and transcendent horizon is expressed in religious teachings which speak of an eternal divine spark or the image of God as ultimate basis of the human being. This spiritual basis of the human, which is a challenge and call towards spiritual transformation and fulfilment, can be taken as the ultimate source of all human dignity, as the reason for the intrinsic value of each human person, which we must profoundly respect and respond to. Our secular declarations about human equality and human rights to a fully lived and fully realized humanity are in the last resort derived from this teaching about the spiritual nature of the human being.

Explorations into and experiments with spirituality will always be tentative and in need of further elaboration. In a truly postmodern vein the spiritual project remains an ongoing one, always somehow incomplete. But the connection between spirituality and postmodernism is important for several reasons: it affirms the possibility of spirituality in a secular society; it recognizes spirituality as an open-ended quest with the potential for considerable further development; it acknowledges the transformative potential of spirituality for contemporary consciousness and culture. Arguments exist both *for* and *against* the significance of postmodern thought for spirituality. To engage with them requires further re-examination and critical reflection on the meaning of spirituality itself. Samuel Rayan has said: 'Spiritual life is human life, the whole of human life inspired and led by the Spirit.'[29] To make sense of such a statement invites another essay.

Notes

1. M. Joy, 'Sainthood or heresy: contemporary options for women' in Morny Joy and Penelope Magee (eds), *Claiming Our Rites: Studies in Religion by Australian Women Scholars* (Adelaide: Australian Association for the Study of Religions, 1994), pp. 117–33. See also Andrea Günter (ed.), *Feministische Theologie und postmodernes Denken* (Stuttgart: Kohlhammer, 1996).
2. See P. Sheldrake, *Spirituality and History: Questions of Interpretation and Method* (New York: Crossroad, 1992); also the section on 'Spirituality' by various authors in P. Byrne and L. Houlden (eds), *Companion Encyclopedia of Theology* (London and New York: Routledge, 1995), pp. 511–686; also J. Cheslyn, G. Wainwright and E. Yarnold (eds), *The Study of Spirituality* (London: SPCK, 1986).
3. The great diversity of spiritualities is clear from the many publications in the series *Classics of Western Spirituality: A Library of Great Spiritual Masters* (1978–), editor-in-chief R. J. Payne (New York: Paulist Press/London:

SPCK); and also the series *World Spirituality: Encyclopedic History of the Religious Quest* (1986–), general editor E. Cousins (New York: Crossroad/ London: Routledge & Kegan Paul, also SCM Press). Particularly relevant for the understanding of spirituality within contemporary culture are vols 21 and 22 of this series: A. Faivre and J. Needleman (eds), *Modern Esoteric Spirituality* (New York: Crossroad, 1995) and Peter Van Ness (ed.), *Spirituality and the Secular Quest* (New York: Crossroad, 1996) This last volume looks at the precursors and beginnings of secular spirituality, and then examines spirituality within the context of both modernity and contemporary postmodernism.

4. See the challenging reflections by Tom W. Boyd, 'Is spirituality possible without religion? A query for the postmodern era' in Ann W. Astell (ed.), *Divine Representations: Postmodernism and Spirituality* (New York and Mahwah, NJ: Paulist Press, 1994), pp. 83–101.

5. Boyd, 'Is spirituality possible?', p. 83.

6. See note 4 above.

7. Elena Lugo, 'Reflections on philosophy, spirituality, and mariology' in Astell, *Divine Representations*, pp. 248–66. The quotations (her italics) are on p. 252.

8. Anna S. King, 'Spirituality: transformation and metamorphosis', *Religion*, 26.4 (October 1996), pp. 343–51. The quotation is on p. 343.

9. I have discussed this understanding of spirituality, in the context of contemporary feminism, at greater length in U. King, *Women and Spirituality: Voices of Protest and Promise* (London: Macmillan, 1993).

10. S. Schneiders, 'Spirituality as an academic discipline', *Christian Spirituality Bulletin*, 1.2 (Fall 1993), pp. 10–15. The quotation is from p. 11.

11. Schneiders, 'Spirituality'.

12. L. Dupré and D. E. Saliers (eds), *Christian Spirituality: Post-Reformation and Modern* (London: SCM, 1989), p. xiii.

13. See P. Berry and A. Wernick (eds), *Shadow of Spirit: Postmodernism and Religion* (London and New York: Routledge, 1992).

14. For some of the issues associated with the study of spirituality see Bradley C. Hanson (ed.), *Modern Christian Spirituality: Methodological and Historical Essays* (American Academy of Religion, Studies in Religion Number 62; Atlanta, GA: Scholars Press, 1990). See also the excellent articles in the *Christian Spirituality Bulletin, Journal of the Society for the Study of Christian Spirituality*, published by the Department of Theological Studies, Loyola Marymount University, Los Angeles, CA 90045, USA.

15. 'Teaching spirituality', *The Way Supplement*, 84 (Autumn 1995). Available from The Way Publications, 114 Mount Street, London W1Y 6AN.

16. See note 1 above.

17. See J. R. Hinnells (ed.), *A New Handbook of Living Religions* (Oxford: Blackwell, 1997; London: Penguin Books, 1998).

18. See note 3 above.

19. See General Preface to the Series *World Spirituality* (note 3 above). The quotation is taken from vol. 16, B. McGinn and J. Meyendorff (eds),

Christian Spirituality: Origins to the Twelfth Century (London: Routledge & Kegan Paul, 1986), pp. xiiif.

20. In Hanson, *Modern Christian Spirituality*, pp. 15–37.
21. Hanson, *Modern Christian Spirituality*, p. 33.
22. Hanson, *Modern Christian Spirituality*, p. 35.
23. See Clive Beck, 'Education for spirituality', *Interchange*, 17.2 (Summer 1986), pp. 156–8.
24. Published in 1997, these are available from the Christian Education Movement, Royal Buildings, Victoria Street, Derby DE1 1GW, England.
25. P. Teilhard de Chardin, *Human Energy* (London: Collins, 1969), p. 93.
26. I have discussed Teilhard's approach to spirituality at length in U. King, *Christ in All Things: Exploring Spirituality with Teilhard de Chardin*, (Maryknoll, NY: Orbis Books/London: SCM Press, 1997) and in *The Spirit of One Earth: Reflections on Teilhard de Chardin and Global Spirituality* (New York: Paragon House, 1989).
27. See S. Rayan 'The search for an Asian spirituality of liberation' in V. Fabella, P. K. H. Lee and D. Kwang-sun Suh (eds), *Asian Christian Spirituality: Reclaiming Traditions* (Maryknoll, NY: Orbis Books, 1992), pp. 11–30.
28. Fabella *et al.*, *Asian Christian Spirituality*, p. 3.
29. Rayan in Fabella *et al.*, *Asian Christian Spirituality*, p. 20.

7

The other Enlightenment project

Buddhism, agnosticism and postmodernity

Stephen Batchelor

Buddhism

The metaphor often used to describe Buddhism is that of a 'path'. Buddhism regards itself as the 'central path' (or the 'Middle Way'). But this is a fluid notion that can be continuously expanded. In the Buddha's first discourse it is presented as a moral resolve to avoid the extreme behaviours of indulgence and mortification. By the time of Nagarjuna – some six hundred years later – it has become a philosophical perspective that avoids the pitfalls of asserting either Being or Nothing as absolutes. In both cases it remains a metaphor: a device that creatively imagines a link between an everyday reality (a road, a street, a highway) and an organizing principle in a system of thought and practice. While Buddhist orthodoxies have sought to fix this link with dogmatic definitions of 'path', the ambiguity and contingency of its metaphorical nature keep breaking out in playful irreverence.

This is noticeable in Ch'an (Zen). A monk visits the Ch'an Master Chao-chou and asks: 'Where is the great way?' (Now to complicate matters, remember that the Sanskrit word *marga* [path] was translated by the Chinese *tao*, which in English we prefer to render as 'the Way' (replete with definite article and capital to lend it spiritual legitimacy, forgetting

the absence of definite articles or capitals in either Sanskrit or Chinese).)
Having fallen for this linguistic sleight of hand myself, I was able to be
surprised while standing on a street corner in Hong Kong and reading on
the street sign 'squiggle' 'squiggle', followed by one of the few Chinese
characters I could recognize, 'tao' – and beneath it in English 'Prince
Edward Road'. 'Where is the great way?' asks the monk. And Chao-chou
replies: 'Go back to the lights, turn left and it's the second on the right' (or
words to that effect).

I was once walking along the coastal path between Kingswear and
Brixham in South Devon. The footpath threaded through a patch of
woodland on the cliff edge and in post-monastic fashion I contemplated
the track about six feet in front of me. I was suddenly hit, like a soft blow
in the stomach, by what it meant for this thing to be a path. It was a path:
(1) because it led somewhere; (2) because it was free from obstruction; and
(3) because it was used by others. In what sense is the Buddhist 'path'
comparable to these aspects of a footpath? How could I link this visceral
insight of walking on a path with the metaphor of 'path' as spoken of in
Buddhism? To what extent did my internalized Buddhist idea of a 'path'
contribute to my experiencing this actual path in such a way? Might this
be an instance of how an idea from another culture is digested?

A path is most explicitly experienced as such when you find it again
after having lost it. When driving at a constant 70 mph along a motorway,
we are oblivious to the path-like nature of the experience. Like a
telephone, or a hand, we tend only to notice a path when we lose it or it
breaks down. At the moment of finding it again or recovering its use, we
experience exhilaration, gratitude and relief – but no sooner have these
feelings surfaced than we forget the startling, gift-like nature of the thing
and once more take it for granted.

At the moment of its recovery, a path reveals itself. Even if we haven't a
clue where it will lead, we know it will lead somewhere – which is infinitely
preferable to the terror of being lost. And simultaneous with the recovery
of purpose and direction, we recover freedom of movement. A path is a
negation; it is what it is due to the *absence* of obstruction. Being lost
entails not only loss of direction but also loss of the freedom to move. We
get entangled in brambles and undergrowth, stuck in gullies, bogged down
in sand and mud. A path is nothing but a stretch of ground from which
such obstacles have either been removed or circumvented. And
simultaneous with the recovery of direction and freedom, we recover
community. For recent footprints show that others have followed the

same track. A path is witness to the presence of creatures like ourselves, while to be lost is to be terribly alone. Even if the path is deserted, even if no one has passed by in days, we are reconnected to the human (and animal) community. And simply by walking along it, we too maintain it for those who will come later. Being on a path implies both indebtedness to those who have preceded us and responsibility for those who will follow.

Do these implicit elements of a path illuminate the metaphor of 'path' in Buddhism? How does the central path embody purposeful direction, unobstructed freedom of movement and realization of community? There are parallels with the doctrine of 'taking refuge in the three Jewels'. The three Jewels (Buddha, Dharma and Sangha) are the primary, non-negotiable values in which commitment to a Buddhist way of life is rooted. A Buddhist is even defined as a person who consciously commits himself or herself to these values.

'Buddha' here refers not to the historical figure of Gautama, but to the awakened perspective on life (enlightenment) realized by Gautama. It is the goal, the destination of the path. Just as walking along a path draws one to an as yet unknown but intimated destination, so the practice of Buddhism draws one to an as yet unknown but intimated meaning. Engaging in the practice grants one confidence in the direction and purpose of one's life. 'Dharma' refers not only to the teaching of Gautama but more crucially to the application of that teaching in the world. It is equivalent to the act of walking along the path. Like walking, it requires a rhythmic and unimpeded pace, unobstructed by the thickets of hesitation, aggression, attachment, restlessness and lethargy. And 'Sangha' means community. This practice entails participation in a communal endeavour. It cannot take place in isolation. For we belong to a tradition; we follow in the footsteps of those who have preceded us. But this tradition evolves. The path is maintained for those who will come later only by what we do now. In practising this way of life, we are simultaneously indebted to and responsible for a community of which we are a part.

So 'taking refuge in the three Jewels' ceases to be merely the formal act of admission to the Buddhist religion, and becomes instead a metaphor of sustained authenticity in treading the path. ('Jewel' in Sanskrit, by the way, is *ratna*, the common word for a precious gem. When it came to be translated into Tibetan, instead of the common word for jewel, the Tibetans chose (or coined?) the term *dkon mchog* – literally 'supreme rarity'. So the 'three Jewels' become the 'three Supreme Rarities'. 'Supreme Rarity' was subsequently used by Christian missionaries in the nineteenth century to translate 'God'.)

Yet this path is not (like an ordinary path) something apart from oneself on which one treads. One creates this path within the contours of one's own internal and communal landscape. It is like a thread weaving its way through the unfolding fabric of experience. A many-stranded thread, though, irreducible to any particular activity (like meditation). Embracing one's vision, ideas, speech, action, livelihood, resolve, mindfulness and concentration, it encompasses the complexity of being in a world.

Over time, metaphors undergo shifts of nuance and association. Is it still possible to understand the metaphor of path today as it would have been understood in the societies of Asia where it originated? What does a path mean for someone used to the rectilinear grid of a modern city? Probably little more than one of several possibilities for recreation. In an urban environment paths have become a functional network of streets that go everywhere and nowhere, whose macadam surface is welded to the concrete and brick on either side. Wilderness has been either sealed over or trapped within parks. Elsewhere it is mapped, owned, legislated, fenced off, monitored from the air, criss-crossed with roads.

In those traditional societies where this metaphor of path evolved, wilderness was dangerous and unknown. You would not walk alone on the paths that threaded through it. You would travel in well-organized caravans, in the company of those you trusted, armed to the teeth. Paths were rare and one's survival depended on them. But this has changed. Today wilderness itself has become a 'Supreme Rarity', a value in danger of being lost, the survival of which is under threat. While path (in its contemporary guise of roads, railways, air lanes, the information superhighway) is becoming a metaphor of domination rather than freedom.

The large authoritarian institutions that Buddhist societies have created reflect the clumsy, slow-moving but protective caravans that crossed the forests, steppes and deserts of Asia. Today the individual in search of awakening may well start out on those well-trodden and familiar roads but, growing in self-confidence, may want to branch off on to footpaths and seek indistinct trails that peter out. Such a person longs not for the security of the path but for those unknown places where there is little trace of marauding humanity. He or she may be more deeply inspired by the metaphor of open, untrammelled wilderness rather than that of a path.

So might we discern a trend in Buddhism of moving away from dependence on organized religious institutions towards a more individuated form of practice, in which each person finds his or her own way within the *dharmadhatu*: the 'Dharma realm'? A way of life that subverts the traditional legitimating myth of 'path' with a myth of recovered wilderness? After centuries in premodern societies, Buddhism finds itself abruptly catapulted into postmodern societies, where even its central metaphor of 'path' is questionable.

Agnosticism

The term 'agnostic' was coined by Thomas Huxley in the 1880s as a joke. As the member of a small philosophical circle, he felt out of place with people who could so easily identify themselves with a particular persuasion. So he decided to call himself 'Agnostic' in order that he too, as he said, 'could have a tail like all the other foxes'. 'It came into my head', he recalled, 'as suggestively antithetical to the "Gnostic" of Church History who professed to know so much about the very things of which I was ignorant.'[1] He nonetheless came to see it as demanding as any moral, philosophical or religious creed. But instead of a creed, he saw it as a *method* realized through 'the vigorous application of a single principle', positively expressed as: 'follow your reason as far as it will take you', and negatively as: 'do not pretend that conclusions are certain which are not demonstrated or demonstrable'.[2] He called it the 'agnostic faith'.

Whatever Huxley's motives in coining the term, it caught on. Within less than twenty years it was being applied to Buddhism by Ananda Metteyya (Allan Bennett), the first Englishman to take the vows of a Buddhist monk. Bennett had been ordained in Burma in 1901 and set out to promote the Dharma in the West via *Buddhism: An Illustrated Review*, a magazine he edited in Rangoon. The October 1905 issue quotes from a letter he wrote to the 1904 Free Thought Congress (a celebration of the pro-scientific/anti-religious position inspired in large measure by Huxley): 'The position of Buddhism on these vital problems', writes Bennett, 'is exactly coincidental, in its fundamental ideas, with the modern agnostic philosophy of the West ...'[3] The idea is further developed in the same issue in an article 'Buddhism: an agnostic religion' by Professore Alessandro Costa.

A key source for Bennett's and Costa's view of the agnostic nature of Buddhism would doubtless have been this famous passage from the *Culamalunkya Sutta* in the *Majjhima Nikaya*:

> Suppose, Malunkyaputta, a man were wounded by an arrow thickly smeared with poison, and his friends and companions brought a surgeon to treat him. The man would say: 'I will not let the surgeon pull out the arrow until I know the name and clan of the man who wounded me; whether the bow that wounded me was a long bow or a crossbow; whether the arrow that wounded me was hoof-tipped or curved or barbed.'
>
> All this would still not be known to that man and meanwhile he would die. So too, Malunkyaputta, if anyone should say: 'I will not lead the noble life under the Buddha until the Buddha declares to me whether the world is eternal or not eternal, finite or infinite; whether the soul is the same as or different from the body; whether or not an awakened one continues or ceases to exist after death', that would still remain undeclared by the Buddha and meanwhile that person would die.[4]

Over the course of its history, however, Buddhism has tended to lose its agnostic dimension through becoming institutionalized as a religion with dogmatic belief systems. Periodically (as with Zen and Tantra) this process has been challenged and even reversed, but in traditional Asian societies this never lasted long. The power of organized religion has swiftly reasserted itself – usually by subsuming rebellious ideas into the canons of a revised orthodoxy.

Consequently, as the Dharma emigrates westward, it is treated as a religion – albeit an 'Eastern' one. The very term 'Buddhism' (an invention of Western scholars for which there is no exact equivalent in Asia) suggests that it is a creed to be lined up alongside other creeds. This perception of Buddhism as a religion obscures and distorts the encounter of the Dharma with secular, agnostic culture. Yet could it be that the Dharma might in fact have more in common with Godless secularism than with the bastions of religion? Might agnosticism serve as a more fertile common ground for dialogue than any attempt to make Buddhist sense of Allah?

Today the force of the term 'agnosticism' has been lost. It has come to legitimate an avoidance of the existential questions posed by birth and death. Just as the modern agnostic tradition has tended to lose its confidence and lapse into scepticism, so Buddhism has tended to lose its critical edge and lapse into religiosity. What each has lost, however, the other may be able to help restore. In its encounter with secular culture, the Dharma may recover its agnostic imperative, while agnosticism may be helped to recover its soul.

So what would be the features of an 'agnostic Buddhist'? Such a person would not regard the Dharma as a source of 'answers' to questions of where we came from, where we are going, what happens after death. He or she would seek such knowledge in the appropriate domains: astrophysics, evolutionary biology, neuro-science, etc. An agnostic Buddhist would therefore not be a 'believer' with claims to revealed information about supernatural or paranormal phenomena, and in this sense would not be 'religious'. An agnostic Buddhist would look to the Dharma for metaphors of existential *confrontation* rather than metaphors of existential *consolation*. He or she would start by facing up to the primacy of anguish and uncertainty (*dukkha*), then proceed to apply a set of practices to understand the human dilemma and work towards a resolution. An agnostic Buddhist would eschew atheism as much as theism, and would be as reluctant to regard the universe as devoid of meaning as endowed with meaning. (For to deny either God or meaning is surely just the antithesis of affirming them.) Yet such an agnostic stance would not be based on disinterest. It would be founded on a passionate recognition that *I do not know*. It would confront the enormity of having been born instead of reaching for the consolation of a belief. It would strip away, layer by layer, the views that conceal the mystery of being here at all.

The process of stripping away consolatory illusions by holding true to *agnosis* (not-knowing) leads to what could be called 'deep agnosticism'. A Zen koan (case 41 of the *Gateless Gate*) illustrates this well. It reads:

Bodhidharma sat facing the wall. The second patriarch, standing in the snow, cut off his arm and said: 'Your disciple's mind is not yet at peace. I beg you, Master, give it rest.' Bodhidharma said, 'Bring me your mind and I will put it to rest'. The patriarch replied, 'I have searched for the mind but have never been able to find it'. Bodhidharma said, 'I have finished putting it to rest for you'.[5]

This deep agnosticism is further evident in such formal Ch'an concepts as *wu-hsin* (no mind) and *wu-nien* (no-thought) (as well as the popularized

'Don't Know Mind' of the Korean Son Master Seung Sahn). It also reflects the Sixth Ch'an Patriarch Hui-neng's initial insight as a young boy when, after receiving payment for some firewood, he chanced across a man reciting the *Diamond Sutra*. According to tradition, it was upon hearing the words 'must produce a mind that stays in no place'[6] that Hui-neng was suddenly awakened.

As one of the best known texts of the *Perfection of Wisdom* (*Prajnaparamita*) literature of Mahayana Buddhism, the *Diamond Sutra* takes as its central theme the idea of emptiness (*sunyata*). 'Emptiness' is a deliberately unappetizing term used to undercut yearnings for religious, psychological or metaphysical consolation. Although a noun, it does not in any way denote a thing or state. It is not something one 'realizes' in a moment of mystical insight that 'breaks through' to a transcendent reality concealed behind yet mysteriously underpinning the empirical world. No do things 'arise' from emptiness and 'dissolve' back into it as though it were some kind of formless, cosmic stuff.

So what is emptiness? According to the second-century CE philosopher Nagarjuna: 'Whatever is contingently emergent is said to be emptiness.'[7] Emptiness is the simple negation of any intrinsic, non-contingent identity in either oneself or anything else. Although the restless mind of Bodhidharma's disciple appeared to exist in and of itself and be tormented by an anguish fused with its own self-identity, by enquiring deeply into its nature, he found nothing he could put his finger on and say 'this is it!' Emptiness is the infinite unfindability of things. But this does not mean that nothing exists; it only implies that the deeper one delves into the heart of things, the more their utter contingency becomes apparent. Rather than being confined as fixed essences, things are released as changing, processual events configured by an unprecedented and unrepeatable matrix of causes, conditions components as well as conceptual and linguistic conventions.

Nagarjuna continues: 'Emptiness is contingently configured; it is the central path.'[8] So emptiness is as contingent as anything else; it has no privileged ontological status. Even more surprising is Nagarjuna's equating of emptiness with that key metaphor of the Buddhist enlightenment project: the central path. In 1397, while in a hermitage in the hills north of Lhasa, the Tibetan philosopher Tsongkhapa commented on this passage. 'Emptiness', he explains, 'has relinquished the extremes of Being and Nothing. Thus it is both the centre itself and the central path. *Emptiness is the track on which the centred person moves.*'[9]

Track? The Tibetan word Tsongkhapa uses for 'track' is *shul*, a somewhat obscure term defined by the dictionary as *rjes*, which means an 'impression', i.e. a mark which remains after that which made it has passed by – a footprint, for example. In other contexts, *shul* is used to describe the scarred hollow in the ground where a house once stood; the channel worn through rock where a river runs in flood; the indentation in the grass where an animal slept last night. All these are *shul*: the impression of something that used to be there.

A path is a *shul* because of its essentially negative nature: it is an impression in the ground left by the regular tread of feet, a passage which is clear of obstruction. So we can translate *shul* as 'track', which also in English means a path as well as an impression left by an animal or person. To experience the 'track-like' nature of emptiness would be like recovering a path that had been lost, or stumbling into a clearing in the forest, where suddenly you can move freely and see clearly. To know emptiness is to experience the shocking absence of what normally determines the sense of who we are. It may only last a moment, before the habits of a lifetime reassert themselves and close in once more. But for that moment, one witnesses oneself and the world as immediate, vivid, open and vulnerable.

This free and open space is the very centre of Dharma practice. As Tsongkhapa says, it is both the centre *and* the central path. It is both wilderness *and* track. A life centred in awareness of emptiness is a way of being in this changing, shocking, painful, joyous, frustrating, awesome, stubborn and ambiguous reality. Emptiness is a way of being that leads not beyond this reality but into its heart. Rather than a state of transcendent, mystical absorption, it is a dynamic, processual experience: the track on which the centred person *moves*.

As a negation, emptiness can offer no definitive, positive revelation of Reality. As this awareness becomes stiller and clearer, things become not only more vivid but also more baffling. The more deeply we know something in this way, the more deeply we do not know it. The ultimate ambiguity of experience is that it is simultaneously knowable *and* unknowable. No matter how well one may know something, at the same time one has to confess '*I don't really know what this is*'. One has to let go of the insistence to pin things down in a categorical way. One is invited to encounter their mystery.

Such unknowing is the tap-root of deep agnosticism. When even the concept of emptiness is suspended, the mind has nowhere to rest. And we are free to begin a radically other kind of questioning: a perplexity which is already present within unknowing itself. When we find ourselves baffled and puzzled by things, they present themselves as questions. Habitual assumptions and descriptions suddenly fail and one hears one's stammering voice cry out: 'What is this?' Or simply: 'What?' or 'Why?' Or perhaps no words at all, just '?' Such perplexity is neither frustrated nor merely curious about a specific detail of experience. It is an intense, focused questioning into what is unfolding at any given moment. It is the engine that drives one into the heart of what is unknown.

This perplexed questioning is another way of understanding the centre and the central path. In refusing to be drawn into the answers of 'yes' or 'no', 'it is this', or 'it is that', it lets go of the polarities of affirmation and negation, something and nothing. Like life itself, it just keeps going, free from the need to hold to any fixed position – including those of Buddhism. It prevents awareness from becoming a passive, routinized stance, which may accord with a belief system but renders experience numb and opaque. Perplexity keeps awareness on its toes. It reveals experience as transparent, radiant and unimpeded. To give Tsongkhapa a Zen twist: *Perplexity is the track on which the centred person moves.*

Postmodernity

A postmodern world that takes for granted the plurality and ambiguity of perception, the fragmented and contingent nature of reality, the elusive, indeterminate nature of self, the arbitrariness, inauthenticity and anguish of human existence, would seem to fit Buddhism like a glove. Yet this is nothing new. Western advocates of Buddhism, from Schopenhauer onwards, have all tended to be impressed by the compatibility of its doctrines with their own way of seeing the world.[10] Kantians saw the view of Kant in Buddhism, logical positivists those of Bertrand Russell, just as today deconstructionists behold the unravellings of Jacques Derrida. Within the last hundred years the teachings of the Buddha have confirmed the views of theosophists, fascists, environmentalists and quantum physicists alike. Then is Buddhism just an exotic morass of incompatible ideas, a 'Babylon of doctrines' as the sixteenth-century missionary Matteo Ricci suspected? Or is this another illustration of the Buddha's parable of the blind men who variously interpret an elephant as a pillar, a wall, a rope or a tube depending on which bit of the animal's anatomy they clutch? They may well be as many kinds of Buddhism as there are ways the Western mind has to apprehend it. In each case 'Buddhism' denotes something else. But what is it really? The answer: nothing you can put your finger on. To fix the elephant in either time or space is to kill her. The elephant is both empty and perplexing. She breaths and moves – in ways no one can foresee.

This fluidity has enabled Buddhism throughout its history to cross cultural frontiers and adapt itself creatively to situations quite different from those in its lands of origin on the Indian sub-continent. (The most striking example being that of its movement nearly two thousand years ago to China.) This creative process requires Buddhism to imagine itself as something different. It entails adopting compatible elements from the new host culture while at the same time critiquing elements of that culture which are at odds with its own Buddhist values. So it is hardly surprising that Buddhists today would instinctively home in on elements of postmodernity that resonate with their own understanding of the Dharma. The danger is that, for the sake of appearing 'relevant', they sacrifice the equally vital need to retain a lucid, critical perspective.

The element of postmodernity that potentially promises Buddhist voices access to contemporary culture is implicit in Jean-François Lyotard's simplified but seminal definition of 'postmodern' as 'incredulity toward grand narratives'.[11] The grandest of all these grand narratives for Lyotard and others is the European Enlightenment Project itself: the certainty of human progress through reason and science, which began in the eighteenth century. As soon as conviction in this myth wavers, a host of other assumptions are thrown into question. Through focusing on change and uncertainty rather than assured continuity, through emphasizing contingency, ambivalence and plurality, postmodern thinkers have come to hear voices of the Other: those the Enlightenment Project has either suppressed, ignored, or disdained: women, citizens of the Third World, non-European systems of thought such as Buddhism.

As a Buddhist I find myself reading erudite texts on themes such as the nature of the 'self', which explore ideas quite familiar to me as a Buddhist yet fail to make even a passing reference to the fact that this kind of analysis and discourse has been pursued in Asia for more than two thousand years. I sense at these times what women must feel about texts that blithely assume a male perspective as normative. The habit of treating the 'East' as Other is a deeply engrained European trait that goes back at least as far as Euripides and is ironically perpetuated even by postmodern writers. Yet there are signs of change. After the usual Eurocentric analysis, Galen Strawson concludes in a recent article, 'The sense of the self': 'Perhaps the best account of the existence of the self is one that may be given by certain Buddhists.'[12] Note the hesitation: 'Perhaps ...,' '... may be ...,' '... certain Buddhists ...' (not all of them of course).

Whatever features of postmodernity may be apparent in Buddhism, it would be foolish to describe Buddhist thought as 'postmodern' – for the simple reason that Buddhism has undergone no phase of modernity to be 'post' of. Buddhist cultures have evolved according to the grand narrative of their own Enlightenment Project. Consequently, two broad but opposing trends can be seen in the way Buddhism encounters contemporary Western culture.

In recognizing, on the one hand, the breakdown of the grand narratives of the West, Buddhists might seek to replace them with their own grand narrative of enlightenment. This is explicit in the stated goals of at least two of the most successful Buddhist movements in Britain today: the Friends of the Western Buddhist Order (FWBO), who aim to create a 'New Society' founded on Buddhist principles, and Soka Gakkai International (SGI), who seek to realize 'Kosen Rufu' – the world-wide spread of Nichiren Daishonin's Buddhism.[13] Although both organizations are contemporary reformed Buddhist movements, from a postmodern perspective they remain entranced by the legitimating myth of a grand narrative that promises universal emancipation. If a defining trait of our times is indeed widespread loss of credibility in such narratives and their inability any longer to compel consensus, then such ambitions may be doomed to frustration.

Yet, on the other hand, if Buddhists find themselves in sympathy with postmodern incredulity towards grand narratives, then they might be compelled to imagine another kind of Buddhism altogether. They will try to rearticulate the guiding metaphors of Buddhist tradition in the light of postmodernity. An attitude of incredulity would itself tend to resonate more with the metaphor of wilderness than with that of path, with the possibilities of unbounded landscape as opposed to the secure confinement of a highway.

The key notion in such an endeavour would be 'emptiness'. For here we have a notion that shares with postmodernism a deep suspicion of a single, non-fragmentary self, as well as any 'transcendental signified' such as God or Mind. It too celebrates the disappearance of the subject, the endlessly deferred play of language, the ironically ambiguous and contingent nature of things. Yet in other respects it parts company with the prevailing discourses of postmodernity. Meditation on emptiness is not a mere intellectual exercise, but a contemplative discipline rooted in an ethical commitment to non-violence. It is not just a description in unsentimental language of the way reality unfolds, it offers a therapeutic approach to the dilemma of human anguish.

Proponents of the doctrine of emptiness, at least from the time of Nagarjuna, have been subjected to the same kind of criticism as postmodernists receive today. They too have stood accused of nihilism, relativism, and undermining the basis for morality and religious belief. And not only from non-Buddhists; the concept of emptiness is still criticized within the Buddhist tradition itself.[14] The history of the idea of emptiness has been the history of the struggle to demonstrate that far from undermining an ethical and authentic way of life, such a life is actually realized through embracing the implications of emptiness.

The emptiness of self, for instance, is not the denial of individual uniqueness, but the denial of any permanent, partless and transcendent basis for individuality. The anguish and uncertainty of human existence are only exacerbated by the pre-conceptual, spasm-like grip in which such assumptions of transcendence hold us. While seeming to offer security in the midst of an unpredictable and transient world, paradoxically this grip generates an anxious alienation from the processes of life itself. The aim of Buddhist meditations on change, uncertainty and emptiness is to help one understand and accept these dimensions of existence and thus gently lead to releasing the grip.

By paying mindful attention to the sensory immediacy of experience, we realize how we are created, moulded, formed by a bewildering matrix of contingencies that continually arise and vanish. On reflection, we see how we are formed from the patterning of the DNA derived from our parents, the firing of a hundred billion neurons in our brains, the cultural and historical conditioning of the twentieth century, the education and upbringing given us, all the experiences we have ever had and choices we have ever made. These processes conspire to configure the unrepeatable trajectory that culminates in this present moment. What is here now is the unique but shifting impression left by all of this, which I call 'me'.

Moreover, this gradual dissolution of a transcendental basis for self nurtures an empathetic relationship with others. The grip of self not only leads to alienation but numbs one to the anguish of others. Heartfelt appreciation of our own contingency enables us to recognize our inter-relatedness with other equally contingent forms of life. We find that we are not isolated units but participants in the creation of an ongoing, shared reality.

A postmodern perspective would question the mythic status of Buddhism and Agnosticism. In letting go of 'Buddhism' as a grand, totalizing narrative that explains everything, we are freed to embark on the unfolding of our own individuation in the context of specific local and global communities. We may find in this process that we too are narratives. Having let go of the notion of a transcendental self, we realize we are nothing but the stories we keep telling ourselves in our own minds and relating to others. We find ourselves participating in a complex web of narratives: each telling its own unique story while inextricably interwoven with the tales of others. Instead of erecting totalitarian, hierarchic institutions to set our grand narratives in brick and stone, we look to imaginative, democratic communities in which to realize our own *petits récits*: small narratives.

Such a view is inevitably pluralistic. Instead of seeing itself in opposition to other grand narratives that seem to contradict or threaten it, Buddhism remembers how in its vital periods it has emerged out of its interactions with religions, philosophies, and cultures other than its own. This reminds one of the traditional Hua-yen image of the Jewelled Net of Indra: that vast cosmic web at the interstices of which is a jewel that reflects every other jewel. Today this image suggests the biosphere itself: that vast interdependent web of living systems that sustain each other in a miraculous whole. Which brings us back to the metaphor of wilderness as an image of a postmodern, postpath practice of Buddhism.

Acknowledgement

The second section of this chapter draws on material from my book *Buddhism Without Beliefs: A Contemporary Guide to Awakening* (London: Bloomsbury, 1997).

Notes

1. From T. H. Huxley's essay 'Agnosticism' (1889) included in *Science and the Christian Tradition* (London: Macmillan, 1904), p. 239.
2. Huxley, 'Agnosticism', pp. 245–6.
3. *Buddhism: An Illustrated Review*, II.1 (Rangoon, October 1905), p. 86.
4. Abridged from *Culamalunkya Sutta* (*Majjhima Nikaya* 63), trans. Nanomoli Thera and Bhikkhu Bodhi, *The Middle Length Sayings of the Buddha* (Boston: Wisdom, 1995), pp. 534–6.

5. Koun Yamada, *Gateless Gate* (Los Angeles, 1979), p. 208.
6. Philip B. Yampolsky, *The Platform Sutra of the Sixth Patriarch* (New York: Columbia University Press, 1967), p. 94.
7. Nagarjuna, *Mulamadhyamakakarika* XXIV:18a–b. My own translation from the Tibetan: /*rten cing 'brel bar 'byung ba gang*//*de ni stong pa nyid du bshad.*
8. Nagarjuna, *Mulamadhyamakakarika* XXIV:18c–d. My own translation from the Tibetan: /*de ni brten nas gdags pa ste*//*de nyid dbu ma'i lam yin no.*
9. Tsongkhapa, *rTsa she tik chen rigs pa'i rgya mtsho* (Sarnath, 1973), p. 431. The Tibetan reads: … *stong pa nyid de ni yod med kyi mtha gnyis spangs pas dbu ma dang de'i lam ste dbu ma pas bgrod pa'i shul yin no.*
10. See Andrew P. Tuck, *Comparative Philosophy and the Philosophy of Scholarship: On the Western Interpretation of Nagarjuna* (New York/Oxford: OUP, 1990).
11. Jean-François Lyotard, *The Postmodern Condition: A Report on Knowledge,* trans. Geoff Bennington and Brian Massumi (Manchester: Manchester University Press, 1986), p. xxiv. I have translated Lyotard's *grands récits* as 'grand narratives' rather than 'meta-narratives' as found in this English translation.
12. Galen Strawson, 'The sense of self', *London Review of Books* (18 April 1996), pp. 21–2.
13. For further information on these organizations, see Stephen Batchelor, *The Awakening of the West: The Encounter of Buddhism and Western Culture* (London: Thorsons, 1994).
14. See, for example, S. K. Hookham, *The Buddha Within: Tathagatagarbha Doctrine According to the Shentong Interpretation of the Ratnagotravibhaga* (Albany: State University of New York Press, 1991).

8

Faith in the future?

Islam and postmodernity

Martin Forward

Modernity has been a problematic historical and ideological era for Islam. The historical era in which modernism flourished was, for most Muslims, inextricably linked with the imperial system. Large tracts of the Muslim world were ruled by Christian powers: the British, the French, or the Dutch. Yet, in its origins, Islam was a successful political polity. Thus, Islamic Law developed strategies for coping with the treatment of minority groups within the territories in which Muslims were numerically superior or politically dominant. However, it has advanced much less defined guidance for situations in which Muslims are in a minority, either in numbers or else in civic authority. Modernism has therefore been associated in the mind of Muslims with their political, social and economic subservience to other religio-cultural entities.

If the agents of modernism had made Muslims wary of its potential benefits, many of its chief concerns have also been profoundly inimical to the teachings and dogmas of Islam, especially modernism's ideological interrogation of traditional religious dogmas. In particular, the central Islamic conviction in the Qur'an's divine origin has resisted modernist convictions that scripture can either be treated as any other book from the past might be, and even be judged and found wanting in comparison with other works that have survived the erosions of time.

Nevertheless, the political dominance of the modernist and moderniz- ing West created a small class of Muslims who were deeply influenced by its presuppositions and by the economic rewards it held out to those who worked as its agents, or who felt that Islam could only regenerate itself by creatively engaging with modernism, taking what was perceived to be good and condemning what was regarded as base. Not least in British India, the modernist movement was embraced by a small number of Muslim intellectuals from the middle years of the nineteenth century.

Even so, because of Islam's suspicion of modernism, many nineteenth- and twentieth-century Western proponents of modernism have depreciated Islam as a backward-looking religion, an agent of religious, social and economic repression. In more recent years, the rise of Islamic 'fundamentalism' has intensified this interpretation among critics of traditional forms of Islam. It is therefore arguable that Islam cannot flourish in a modernist milieu, but only in one where other historical and ideological forces permit a less fractious relationship between Muslims and the West.

Is postmodernism a more friendly environment than modernism for Muslims? This would depend on whether postmodernism is a genuinely new and global phenomenon, which treats all comers on an equal basis, or is simply the tired petering out of the parochial and often inequitable Western concept of modernity. The distinguished Islamicist Wilfred Cantwell Smith has written of postmodernity:

> Has anyone with new ideas since the Stone Age not been 'postmodern' in this new sense of moving beyond what in his or her recent past had been perceived as modern? Furthermore, the 'postmodern' concept is intolerably provincial, dismissing the recent history of all cultures other than the West's.[1]

It is clearly Smith's view that postmodernity is inextricably linked to modernity and is excessively parochial. Time will tell whether he is right to be so dismissive.

Ameer Ali

This chapter looks at one important Indian Muslim modernist figure, Syed Ameer Ali. (I have spelled Ameer Ali's name in the anglicized way he did, a small but not insignificant illustration of the importance to him of his Western-style education.) It then looks at Akbar Ahmed's cautious defence of postmodernism against modernism; he is a contemporary

Pakistani Muslim social anthropologist and Cambridge don, and one of the comparatively few Muslim scholars not simply to dismiss post-modernism as a parochial Western obsession. Our purpose is to consider aspects of Islam's engagement with modernism and postmodernism.

Ameer Ali (6 April 1849–3 August 1928) was a man of many parts: he was a distinguished lawyer, becoming a judge of the Bengal High Court in 1890; a politician whose moment of glory was when, as secretary of the London branch of the Muslim League, he represented Muslim demands to the Secretary of State, Lord Morley, prior to the Morley–Minto Act of 1909; a philanthropist who founded the British Red Crescent Society in 1897 to succour the wounded in the Graeco-Turkish war. Perhaps he is best remembered now for his life of the prophet Muhammad, which was first published as *A Critical Examination of the Life and Teachings of Mohammed* in 1873, when he was a student in London. An expanded form was published from London in 1891 as *The Life and Teachings of Mohammed or The Spirit of Islam*, which was revised as *The Spirit of Islam* in 1902 (published in Calcutta) and revised again in 1922 (published in London).

Ameer Ali was a first-generation Anglo-Muhammadan, versed in both Islamic learning and Western lore. He was therefore one of the first Muslim 'modernists', that group which attempted, however cautiously, to interpret Islam in ways congruent with current Western intellectual assumptions. He was born at Chinsura in Bengal, the fourth of five sons of Saadat Ali, whose grandfather came to India from Persia in Nadir Shah's invasion of 1739. Saadat Ali had trained as a *hakim* (a Muslim physician) but was possibly wealthy enough not to need to practise his profession after his marriage. Ameer Ali recollected that 'we were not rich but in comfortable circumstances'.[2] The family claimed descent from the prophet Muhammad through his daughter Fatima. Ameer Ali therefore took the title of Saiyid (anglicized as Syed), a word he explained was 'used to signify deference and respect to a descendant of the Prophet'.[3] This title was particularly important to him because he was a 'twelver' Shia (i.e. a member of the *ithna 'ashariyya*, who accept a line of twelve imams – descendants of the prophet Muhammad through his daughter Fatima, personalities whom Shia Muslims believe to have been the legitimate leaders of the Islamic community in their time – ending with Muhammad al-Muntazar 'the awaited' who, it is believed, went into occultation 874 but who will appear at a pre-ordained time to fill the earth with justice.

Saadat Ali was a devout Muslim, engaged upon writing a life of the prophet Muhammad when in 1856 he died of cholera.[4] He insisted upon a Muslim education for his sons, who were instructed by a *maulvi* in Persian and Urdu in the evening after school. Religious observance was, however, less punctiliously demanded of them; they attended only the evening prayers. Ameer Ali recorded that his mother 'was strict in the observance of the prescribed prayers' although she allowed the women of her household to neglect them if about their secular duties.[5] In his memoirs there is no mention of any of the family or servants observing Ramadan, the month of fasting. Many years later, he wrote that fasting 'for the student (who is engaged in the pursuit of knowledge – the Jihad ul-Akbar) ... is disallowed',[6] thus excluding himself from its demands. There is no evidence whether Ameer Ali ever undertook the *hajj*, the annual pilgrimage to Mecca; it seems unlikely that he would have done so without mentioning it somewhere in his writings. Presumably his family's 'comfortable circumstances' enabled them to devote themselves to *zakat* (almsgiving). Although the consensus of Muslims is that the performance of prayer, pilgrimage, fasting and almsgiving is a divine commandment to be obeyed, Saadat Ali's family were not so much lukewarm believers as devout Muslims struggling to seek out the relevance of Islam to their situation.

The situation was one that put many Muslims in British India at a disadvantage, religiously, politically and economically. By the time of Ameer Ali's birth, the British were the effective rulers of large tracts of north India. After 1835 in British India, Persian, the language of the Muslim élite, was progressively demoted from its status as the official language of higher education and government. Urdu became the language of government below the top levels, at least in Punjab, the United Provinces and Bihar until 1881.[7] Knowledge of English became increasingly important as the passport to remunerative employment. The possibility of a Western-style education was opened up to some Indians. Saadat Ali was persuaded by Dr Malet, then judge (possibly a district judge) of Orissa, and Dr Mowat, then Director of Public Instruction in Bengal, to give his sons an English education. Ameer Ali wrote that 'Although in those days English was not in favour with Moslems, my father felt the time was coming when it would be an important factor in the growth of the people'.[8] Thus, Ameer Ali in his youth read Gibbon, Milton, Keats, Shelley, Byron, Dr Johnson, Dickens and other English writers.[9]

When he went to college at Hooghly, one of his mentors was Maulawi

Karamat Ali (1796–1876), 'the venerable and venerated Mutawalli of the Shiah religious institution at Hooghly'.[10] Ameer Ali claimed that:

> whatever knowledge of Moslem philosophy I happen to possess, I owe to that truly great man. Every Sunday morning Moulvi Obaidollah, the Persian Professor, and I breakfasted with the Syed and scarcely ever left before 1 o'clock. We ranged over the whole region of Oriental history and philosophy.[11]

Karamat Ali had been in the service of the East India Company and had represented the Company at the court of Amir Dost Mohammed Khan at Kabul prior to his appointment as the mutawalli of the Hooghly imambara. He was in favour of British rule in India, and interpreted Muslim theology and practice so as to legitimize that rule. Indeed, his appointment at Hooghly from 1837 until his death in 1873 was in the gift of the British.[12] His book, the *Makhaz-i-Uloom*, which was translated by Obaidollah and Ameer Ali in 1867, was written as an essay for a prize offered by the British government official Sir C. E. Trevelyan (1807–86).[13] Ameer Ali's mentor would not have led him to question the legitimacy of British rule in India. Instead, he helped him to see Islam as justifying the *status quo*. Furthermore, Saadat Ali's relations with the British led his family to justify and support British rule in India. Waris, his eldest son, helped to restore order in the Shahabad district of Bihar in the aftermath of what Ameer Ali called 'the great Sepoy Revolt'.[14] Ameer Ali recorded this act without any recognition of the fact that some Muslims could regard such assistance as a disloyal act to Islam. Thus Ameer Ali's childhood and adolescence were influenced at home and at college by an interpretation of Islam which sought to accept and legitimate British rule in India, with a view to Muslims profiting from collaboration with the Raj.

Ameer Ali, a first-generation Anglo-Muhammadan, proud of his descent from the Prophet as a Saiyid ('prince', 'lord', 'chief', 'owner'), sought acceptance from the British social élite also. Yet Ameer Ali was not well thought of by the British ruling classes. To give one particular example, why was he elevated to the Privy Council? Not, it would seem, because the British Government, in whose gift the appointment was, considered him a natural ally. After Ameer Ali retired to England with his English wife and two sons in 1904, he launched the London branch of the Muslim League and became, at least in 1909, a central figure in the negotiations about forthcoming political reforms in India with the Secretary of State for India, Lord Morley. He led a deputation to Morley on 27 January 1909 and read a speech in which he claimed that the committee of the London Muslim League spoke 'on behalf of the Musulmans of India'.[15] The following day, Morley wrote to the Viceroy, Lord Minto, that

> Amir Ali, the head of them, is a vain creature, with a certain gift of length, and I believe that I could convert him from the Crescent to the Cross, if only I would make him a K.C.S.I. [Knight Commander of the Star of India].[16]

This is hardly an unbiased judgement, but it is certainly true that Ameer Ali was ambitious and wanted to be rewarded by the British Government. Writing of Millicent Fawcett (1847–1929), in her time a famous campaigner for women's rights, Ameer Ali recorded that 'on the 1st January 1925 a D.B.E. was conferred on her' and immediately offered the acid judgement: 'it cannot be said any more that the British Government never recognises honest, unselfish labour in the advancement of the public weal'.[17] Even more caustic was his comment on the Hindu nationalist Surendranath Banerji (1848–1925):

> he had said in one of his speeches to students that he would shake the foundations of British Rule; and he fully justified his threat until the Government realised the merits of having its foundations shaken by rewarding him with a knighthood.[18]

No doubt the British Government elevated Ameer Ali to the Privy Council for the same reason it honoured Surendranath Banerji with a knighthood: in the hope that such a prize would stop him 'rocking the boat' of imperial rule. Officials and other influential British supporters of the Raj wanted educated Indians as agents, clients or collaborators; not as freely admitted equals. In fact, he was appointed despite the opposition of King Edward VII.[19] There was nothing personal in this: the king opposed the proposals for two Indians to become members of the Viceroy's Council on the grounds that 'however clever the Native might be and however loyal you and your Council might consider him to be, you never could be certain that he might not prove to be a very dangerous element'.[20]

Significantly, Ameer Ali's desire to be accepted by British polite society meant that he could not hope to possess the regard and confidence of all of his co-religionists, because the Raj set even the relatively few Western-educated Muslims in competition with each other for jobs and other crumbs that fell from the imperial table. In fact, he was ill equipped to interpret or re-interpret Islam to his Indian co-religionists. His Shia background as well as his anglicized lifestyle would not have inclined the majority of them, who were Sunni Muslims, to regard him as a religious leader. Indeed, his knowledge even of his own branch of Islam was eccentric: he wrote that 'the term "Shiah" is applied nowadays exclusively to the followers of the twelve Apostles of the House of Mohammed',[21] a quite untrue assertion.

During his student days in London, he met Sir Saiyid Ahmad Khan (1817–98), the greatest of those Indian Muslims of his day who tried to convince Muslims that the British were in India to stay for at least the foreseeable future, and that the regeneration of Indian Islam must therefore occur under British patronage.[22] But Ameer Ali was more élitist than Sir Saiyid. In his preface to the 1902 edition of *The Spirit of Islam*, he wrote:

> I have deliberately adopted the English language for my thoughts and views to Islamists as well as to others. English now exercises the same unchallenged sway over a greater part of the globe as Arabic did in Asia, Africa and Spain for nearly seven centuries. It is the language of culture and civilised progress. In India it has become within the last thirty years, the ordinary vehicle of literary thought.[23]

English had become nothing of the sort. Among educated Indian Muslims (themselves a very small proportion of Muslims in India), many more would have been able to read the Urdu of Sir Saiyid and his disciples than Ameer Ali's English. His total adoption of English to communicate his thoughts blinded him to or led him to ignore creative reconstructions of Islam published in Urdu. If his works betray little awareness of the work of Sir Saiyid and his followers to reform Indian Islam, they show none at all of the teachings of Saiyid Ahmad of Rai Bareilly (1786–1831), or of Maulana Muhammad Qasim Nanowati (1832–80) who in 1867 raised a small *maktab* or school at Deoband to the status of a *dar al-'ulum* ('the abode of sciences' – a Muslim establishment for higher religious learning). Both the Barelvi and Deobandi movements became enormously influential in the development of South Asian Islam during Ameer Ali's lifetime and thereafter, but because they govern people who speak the vernacular, they passed him by.

Most of the British officials by whom he aspired to be praised, accepted and honoured were at least nominal Christians or, even when they were atheists as was Lord Morley, lived in a country in which a form of Christianity was by law the established religion. Because of their antipathy towards Islam, Ameer Ali was driven to defend it in terms which they, as well as he, could understand.

His first book had been written in order to refute what he believed were mistaken Christian impressions about Islam. In his memoirs, he recalled an incident during his student days in London (1869–73) when:

> Henry Channing lent me for perusal Clark's *Ten Great Religions* and when I referred to the errors with which the book teemed, he asked me to write something on the subject. This was the genesis of my first book *The Critical Examination of the Life and Teachings of Mohammed*.[24]

That Ameer Ali was particularly intent upon correcting distorted interpretations of Islam can be inferred from the title of his work. This is also made plain by the preface in which he recorded his approval of 'the gradual enlightenment of the human mind which is shown strikingly in the silent change which is taking place in Christendom towards a moral liberal conception of the grand work achieved by the Arabian prophet in the seventh century'. He praised in particular the works of Caussin de Perceval, Sedillot, Oelsner, Deutsch, Barthélemy St Hilaire, Davenport and Higgins and Carlyle 'for their attempts to free Islam from the abuses of its ecclesiastical enemies'.[25]

One of the enemies whom he had in mind was Sir William Muir (1819–1905), whose *Life of Mahomet* (1858–61) impugned the integrity of the prophet. Ameer Ali claimed that:

> Muir's life ... requires a refutation of every false theory and apocryphal story stated in it. The motive, however, with which this work was undertaken would lead impartial minds to doubt the author's perfect freedom from bias against Islam. He has candidly admitted in his preface that it was undertaken to help a Christian missionary [Carl Pfander (1803–65)] in his controversial war with the Muslims in India.[26]

Ameer Ali singled out the works of Muir because he was a person of distinction in British India. He served in the government of the North-Western Provinces at Agra, eventually becoming Lieutenant Governor in 1868, in a position to influence against Islam the 'class' of Western-educated Indian Muslims to which Ameer Ali belonged.

Was Ameer Ali's interpretation of Christianity any less polemical than Christian interpretations of Islam? In Appendix 2 of the 1902 edition of *The Spirit of Islam*, he wrote that:

> it is a matter for regret that European scholars, generally speaking, should persist in comparing the lowest form of Islam with the highest form of Christianity. All religions have different phases, they vary according to the climatic and economic conditions of the country, the environment and the people, their national character-istics and a multitude of other causes. To compare modern idealistic Christianity with a debased form of Islam is an insult to common sense and intelligence.[27]

Yet it is a matter of fact that Ameer Ali often compared his own favourable interpretation of Islam with a depreciatory assessment of a lower, if not 'the lowest', form of Christianity. This biased comparison of the two religions was a feature of his controversy in print with Canon Malcolm MacColl (1831–1907). The controversy began with a review of eight books, including the 1891 edition of *The Spirit of Islam*, written anonymously by MacColl in the July 1895 edition of the *Quarterly Review* (not *The Nineteenth Century*, as Ameer Ali's memoirs state[28]). The bulk of the review adversely commented on Ameer Ali's interpretation of Islam. Ameer Ali wrote a reply in the September 1895 edition of *The Nineteenth Century*. MacColl answered this, again anonymously, in the October 1895 edition of the *Fortnightly Review*, eliciting a response in the November 1895 issue of *The Nineteenth Century*. MacColl wrote yet another article for the December 1895 issue of the *Fortnightly Review*, this time under his own name, but evoked no further response from Ameer Ali.

MacColl wished to prove 'the chronic mistake of European dealings with Turkey',[29] and his hostility towards Ameer Ali's book encouraged him (or was an excuse for him) to present his view of Islam as a religion which 'must eventually destroy, or be destroyed by, the civilization on which it fastens'.[30] The other works he reviewed were less important to his argument. Since one dated back to 1791, he was obviously interested not so much in an orthodox book review as in pressing others' works into a mould of his thesis. Both writers condemned the intemperate tone of the other's contributions.[31] Both employed analogous modes of argument, for example, the claim that progress was encouraged by and achieved in his own religion and not the other's.[32] Indeed, the controversy raised a large number of issues including: the importance of 'principles' or more practical action and legislation in improving human conduct; each religion's treatment of women and of members of other religions; each religion's attitude towards Jesus and Muhammad; the role of scripture in the development of religion; and the reasons for Islam's plight as a religion in the nineteenth century.

One of the issues raised by both men was the burning of the Alexandrian library. MacColl quoted Abulpharagius's *Compendious History of Dynasties* and also other 'historians' to prove his contention that the Caliph Umar was responsible for the event. This contention was part of a wider argument by the Canon that 'the Koran ... supersedes all other literature, making all previous or subsequent learning ... either superfluous or pernicious'.[33] This was, he averred, a Muslim conviction that (in his opinion) led to Umar's order to burn the library, an example of 'the typical attitude of Islam towards Literature and science'.[34] However, this is a large argument to base on a controversial event, and illustrates MacColl's merits as a polemicist rather than a historian. Equally, Ameer Ali's defence of Islam on this point was not a careful survey of the historical records, but consisted in an unsubstantiated assertion that the library was burnt in the time of Julius Caesar. He added that 'if anything remained, it was destroyed by Theodosius and the saintly murderer of Hypatia and his myrmidons'.[35] Ameer Ali was often given to dwelling upon some of the more scandalous and bloody aspects of Church history, implying how far removed Christianity had become from the teachings of Jesus.[36] He judged, again giving no evidence, either that the 'authorities' quoted by MacColl are poor historians, or else that their material is 'irrelevant' to MacColl's thesis.[37]

The fact that great issues hung for both men upon the impossible task of establishing the truth of events of relatively minor importance, such as the destruction of the Alexandrian library, shows that Ameer Ali's and Malcolm MacColl's commitment to their respective cause outweighed their talents as objective historians. One of MacColl's assertions particularly reveals his unconvincing and unfair comparison of Christianity and Islam:

> When Muslims slay and outrage Christians they act in accordance
> with their law and with the precepts and example of their Prophet.
> When Christians act similarly they violate the precepts of their
> religion and go against the teaching and practice of their master.[38]

He based his claim on the massacres of Christians 'perpetrated at
intervals of about ten years in Turkey' which, he claimed, were not
denounced by Muslims, as were Christian crimes (such as the massacre
of Glencoe and the cruelties of Culloden – parochial examples for a Scot
to offer) by Christians.

Ameer Ali's interpretation of Islam in relation to Christianity yields
the extremely important fact that he was far more at home in Western
intellectual assumptions of his day than in Islamic scholarship. For
example, his description of a truly progressive religion owes far more to
nineteenth-century European anthropological and theological hypo-
theses (now somewhat tarnished) than to Islamic beliefs about revelation
and servanthood. To be sure, Ameer Ali was anxious to offer an
interpretation of Islam that was consonant with ideas of rationalism and
progress. Nevertheless, he was more of an apologist and polemicist for
Islam to a Western audience than a creative reinterpreter of Islam to
other Muslims.

From our perspective, Ameer Ali's life and career illuminate certain
problems about the Muslim modernist movement in South Asia. Arising
as it did within the British imperial system in the wake of the failure of the
uprising of 1857 which convinced many Muslims that there was no real
hope of a restoration of Mughal or any other Muslim rule, it was bound
to seem a betrayal of Muslim history, culture, language and religion to
many other Muslims. During most of Ameer Ali's lifetime, the British
were neither flexible nor secure enough to want Indians, even Indian
intellectuals, as colleagues rather than as collaborators. Twenty years
after Ameer Ali's death, the end of the British Raj came more quickly
than he or many of his contemporaries could have believed possible. The
modernist movement has therefore been tainted by association with
imperialism, and has run its course in South Asia. It is intriguing to
speculate whether it, as opposed to or in co-operation with other forms of
Islamic revivalism, can be renewed in a more clear-sighted and lasting
form than Ameer Ali attempted.

Akbar Ahmed

Perhaps a more propitious and realistic option for Islam is to engage with postmodernism, not with modernism. In Akbar Ahmed's view:

> Nafees [his young daughter] will live, as a Muslim, in the postmodern world which is just beginning to shape our lives; therein lies the Muslim predicament: that of living by Islam in an age which is increasingly secular, cynical, irreverent, fragmented, materialistic and, therefore, for a Muslim, often hostile. However, postmodernism also promises hope, understanding and toleration – and this is where it connects with Islam. In an age of cynicism and disintegration Islam has much to offer.[39]

Although Ahmed is friendly towards certain aspects of the West, specifically citing democracy, human rights and literacy, he sees at its heart a fundamental moral vacuum that Islam can fill.[40] His interpretation of Islam does not shirk from serious criticism of its contemporary practices,[41] yet for him the Islamic ideal is more important than Islamic practice. He writes that 'The modern period had led Muslims into a cul-de-sac ... They ... saw it [modernity] as "a Western project". The reality of Muslim life was a far cry from the edifying and noble Islamic ideal.'[42] The impression is that, though a far less passionate polemicist than Ameer Ali, Akbar Ahmed's instincts, like those of his distinguished predecessor, are to defend an ideal of Islam, but to condemn the practices of the West, whilst wanting to own and appropriate part of its heritage. This 'pick and choose' approach could be interpreted as a standard postmodern response, but will it do? After all, Ahmed's deep and moving commitment to Islam seems to run counter to one of his definitions of postmodernism, which presupposes:

> A questioning of, a loss of faith in, the project of modernity; a spirit of pluralism; a heightened scepticism of traditional orthodoxies; and finally a rejection of a view of the world as a universal totality, of the expectation of final solutions and complete answers ... For postmodernists, ideology, Marxist or Buddhist, is just one brand of many available in the shopping mall.[43]

Maybe, in his defence of Islam as a total way of life, Ahmed is deliberately challenging the parochial, Western nature of postmodernism. Yet because that is, in his view, only one aspect of it, he feels able to draw on its more positive features. Embedded in his book are suggestions that Islam has its own, non-Western, authentic resources with which to respond to each and every situation. In particular, he sees the qur'anic concept of balance (*adl*) as essential to understanding the Islamic vision:

> Balance is essential to Islam and never more so than in society; and the crucial balance is between *din* (religion), and *dunya* (world); it is a balance, not a separation, between the two. The Muslim lives in the now, in the real world, but within the frame of his religion, with a mind to the future after-life. So, whether he is a business man, an academic or a politician, he must not forget the moral laws of Islam. In the postmodern world *dunya* is upsetting the balance, invading and appropriating *din*.[44]

This response is, characteristically for a Muslim, deeply qur'anic in its origin: *adl* occurs twelve times in the Qur'an, including some important passages.

Revelation and postmodernity

Consequently, it may be more appropriate for Muslims to renew their tradition from within, rather than combining that response with insights from a fractured and fragmented Western, post-imperial philosophical and historical heritage. Indeed, in one specific and, for Muslims, crucially important area, the presuppositions of modernity and postmodernity run counter to traditional Islamic teaching: the form of the Muslim commitment to the Qur'an is powerfully contentious in a postmodern world. Ahmed recounts a story:

> 'You keep on saying to Akbar ... why don't you accept the human origin of your religion? Well, he can't', Ernest Gellner [formerly Professor of Social Anthropology at the University of Cambridge] said sharply, coming to my rescue, in a television discussion on Islam. 'Islam has not', he further explained, 'been secularized. This is the great mystery about it. All the other world religions have been softened, have permitted ambiguities of meanings.' Gellner was right. For those who believe in Islam, the choice is between being Muslim and being nothing: there is no other choice.[45]

Gellner supports a common Muslim view, but whether it is right, or simply a matter of unexamined but widespread belief and assertion, is debatable. After all, subtlety, ambiguities of meanings, and pluralism of commitments are not unknown within Islam. What is clear, however, is how few Muslims have felt able to question the Qur'an's status as the exact and unambiguous Word of God. In differentiating Semitic from Greek views about God, Ahmed writes that 'God on high spoke through chosen prophets and the divine words were embodied in holy books: the Jewish and Christian scriptures and the Qur'an'.[46] Some Jews and Christians have reinterpreted how God is revelatory in their scriptures, not so as to exclude divine participation in the process, but so that human contributions can also be upheld. This has not been a route trodden by many Muslims.

Unlike the vast majority of Muslims, including Akbar Ahmed, Ameer Ali ventured an interpretation of revelation that acknowledged the place for prophetic participation. In discussing the conception of future rewards and punishments, his attempt to prove Muhammad's a more reasoned and reasonable view than Jesus's shows how unconventional were his own views about revelation:

A careful study of the Koran makes it evident that the mind of Mohammed went through the same process of development which marked the religious consciousness of Jesus ... The various chapters of the Koran which contain the ornate descriptions of paradise, whether figurative or literal, were delivered wholly or in part at Mecca. Probably in the infancy of his religious consciousness Mohammed himself believed in some or other of the traditions which floated around him. But with a wider awakening of the soul, a deeper communion with the Spirit of the Universe, thoughts which bore a material aspect at first became spiritualised.[47]

Ameer Ali's view of the provenance of the Qur'an, associating it with the mind of Muhammad, a view which he never changed,[48] is quite unacceptable to orthodox Muslim belief. What is particularly telling is that this interesting association is not justified or developed in any way. He seems to assume that everyone will know about and accept this interpretation. He hardly reveals a clear and open desire to reinterpret his own tradition creatively and provocatively.

What exactly was Ameer Ali doing, then? It is extraordinary that he did not admit the singularity and unorthodox nature of his conviction, if only as a prelude to making his case for arguing that it (or some of it) expresses the mind of Muhammad. Thus, though it is possible that he was trying, clumsily and simplistically, and with too much reliance upon nineteenth-century European notions of the progressive development of humankind, to restate orthodox views in ways that his audience could appreciate and affirm, it is also arguable that he was, in crucially important respects, ignorant of what constitutes orthodox Islamic belief. At any rate, the fact that few Muslims picked him up on this point over the half-century in which he continued to make it, shows how few read him carefully. The Punjab Mohammedan Tract and Book Depot published three anonymous essays in 1893, the second of which attacked his opinion about the provenance of the Qur'an. The author wrote that

> the principal mistake under which Sir [sic] Say-yad Amirali seems to be labouring is this, that according to him it is the Prophet that conceives and works out a scheme, whereas Islam teaches that it is The Lord, who in his mercy from time to time, inspired some of his best persons to bear his messages to the people.[49]

Apart from this reference, it is hard to find an orthodox Muslim, contemporary with Ameer Ali, who read and took issue with his writings.

The issue of the provenance of the Qur'an has remained the great unexamined question by most Muslims. This seems non-negotiable. If so, then it is difficult to imagine that Muslims can agree with the assumption or even assertion of a postmodern world that all old certainties are questionable and, indeed, suspicious. However, even if most Muslims, like Akbar Ahmed but unlike Ameer Ali, hold fast to the divine *origin* and *transmission* of the Qur'an, some have provided innovative ways of understanding the human *reception* and *meaning* of it. These may, in future, open up new possibilities of responses from scholars who advocate a more critical engagement with the understanding of sacred texts.

It would be possible to argue that the revelation can be, in certain senses, both God's and his prophet's, a point which a later modernist, Fazlur Rahman (1919–87), was to make,[50] extremely controversially, as it turned out. Or else one might take the explorations of Mohammed Arkoun, an Algerian at present teaching at the Sorbonne, a little further than he does. He has called for an analysis of the Qur'an's religious language, and that of the Hebrew Bible and the Gospels, 'as examples of a more general linguistic phenomenon, religious discourse'.[51] Most radical Muslim thinkers are reluctant to follow through the questions of historicity that their questionings imply. The Indian lawyer and diplomat Asaf Fyzee pointed in that direction when he asserted that:

> We cannot go 'back' to the Koran, we have to go 'forward' with it. I wish to understand the Koran as it was understood by the Arabs at the time of the Prophet only to reinterpret it and apply it to my conditions of life and to believe in it, so far as it appeals to me as a twentieth-century man.[52]

For Muslims, as for all major religions, faith in the future must clearly be linked with faith in the past. How far Islam is willing or able to accept the assumptions of a modern, now perhaps postmodern world, is open to question, for reasons this chapter has indicated. Iran and Libya, and other Muslim countries where anti-Western rhetoric runs high, may offer more important bases for authentic reconstructions of Islam than, say, Turkey. But neither Iran nor Libya can entirely avoid the encroaching globalization, based on the achievements of Western modernist and postmodernist history and ideology, any more than Turkey can escape from its Islamic heritage. How, then, will Muslim academics evaluate their religion in, let us imagine, twenty years' time? Will that interpretation be wholly free from Western concerns and insights? Past precedent suggests that Muslims will not, indeed cannot, resist outside influences, but that they will retain traditional views about the central tenets of Islam, and be reluctant to abandon them in the name of an often ephemeral, questionable and externally imposed view of progress, whether couched in the language of modernity or postmodernity.

Acknowledgement

Some of this material has been published previously in an article in *Islam and Christian–Muslim Relations*, 6.1 (1995), and appears here by permission.

Notes

1. W. Cantwell Smith, *What Is Scripture?* (London: SCM, 1993), p. 243.
2. Ameer Ali, 'Memoirs', *Islamic Culture*, V.4 (October 1931), p. 518.

3. Ali, 'Memoirs' (October 1931), p. 513.
4. Ali, 'Memoirs' (October 1931), pp. 520f.
5. Ali, 'Memoirs' (October 1931), p. 518.
6. Ameer Ali, *Islam* (London, 1906), pp. 24f.
7. F. Robinson, *Separatism Among the Indian Muslims: The Politics of the United Provinces' Muslims, 1860–1923* (Cambridge: Cambridge University Press, 1974), pp. 31, 41f.
8. Ali, 'Memoirs' (October 1931), p. 517.
9. Ali, 'Memoirs' (October 1931), pp. 526f.
10. Ali, 'Memoirs' (October 1931), p. 524.
11. Ali, 'Memoirs' (October 1931), p. 528.
12. Ameer Ali, *The Rights of Persia* (London: Central Asian Society, 1919).
13. Keremat Ali, *Makhaz-i-Uloom, or a Treatise on the Origins of the Sciences*, trans. Moulvie Obeyd-Olla and Moulvie Syed Ameer Ali (Calcutta, 1867), preface.
14. In British parlance the Indian Mutiny (1857). Ali, 'Memoirs' (October 1931), p. 519.
15. Ameer Ali, 'Memoirs', *Islamic Culture*, VI.3 (July 1932), p. 341.
16. M. N. Das, *India Under Morley and Minto* (London: 1964), pp. 222f.
17. Ali, 'Memoirs' (October 1931), p. 533.
18. Ameer Ali, 'Memoirs', *Islamic Culture*, VI.2 (April 1932), p. 178.
19. R. B. Haldane, *Memoirs* (London: William Norgate, n.d.), p. 387.
20. Das, *India*, p. 225.
21. Ameer Ali, 'The Caliphate: a historical and juridical sketch', *Contemporary Review*, 107 (June 1915), p. 682.
22. Ali, 'Memoirs' (October 1931), pp. 540f.
23. Ameer Ali, *The Spirit of Islam* (Calcutta, 1902), p. vii.
24. Ameer Ali, 'Memoirs', *Islamic Culture*, VI.4 (October 1932), pp. 539f.
25. Ameer Ali, *A Critical Examination of the Life and Teachings of Mohammed* (London: Williams and Norgate, 1873), pp. viiif.
26. Ali, *Critical Examination*, p. vii.
27. Ali, *Spirit of Islam*, pp. 425f.
28. Ali, 'Memoirs' (April 1932), p. 175.
29. Anon. (actually Canon MacColl), Article X, *Quarterly Review*, 182.CCCLXIII (July 1895), p. 251.
30. MacColl, Article X, p. 234.
31. Anon. (Canon MacColl), 'Islam and its critics: a rejoinder', *Fortnightly Review*, 58.CCCXLVI (October 1895), p. 621; Ameer Ali, 'Islam and Canon MacColl', *The Nineteenth Century*, XXXVIII.225 (November 1895), p. 778.
32. Anon. (July 1895), pp. 220f.; Ameer Ali, 'Islam and its critics', *The Nineteenth Century*, XXXVIII.223 (September 1895), pp. 363ff.
33. Anon. (July 1895), p. 235.
34. Anon. (July 1895), p. 237.
35. Ali, 'Islam and its critics', p. 375.
36. See, for example, Ameer Ali, *The Spirit of Islam* (revised and enlarged edn; (London: Chatto and Windus, 1922), p. 182.

37. Ali, 'Islam and its critics', p. 376.
38. Anon. (October 1895), p. 633.
39. Akbar Ahmed, *Postmodernism and Islam: Predicament and Promise* (London: Routledge, 1992), p. x.
40. Ahmed, *Postmodernism*, pp. 98, 109.
41. Ahmed, *Postmodernism*, pp. 33–46.
42. Ahmed, *Postmodernism*, p. 33.
43. Ahmed, *Postmodernism*, p. 10.
44. Ahmed, *Postmodernism*, p. 48.
45. Ahmed, *Postmodernism*, p. 42.
46. Ahmed, *Postmodernism*, p. 57.
47. Ali, *Critical Examination*, pp. 282f.
48. This passage is also found in Ali, *The Spirit of Islam*, pp. 200f.
49. Anon., Essay 2 upon *Women in Islam* (Lahore: Mohammedan Tract and Book Depot, 1893), p. 32.
50. Fazlur Rahman, *Islam* (Chicago: University of Chicago Press, 1979), p. 31.
51. M. Arkoun, *Rethinking Islam: Common Questions, Uncommon Answers* (Oxford and Boulder, CO: Westview Press, 1994), p. 39.
52. A. A. A. Fyzee, *A Modern Approach to Islam* (Bombay, 1963), p. 101.

9

Judaism and Israel

From faith to practice

Dan Cohn-Sherbok

Next year in Jerusalem! For nearly 4,000 years the Jewish people have kept alive their love of Zion. Sustained through exile and persecution by their hope for the long-awaited Messiah, they remained faithful to the dream of a final ingathering in the land of their ancestors. Yet, in the modern period there has been radical reformulation of this ancient quest. Rather than wait for the miraculous intervention of a Messianic figure, secular Zionists pressed for the creation of a Jewish state in order to solve the problem of anti-Semitism. For such figures as Moses Hess, Leon Pinsker, and Theodor Herzl, the establishment of a homeland was the only solution to the Jewish problem. This shift in orientation, however, has raised fundamental issues about the relationship between religious ideals and political reality. The aim of this chapter is to trace the evolution of secular Zionism, examine the various anti-Zionist movements that emerged in its wake, and focus on the central problems facing the Jewish people now that they have become an empowered nation in the Holy Land.

National consciousness and universalism

Modern secular Zionism begins with the writings of Moses Hess. Born in Bonn, Germany, he published his first philosophical work, the *Holy History of Mankind*, by 'a Young Spinozist', in 1837. By 1840, he had settled in Paris where he became active in socialist circles. From 1842 to

1843 he worked as the Paris correspondent of the *Rheinische Zeitung*, edited by Karl Marx. In 1862 he published *Rome and Jerusalem*, a systematic defence of Jewish nationalism. In this work, he explains that after years of estrangement from the Jewish religion, he returned to his people:

> Once again I am sharing in its festivals of joy and days of sorrow, in its hopes and memories. I am taking part in the spiritual and intellectual struggles of our day, both within the house of Israel and between our people and the gentile world. The Jews have lived and laboured among the nations for almost two thousand years, but none the less they cannot become rooted organically within them. A sentiment which I believed I had suppressed beyond recall is alive once again. It is the thought of my nationality, which is inseparably connected with my ancestral heritage, with the Holy Land and the eternal city, the birthplace of the belief in the divine unity of life and the hope for the ultimate brotherhood of all men.[1]

Anti-Jewish sentiment, he believes, is unavoidable. Progressive Jews think they can escape from Judeophobia by recoiling from any Jewish national expression, yet the hatred of Jews is inescapable. No reform of the religion is radical enough to avoid such sentiments, and even conversion to Christianity cannot relieve the Jew of this disability. 'Jewish noses', he writes, 'cannot be reformed, and the black, wavy hair of the Jews will not be changed into blond by conversion or straightened out by constant combing.'[2] For Hess, Jews will always remain strangers among the nations: nothing can alter this state of affairs. The only solution to the problem of Jew-hatred is for the Jewish people to come to terms with their national identity. According to Hess, the restoration of Jewish national-ism will not deprive the world of the benefits promoted by Jewish reformers who wish to dissociate themselves from the particularistic dimensions of the Jewish heritage. On the contrary, the values of universalism would be championed by various aspects of Judaism's national character. Judaism, he contends, is the root of the modern universalist view of life. Until the French Revolution, the Jewish people were the only nation whose religion was both national and universalist. It is through Judaism that the history of humanity can become sacred, namely a unified development which has its origin in the love of the family. This process can be completed only when the members of the human race are united by the holy spirit.

Such a conception of history is grounded in the Jewish messianic vision of God's Kingdom on Earth. From the beginning of their history, Hess notes, the Jews have been bearers of the faith in a future messianic epoch. This conviction is symbolically expressed through Sabbath observance.

> The biblical story of the creation is told only for the sake of the Sabbath ideal. It tells us, in symbolic language, that when the creation of the world of nature was completed, with the calling into life of the highest organic being of the earth – man – the Creator celebrated his natural Sabbath, after the completion of the task of world history, by ushering in the messianic epoch.[3]

Biblical Sabbath precepts thus inspire Jews with a feeling of certainty that a divine law governs both the world of nature and the world of history. This belief, rooted in the spiritual life of the Jewish nation, points to a universal salvation of the world. What is required today, Hess asserts, is for Jewry to regenerate the Jewish nation and to keep alive the hope for the political rebirth of the Jewish people.

In the light of these observations, Hess asserts that a Jewish renaissance is possible once national life reasserts itself in the Holy Land. In the past, the creative energies of the people deserted Israel when Jews became ashamed of their nationality. But the holy spirit, he writes, will again animate Jewry once the nation awakens to a new life. The only question remaining is how it might be possible to stimulate the patriotic sentiments of modern Jewry as well as liberate the Jewish masses by means of this revived nationality loyalty. This is a formidable challenge, yet Hess contends that it must be overcome. Although he recognizes that there could not be a total emigration of world Jewry to Palestine, the existence of a Jewish state will act as a spiritual centre for the Jewish people and for all of humanity.

Autoemancipation

The Russian pogroms of 1881 had a profound impact on another early Zionist thinker, Leon Pinsker, driving him from an advocacy of the ideas of the Enlightenment to the determination to create a Jewish homeland. Born in Russian Poland in 1821, Pinsker attended a Russian high school, studied law in Odessa, and later received a medical degree from the University of Moscow. Upon returning to Odessa, he was appointed to the staff of the local city hospital. After 1860, Pinsker contributed to Jewish weeklies in the Russian language and was active in the Society for the Spread of Culture among the Jews of Russia. However, when Jews were massacred in the pogroms of 1881 he left the Society, convinced that a more radical remedy was required to solve the plight of Russian Jewry. In 1882 he published *Autoemancipation*, a tract containing similar themes to those contained in Hess's writings. He subsequently became the leader of the Hibbat Zion movement, and in 1884 convened its first congress. In *Autoemancipation*, Pinsker asserts that the Jewish problem is as unresolved in the modern world as it was in former times. In essence, this dilemma concerns the unassimilable character of Jewish identity in countries where Jews are in the minority. In such cases there is no basis for mutual respect between Jews and non-Jews. This situation is aggravated by the fact that the Jewish people do not feel a need for an independent national existence; yet without such a longing, there is no hope for a solution to Jewish misery.

Among the nations, Pinsker argues, the Jews are like a nation long since dead: the dead walking among the living. Such an eerie, ghostly existence is unique in history. The fear of the Jewish ghost has been a typical reaction throughout the centuries and has paved the way for current Judeophobia. This prejudice has through the years become rooted and naturalized among all the peoples of the world. Such Jew-hatred generated various charges against the Jewish people; throughout history they have been accused of crucifying Jesus, drinking the blood of Christians, poisoning wells, exacting usury, and exploiting peasants. Such accusations are invariably groundless; they were trumped up to quiet the conscience of Jew-baiters. Thus Judaism and anti-Semitism have been inseparable companions through the centuries and any struggle against this aberration of the human mind is fruitless.

Unlike other peoples, the Jew is inevitably a stranger. Having no home, he can never be anything other than an alien. He is not simply a guest in a foreign country; rather, he is more like a beggar and a refugee. The Jews are aliens, he states, who can have no representatives because their home has no boundaries behind which they can entrench themselves, their misery also has no bounds. It is a mistake, Pinsker continues, to think that the legal emancipation of Jewry will result in social emancipation. This, he believes, is impossible. The isolation of the Jew cannot be removed by any form of official emancipation since the Jew is eternally an alien.

Such natural antagonism between Jew and non-Jew has resulted in a variety of reproaches levelled by both parties at one another. From the Jewish side, appeals to justice are frequently made to improve the condition of the Jewish community. In response, non-Jews attempt to justify their negative attitudes by groundless accusations. A more realistic approach, however, would involve the recognition that the Jewish people have no choice but to reconstitute themselves as a separate people.

The Jewish struggle to attain this goal has an inherent justification that belongs to the quest of every oppressed people. Although this endeavour may be opposed by various quarters, the battle must continue: the Jewish people have no other way out of their desperate position. There is a moral duty to ensure that persecuted Jews, wherever they live, will have a secure home. In this respect, it is a danger, Pinsker states, for Jews to attach themselves only to the 'Holy Land'. What is required is simply a secure land for the Jewish people:

> We need nothing but a large piece of land for our poor brothers; a piece of land which shall remain our property, from which no foreign master can expel us ... Perhaps the Holy Land will again be ours. If so, all the better, but first of all, we must determine ... what country is accessible to us, and at the same time adapted to offer Jews of all lands who must leave their homes a secure and unquestioning refuge which is capable of being made productive.[4]

The Jewish state

More than any other figure Theodor Herzl has become identified with modern secular Zionism. Born in Budapest, Hungary, in 1860, he was the only son of a rich merchant. After studying at a technical school and high school in Budapest, he went with his family to Vienna where he enrolled in the law faculty of the university. In 1884 he received a doctorate and worked for a year as a civil servant; subsequently he wrote plays, and in 1892 was appointed to the staff of the *Neue Freie Presse*. As its Paris correspondent, he witnessed the Dreyfus Affair and became convinced that the Jewish problem could only be solved by the creation of a homeland for the Jewish people. In May 1895 Herzl requested an interview with Baron Maurice de Hirsch to interest him in the establishment of a Jewish state. When the Baron expressed little sympathy for the project, Herzl hoped the Rothschilds would be more receptive and wrote a

65-page proposal outlining his views. This work was an outline of his *The Jewish State* which appeared in 1896; this was followed by a utopian study, *Old-New Land* (*Altneuland*), published in 1902.

Herzl's analysis of modern Jewish existence was not original – many of his ideas had been aired in the writings of Hess and Pinsker. Yet what was novel about Herzl's espousal of Zionism was his success in stimulating interest and debate about a Jewish state in the highest diplomatic and political circles. This was due to both the force of his personality and the passionate expression of his proposals. Convinced of the importance of his views, Herzl insisted that the building of a Jewish homeland would transform Jewish life.

Old prejudices against Jewry, he argues, are ingrained in Western society; assimilation will not act as a cure for the ills that beset the Jewish people. There is only one remedy for the malady of anti-Semitism: the creation of a Jewish commonwealth. In *The Jewish State* Herzl outlines the nature of such a social and political entity. The plan, he maintains, should be carried out by two agencies – the Society of Jews and the Jewish Company. The scientific programme and political policies which the Society of Jews will establish should be carried out by the Jewish Company. This body will be the liquidating agent for the business interests of departing Jews, and will organize trade and commerce in the new country. Given such a framework, immigration of Jews will be gradual. Initially, the poorest will settle in this new land. Their tasks will be to construct roads, bridges, railways, and telegraph installations. In addition, they will regulate rivers and provide themselves with homesteads. Through their labour, trade will be created, and, in its wake, markets. Such economic activity will attract new settlers, and thus the land will be populated.

Those Jews who agree with the concept of a Jewish state should rally round the Society of Jews and encourage its endeavours. In this way they give it authority in the eyes of governments, and in time ensure that the state is recognized through international law. If other nations are willing to grant Jews sovereignty over a neutral land, then the Society will be able to enter into negotiations for its possession. Where should this new state be located? Herzl proposes two alternatives: Palestine or Argentina. Argentina, Herzl notes, is one of the most fertile countries in the world, extending over a vast area with sparse population. Palestine, on the other hand, is the Jews' historic homeland. If the Sultan were persuaded to allow the Jews to repossess this land, the Jewish community could in return undertake the complete management of the finances of Turkey. In this way the Jews could form a part of a wall of defence for Europe and Asia, and the holy places of Christendom could be placed under some form of international extra territoriality. There are therefore advantages for both these options, and Herzl asserts that the Society should take whatever it is given and whatever Jewish opinion favours.

In the conclusion of this tract Herzl eloquently expresses the longing of the entire nation for the creation of such a refuge from centuries of suffering:

> What glory awaits the selfless fighters for the cause. Therefore I believe that a wondrous breed of Jews will spring up from the earth. The Maccabees will rise again. Let me repeat once more my opening words: The Jews who will it shall achieve their state. We shall live at last as free men in our own soil, and in our own homes peacefully die. The world will be liberated by our freedom, enriched by our wealth, magnified by our greatness. And whatever we attempt there for our own benefit will rebound mightily and beneficially to the good of all mankind.[5]

The Orthodox critique

Although some Orthodox Jewish figures endorsed the Zionist movement, Orthodoxy in Germany, Hungary and Eastern European countries protested against this new development in Jewish life. To promote this policy, an ultra-Orthodox body, Agudat Israel, was created in 1912 to unite rabbis and laity against Zionism. Although the Torah maintains that it is the duty of the pious to return to Zion, these Orthodox Jews pointed out that such an ingathering must be preceded by the messianic redemption. Zionism was viewed by these Orthodox critics as a satanic conspiracy against God's will and equated with pseudo-Messianism.

Yet despite such attitudes, Scripture does decree that it is obligatory for Jews to return to the Holy Land, and this prescription called for an Orthodox response. Accordingly, ultra-Orthodox figures differentiated between the obligation to return to the Holy Land and the duty of residing there. Orthodox Jews, they argued, were exempt from actually settling in the land for such reasons as physical danger, economic difficulties, inability to educate the young, etc. In addition, these critics maintained that Zionism was not simply a movement to rebuild Palestine; it was a heretical attempt to usurp the privilege of the Messiah to establish a Jewish kingdom. Further, ultra-Orthodox spokesmen declared that Zionism sought to leave religion out of the national life. As a result, the Jewish state would betray the ideals of the Jewish heritage. Throughout history the nation had been animated by spiritual principles, and refused to perish because of its adherence to traditional precepts. If Israel had endured through thousands of years of persecution, it would be folly to abandon the religious values which kept alive the hope for Jewish survival.

For these reasons Agudat Israel denounced the policies of modern Zionists and refused to collaborate with religious Zionist parties such as the Mizrahi. In Palestine itself the extreme Orthodox movement joined with Agudat Israel in its struggle against Zionism. Frequently its leaders protested to the British government and the League of Nations about the Zionist quest to make a national home in Palestine. Occasionally it even joined forces with Arab leaders. This conflict eventually resulted in the murder of a member of the executive of the Agudat, Jacob Israel de Han. A Dutch Jew by origin, he denounced Zionism in cables to British newspapers, attacking the Balfour Commission and British officers for their seemingly pro-Zionist stance. In 1924 he was assassinated in Jerusalem by the Haganah. For the ultra-Orthodox Jews of Jerusalem de Han became a martyr for the glory of God – this incident illustrated the depths of hatred of Zionism among the right-wing Orthodox.

Eventually, however, these critics of Zionist aspirations modified their position and began to take a more active role in Jewish settlement. This was due to the immigration of members of Agudat Israel to Palestine, as well as the massacre of Orthodox Jews in Hebron, Safed, and Jerusalem during the riots of 1929. None the less, the ultra-right refused to join the National Council of Palestine which had been established in the 1920s. In the next decades the rise of the Nazis and the events of the Holocaust brought about a split in the movement.

Between the end of the war and the founding of the Jewish state a zealous extreme group, the Neturei Karta, in Jerusalem accused the Agudat of succumbing to the Zionists. Headed by Amram Blau and Aharon Katzenellenbogen, these extremists were supported by the followers of rabbis in Brisk (Poland) and Szatmar (Hungary) who had emigrated to America and other Western countries. According to Neturei Karta, those who accepted the Jewish state were apostates, and the rabbis who supported Agudat were viewed as leading the new generation away from Torah Judaism. As a result of these policies, these zealots refused to participate in the War of Independence, demanded the internationalization of Jerusalem under the United Nations, rejected Israeli identity cards, and were unwilling to recognize Israel as a state. Yet despite such attacks, the leaders of Agudat continued to support the creation of a Jewish state and a year before its establishment reached an understanding with Palestinian Zionists concerning such matters as Sabbath observance, dietary laws, and regulations regarding education and marriage. Such a conciliatory policy paved the way for Agudat's participation in Israeli politics and its membership in the United Religious Front.

The liberal critique

Paralleling the Orthodox criticism of Zionism, liberal Jews attacked this new philosophy of Jewish existence for its utopianism. In their view, it was simply impossible to bring about the emigration of millions of Jews to a country which was already populated. In addition, in Western countries nationalism was being superseded by a vision of a global community. It was thus reactionary to promote the establishment of a Jewish homeland. In Eastern Europe, on the other hand, there was still a Jewish national consciousness. Yet Zionism was unable to solve the problem facing Jewry. Multitudes of Jews in Eastern Europe were enduring hardship; only a small minority of these individuals would be able to settle in Palestine. Thus, these liberal propagandists maintained that assimilation alone could be a remedy to the Jewish problem.

In response, Zionists protested that assimilation was undesirable and inevitably impossible; such a stance was influenced by racial theories published during the first two decades before the First World War. According to these writings, distinctive qualities were inherited regardless of social, cultural or economic factors. For the Zionists, the Jewish people constitute an identifiable ethnic group whose identity could not be manipulated through social integration. Anti-Semitism, they argued, could not be eradicated; it was an inevitable response to the Jewish populace, no matter what efforts were made to assimilate Jews into foreign cultures. Further, since Jews were predominantly involved in trade and the professions rather than agriculture and industry, they were bound to be the first targets during times of crisis.

Liberals viewed this interpretation of Jewish history as a distortion of the past. Previously, Jewish emancipation had depended on the goodwill of rulers, but in contemporary society, they stated, it would result from global socio-economic factors. The Zionists disagreed. The lessons of Jewish history, they believed, must guide current Jewish thought and action. Judeophobia is an inherent aspect of modern society, and those who championed liberal ideologies such as socialism would be disappointed. According to Max Nordau, the Zionist literary figure and leader, the Jew is rootless, and in his address to the First Zionist Congress, he discussed the social exclusion of Jews in Western lands. Although Jews were emancipated and enfranchised, they were unable to join gentile clubs and organizations. Everywhere Jews encountered the sign 'No Jews admitted'. Despite the fact that modern Jewry had been assimilated into foreign cultures, they were not fully accepted. Having dissociated themselves from their coreligionists, they were rejected by their Christian neighbours. In spite of fleeing from the ghetto, they were not at home in their adopted countries.

Undeterred by these arguments, liberals were anxious to analyse and refute the principles of Zionism. The German anti-Zionist rabbi Felix Goldman, for example, maintained that Jewish nationalism is a product of the general chauvinistic movement which had poisoned contemporary history, but would eventually be swept away by universalism. The German Jewish philosopher Hermann Cohen stated in a debate with Martin Buber that Zionism rejected the messianic idea, and without this concept there could be no Judaism. The Zionists, he argued, were confused about the national issue. Jews were members of the German nation, even if they had different ethnic origins. Other critics went even further. Ludwig Geiger, the son of one of the founders of liberal Judaism, asserted that Zionists should be deprived of their civic rights.

Political empowerment

With the establishment of the State of Israel, the Jewish people have become a major power after 2,000 years of exile. As we have seen, this was the fervent hope of secular Zionist thinkers. Despite the initial rejection of Zionism by both Orthodox and liberal critics, there is now a general acceptance of the necessity of a Jewish homeland in the Middle East – having endured the horrors of the Holocaust, world Jewry today is united in its commitment to Jewish survival. The rallying call of the Jewish people has become 'Never Again!' But how is the Jewish community to respond to the social responsibilities of political empowerment? In discussing this issue, a number of conservative Jewish writers from across the religious spectrum have stressed that pragmatic considerations must be paramount as the State of Israel struggles to endure against formidable odds. Such a policy of *Realpolitik*, they maintain, will inevitably countenance the occasional use of immoral strategies to achieve desired ends: this is the price of empowerment. According to these pragmatists, if Judaism and the Jewish people are to continue into the twenty-first century, there must be constant vigilance against those forces that seek to undermine the existence of Jewry: anti-Semitism must be countered wherever it exists, no matter what the political, economic, social, spiritual or moral cost may be.

Is such a stance acceptable? As we have seen, secular Zionists such as Hess, Pinsker and Herzl were preoccupied with the protection of the Jewish people from suffering and persecution. Yet, such a concern was animated by an idealistic vision of the Jewish future. For this reason, Herzl wrote the novel *Old-New Land*, in which he discusses the social and economic structure of such a state in Palestine. The foundation of the economy, he contends, should be co-operative. Here he sees the New Israel as realizing the social vision of nineteenth-century European utopian socialism. Another early proponent of Zionism, the Russian essayist Ahad Ha-Am, also stressed the importance of infusing this new Jewish commonwealth with Jewish values – in his view it must embody the religious and cultural ideals of the Jewish past. Without spiritual ideals, he points out, political power may become an end in itself.

After visiting Jewish settlements in Palestine, Ahad Ha-Am wrote an essay, 'Truth from the Land of Israel', filled with his impression of the country. Focusing on the dilemmas faced by Zionism because of the existence of the sizeable Arab population, he declares that it is a mistake to believe that Palestine is devoid of a native population:

> We tend to believe abroad that Palestine is nowadays almost completely deserted, a non-cultivated wilderness, and anyone can come there and buy as much land as his heart desires. But in reality this is not the case. It is difficult to find anywhere in the country Arab land which lies fallow.[6]

What is required, he insists, is a sense of realism. Jews should not regard themselves as superior to the Arab neighbours. Instead, they should perceive that the Arabs are fiercely proud and determined.

Echoing this view, the Jewish philosopher Martin Buber, who emigrated to Palestine in the early part of this century, stressed that the Jews must attempt to live in peace with their Arab neighbours and respect them as human beings. In an 'Open Letter to Mahatma Gandhi' written in 1939, he stated:

We considered it a fundamental point that in this case two vital claims are opposed to each other, two claims of a different nature and a different origin which cannot objectively be pitted against one another and between which no objective decision can be made as to which is unjust, which just. We considered and still consider it our duty to understand and to honour the claim which is opposed to ours and to endeavour to reconcile both claims.[7]

Arguably, such idealism, as expressed by these early proponents of the Jewish state, should act as a warning to those who currently advocate a policy of political pragmatism in Israel, divorced from the religious and spiritual values of the past. Political empowerment should not license actions contrary to the Jewish tradition, nor should it blind the Jewish people to the needs of others who seek to achieve communal autonomy in the land of their ancestors. Political sovereignty in Eretz Israel thus brings with it social and religious duties, and such a shift in attitude calls for a profound change of heart on the part of both Israeli society and world Jewry.

The future of Israel

As we have noted, the Jewish people have longed for a homeland of their own for nearly 4,000 years. From the time of Abraham to the present, this yearning has been at the centre of the Jewish faith. Now that the Jewish nation has re-established itself in Israel after centuries of exile, what of the future? In the light of the events of the twentieth century, it has become extremely difficult for many Jews to believe that God will stand by his people in times of disaster. Increasingly for Jewry a void exists where once the Jewish people experienced God's presence and, as a result, modern Israel has been invested with many of the attributes previously reserved for the Deity. Hence in the post-Holocaust world the traditional conception of a divine Redeemer and Deliverer has been eclipsed by a policy of Jewish self-protection. It is the Holy Land which is viewed as ultimately capable of providing a safe haven for those in need: Israel – not the God of history – is conceived as the protector of the Jewish people.

Such a shift away from theological commitment poses profound difficulties for the future, given the perilous situation of the Jewish state. Over the years Arab anti-Semitism has intensified; even if a Palestinian homeland were created in the Middle East, this would be no guarantee for the survival of modern Israel. The threat of a nuclear holocaust would in all likelihood continue as an ever-present reality. What if Israel were destroyed, and the Jewish state wiped off the map? How could the Jewish community endure yet another tragedy of this order without belief in God and redemption? For those Jews who have substituted the Holy Land for God himself, the destruction of Israel would be the ultimate tragedy.

In substituting the political Israel for traditional religious belief, modern Zionism has turned the story of Jacob wrestling with the angel on its head. According to the Book of Genesis, the patriarch Jacob wrestled with a messenger of God until dawn at the ford of the Jabbok. When this messenger saw that he could not prevail against Jacob, he touched the hollow of Jacob's thigh which was thereby put out of joint. As dawn appeared the messenger said: 'Let me go for the day is breaking.' But Jacob replied: 'I will not let you go, unless you bless me.' And he said: 'What is your name?' He said: 'Jacob.' Then the angel said: 'Your name shall no more be called Jacob, but Israel, for you have striven with God and with men, and have prevailed' (Genesis 32:26–29). This incident was the origin of the name Israel (meaning 'he who struggles with God') which subsequently became the designation of Jacob's twelve sons, and eventually of the entire nation.

Here Jacob struggled, and through God, he became Israel. Yet in the contemporary world it appears that political Israel has prevailed and has become a substitute for God. In the quest to provide a refuge for all who are oppressed and persecuted, the State of Israel has eclipsed religious faith. Such an altered perspective is profoundly disturbing because it provides no religious sustenance for the nation. In the past, Jews viewed God as an all-powerful creator: he is the omnipotent Lord of the universe, capable of doing everything. In his omniscience he is aware of all things that take place in the universe, including the human heart. In addition, God is active in the world's affairs. Not only is he the source of all, he chose the Jews, guides their destiny, and directs all history to its final consummation. As holy, righteous and merciful Lord, he is a loving father to all who call upon him. This view of the Deity, enshrined in the Jewish tradition, has animated the faithful from earliest times.

Through the centuries this belief in the God of Abraham, Isaac and Jacob sustained generations of Jews who suffered persecution and death. As martyrs were slaughtered, they glorified God through dedication to the Jewish faith. These heroic Jews who remained steadfast did not question the ways of God; rather, their deaths testified to their firm belief in a providential Lord of history. In Judaism this conviction gave meaning to the struggle of Jewish warriors, strength of endurance under cruel torture, and a way out of slavery through suicide. By believing in God, the Jewish people have managed to endure centuries of suffering with the assurance of divine deliverance.

Israel may not survive, and if the Jewish people forget God in their passion for the land, then they also will disappear from history. The State of Israel is not an ultimate insurance policy – it is simply a human attempt to bring about the realization for the Jewish yearning for a homeland. Through centuries of hardship, the nation remained faithful to their hope of return. Year by year in the Passover service, they promised themselves: 'Next Year in Jerusalem'. Through their religious faith, the sense of destiny and nationhood was preserved. Since 1948 when Israel became a Jewish state, the hope of a return to the Promised Land became a reality. Yet if Israel is a state like any other, it is subject to the political vicissitudes of all other earthly institutions. The true Israel can only prevail if it continues to wrestle with God. If the Jewish people are to survive into the third millennium, it is not enough for them to assert their identity merely through supporting the State of Israel. The patriarch Jacob himself knew that more was necessary all those years ago when he wrestled with God by the ford of Jabbok. As he limped away from the encounter, he declared: 'I have seen God face to face and still my life is preserved' (Genesis 32:31).

Notes

1. Quoted in Arthur Hertzberg, *The Zionist Idea: A Historical Analysis and Reader* (New York: Schocken, 1959), p. 119.
2. In Hertzberg, *Zionist Idea*, p. 121.
3. In Hertzberg, *Zionist Idea*, p. 131.
4. In Hertzberg, *Zionist Idea*, p. 194.
5. In Hertzberg, *Zionist Idea*, pp. 225–6.
6. Quoted in Shlomo Avineri, *The Making of Modern Zionism: The Intellectual Origins of the Jewish State* (New York: Basic Books, 1981), p. 122.
7. In Hertzberg, *Zionist Idea*, p. 463.

10

Faith, praxis and politics

The South African experience in the period from Gandhi to Desmond Tutu

Martin Prozesky

Ours is a world much more characterized by inequality, injustice, environmental damage and human suffering than by social and environmental well-being. It is therefore a world in need of transformation. I believe that the only structures that have any chance of facilitating such a transformation are our religions, because of their blend of avowed dedication to the highest good, their transnational distribution and their independent organizational capabilities. But in their present inward-looking, highly divided, doctrinally archaic, politically confused and sometimes politically compromised condition, this potential world-saving function cannot happen.

Religion therefore also needs inner transformation in order to direct its energies and vision far more effectively towards world transformation. This suggestion that religious forces can and should be agents of change in the everyday world raises the question of how best to relate the two spheres, faith and politics, particularly as the nation-state diminishes in significance with the rise of a single, world economy with its seemingly all-powerful multi-national corporations.

The present chapter explores the themes of faith, praxis and politics with the world situation just noted firmly in mind. Notwithstanding this larger context, however, special attention is given at the end to South

Africa because it presents us with the world's most recent example of a country attempting to redefine the relationship of religion, spiritual practice and politics in a way that could prevent both the abuse of religion by politicians and the abuse of politics by believers, and open the way to a new era where the spiritual and moral power of religion at its best can act as a much needed light for and critic of the politicians and the captains of industry.

My approach to these matters is primarily analytic, not historical; I will be examining the components of the key terms in my title and correlating them, rather than describing and interpreting the historical development of the relationships between religion and politics. The reference in my subtitle to Gandhi and Tutu indicates that my focus will be on the present century and especially the present time and the future; it means that I have in mind all religions and not just Christianity; and it signals not a series of historical developments but a range of structures in the relations between religion and politics.

It may help readers if the central proposal of this chapter is summarized here. History shows, I contend, periodic upwellings of profound moral criticism directed at key aspects of prevailing religious and political practice. This ethics of power, as I call it, is our best hope of countering the world destruction now taking place, by provoking religious regeneration leading to educational and political counters to the economic imperialism that lies behind the destruction of both human communities and the environment.

Faith and praxis

My exploration starts with four points about faith. The first one is that faith by its nature issues in action or praxis. Nobody has investigated the nature of faith more meticulously and comprehensively than Wilfred Cantwell Smith, so let me cite his definition. Faith is, he writes,

> an orientation of the personality, to oneself, to one's neighbour, to the universe; a total response; a way of seeing whatever one sees and handling whatever one handles; a capacity to live at a more than mundane level; to see, to feel, to act in terms of, a transcendent dimension.[1]

The key words are that faith is a matter of acting in terms of a transcendent dimension; what is believed necessarily affects the actions of the believer, or it is not a genuine religious belief. Why this should be so is obscured by the modern idea of beliefs as poorly attested propositions which are tenuous and marginal to the real-life concerns of people. As Smith has shown in *Faith and Belief*, the work just cited, this is the very opposite of the classical meaning of belief or faith as involving a setting of one's heart upon something transcendent, a deep and fundamental cherishing of that which is believed.

This brings me to my second point about faith. It has been well depicted by John Hick and others as involving the greatest freedom open to the believing person.[2] Like respect and love, faith cannot be coerced. Either it arises freely with glad acceptance in the one who sets his or her heart upon the object of faith, or it is not religious faith at all. I am not of course denying that the object of faith can be experienced so powerfully as to be virtually irresistible to the person having the experience. Yet even here, as some people will know at first hand, believers do not experience the advent of faith as something they do not welcome and want to fight. What happens, rather, is a joyous accepting of or surrendering to what they experience as supremely good, beautiful and true.

My third point is that where faith is real in anybody's life, power is exerted, power being understood as the ability to change what would otherwise have happened, and faith by its nature being something that issues in action or praxis. Perhaps the best example of this reality is the faith that there is a world-transforming, divine love at the heart of things. To have this conviction is not merely to experience caring feelings and intentions towards others; it is to enact the conviction by relating as lovingly as one can to all other beings. Living like this obviously makes a difference to whoever or whatever receives that love, and that means that power has been exercised.

Since faith is something which anybody can experience, the power it carries is potentially a truly democratic power, a power innately vested in everybody. Postmodern insights strongly confirm this point with their emphasis on the dismantling of hierarchies, domination and anything else that takes away or reduces the powers belonging to every person, such as the smothering of personal differences under the blanket of generalities like class or even human nature, or by means of essentialism, with its inevitable locking of one's thinking about people into whatever is deemed to be their alleged (and unchanging) essence.

This brings me to my fourth point about faith. As an orientation of the self at its deepest towards what is taken to be the supremely worthwhile reality, faith is, at its core, a matter of ultimate valuation giving rise to fundamental moral norms of how to live. Thus, it becomes a factor affecting the so-called public space of nature and society, shaped in its effects by the content of the beliefs it enacts. These effects can be both good and ill, both beneficial and harmful. Suppose a group of people believes passionately that there is an almighty deity who has decreed that black people shall serve and be subservient to whites, or women to men, or citizens to their rulers – in short, a group which believes in a domination–subservience model as the God-given way to regulate human affairs. Clearly, for black people, women and citizens generally who resent being dominated, such a faith spells harm, no matter how well intended the upholders of that faith may be. As we all know, the history of religions affords no shortage of such examples and worse ones, for example, the belief that God has commanded us not to suffer a witch to live, or that the chance of saving an immortal soul justifies torturing somebody who believes differently, to death if need be.

Thus my discussion of faith as lived reality in the world emphasizes that it can both humanize and deform, liberate and imprison, bring benefit and bring harm. And this in turn presents us with a problem: how are we to decide what counts as beneficial religion and what counts as harmful religion? What justifies anybody in judging one form of faith good and another bad or even evil?[3] I will suggest an answer later in the chapter after discussing politics.

Politics

When we turn our attention to politics we enter a very different sphere from that of faith with its core of untouchable human freedom. We enter the arena of restrictions on liberty and ultimately also of compulsion, politics being understood as the domain of legislated, coercive power – the power that works preferably by consent but, if necessary, by means of sanctions which can be very unpleasant indeed. If the world over the past few millennia has been profoundly changed by the power of faith, then transformational power is just as evident in politics, if not more so, given the natural differences of physical strength and mental ability among people, whereby some are offered – and make full use of – the opportunity to dominate and exploit others, and given the vast scope that exists for coercive as opposed to persuasive power.

Of course it is also true that political power can be and is used beneficially. In principle, there is no reason why it should not be used beneficially for all people, and I am not suggesting that the exercise of such power is mostly detrimental. What I am doing is drawing attention to a natural potential for domination and harm on the part of those strong, clever and ruthless enough to do so. Political power cannot fail to be irresistibly attractive to such people, just as it also attracts people with humane values like Gandhi or Nelson Mandela. For all who are similarly concerned about the well-being of humanity and nature, the need for restraints on political power is obvious. The concern becomes even more pressing if we interpret political power as including educational and economic power. While these two themes are not explicitly part of my topic, it needs to be said that the greatest threat to human and environmental well-being is now coming from runaway economic activity rather than from politics in the narrower sense, as John Cobb in particular has shown,[4] and that a very significant aspect of the disempowering of the world's people comes from political control over education, very little of which gives learners the means to control their knowledge production and critical competence.

Faith and politics

We are now in a position to appreciate why political power appeals so much to certain believers, and why religion is so attractive an instrument to certain political rulers. Together, these two spheres of human existence have the potential to enlist all the energies and talents of the entire human person: both our freedom, on the one hand, and our potential for domination and subservience, on the other. The result is the closest anybody could get to wielding total power, and we would be very naïve not to recognize the appeal this has for certain people. Those of us who believe that nothing could be worse for human flourishing than total power need to be very alert to, and actively oppose, anything that might promote it.

Another reason why control over religion attracts politicians is that it bestows the potential to control what is believed. To take an extreme but not fictitious example: if a government or ruling élite can control education and information, then it can control what is believed by preventing people finding out about the range of possible objects of their faith, or by stopping them from developing an effective self-criticality in relation to what they already believe. And with control over what is believed comes power over people's values and actions, because, as I pointed out earlier, believing is by its nature also a value-laden act with inevitable practical consequences.

The same situation obtains in connection with religious control of politics. If believers in the unique superiority of a particular creed come to power in a given polity, they will exert much more influence over the laws and thus the praxis of that polity than others, an arrangement that reaches its optimal form in radically theocratic states which do not permit other faiths to be practised. Similarly, if pluralist believers are dominant in politics, they can ensure that no religion has political advantages over others.

The question therefore becomes: how can the praxis that results from both religion and politics, and especially from the two in partnership, bearing in mind the moral ambivalence of that praxis, be optimized to work for the good of all? What does 'the good of all' mean? My answer requires a consideration of what I call the ethics of power.

The ethics of power

I am using the term ethics in an empirical sense. It refers to the fact that human actions are affected by judgements about their perceived moral status – their rightness or wrongness – in the judgement of those concerned. This reality about the way people live also affects politics and religious faith. Both have changed greatly over the past few thousand years – the period about which we have reasonably reliable information – as certain people time and again brought the power of conscience to bear on whatever struck them as morally unacceptable. However, it is not the past that concerns me here, but the present and future.

The moral judgements people make involve, of course, norms or fundamental values. Most of the time for most people these seem to function implicitly rather than consciously or self-critically. We may therefore think of these basic moral norms, these unarticulated notions about right and wrong, as moral axioms which exert very great power because they determine what is regarded as ethical and thus influence what happens under the direction of a sense of morality.

Generating and controlling these moral axioms is thus a crucial component in the power relations of any society. I see little evidence of politics being a genuine source of moral axioms, but there can be no doubting its importance in favouring some rather than other basic values, for example, the positive value ascribed to individual economic success in conservative political theory. Where, then, do the moral axioms operating in people's judgements come from? I make no claim to being able to settle that question metaphysically; what I do think can be substantiated is that religion has been their main empirical source.

What this means is that religion is ultimately much more important than politics as a means of moral direction, being, as it were, the primary historical locus of moral consciousness. (I do not dispute that moral conviction can and does arise in secular people, but secularity is a very recent phenomenon and has grown from moral soil rich in religious nutrients.) We can thus formulate a partial answer to our earlier problem of what it is that makes people judge some things as morally good and others as morally bad: it is primarily the values embedded in their religious traditions. Certainly, religion seems to be the main basis for the extremely high value assigned to compassion and social justice in various traditions. But, on the other hand, it also seems to be the main historic basis for the perception of unquestioning obedience to authority as morally good, a perception many of us would regard as very harmful indeed.

The history of religions also makes it quite clear that religion itself has been extensively reshaped under the impact of ethics. Who can doubt the moral factor in Muhammad's rejection of Meccan religion, or in the biblical picture of Moses, Amos and Jesus, or in the feminist critique of religious patriarchy?

This history of the moral transformation of religion therefore pushes our attention beyond organized religion itself to something more important as the basis of the ethics of power, both political and religious, to a moral demand that appears to well up spontaneously in certain people, for example, in the outrage of Gandhi at racism in South Africa or of women at the sacralizing by powerful males of gender discrimination. Whatever their ultimate source, these judgements about the morality of prevailing political and religious forces have been a world-changing force, redirecting the course of religious as well as political history.

Most important, the content of these periodic episodes of moral criticism has not been static. The ethics of power has not taken the form of a single, timeless, decisive notion about the nature of the good, but has exhibited a sort of punctuated equilibrium down the ages, as powerful moral notions like the ban on human sacrifice or justice for the poor took hold of certain people and energized in them an often heroic contestation of prevailing power relations, leading to major changes followed by periods of relative stability – till the advent of the next critical moral threshold. My suggestion is that we can best understand developments like the Axial Age in the history of religions, the Renaissance, the Reformation, the democratic revolutions of the past few centuries, the erosion of colonialism and imperialism, and the rise of the women's movement, as outcomes of the unfolding ethics of power in which from time to time people come to judge prevailing structures of both faith and politics as morally indefensible.

Why is it important that the actual moral content in these episodes of criticism is not fixed but fluid? It is important because the absence of a fixed content makes this phenomenon available for further development in our time and in the future. It means that there is a counter to even the most powerful of religious and political hegemonies in the form of fresh and ever more inclusive and penetrative moral transformations. Above all, it means that conscience itself can be enlarged, deepened and enriched, in order to bring about future episodes of criticism and transformation in our religions and in our politics.

Much more than merely a sense of radical discomfort at prevailing conditions, this ongoing, open-ended but seldom realized capacity in every person for repeated episodes of devastating, spontaneous moral criticism seems to me to be the single most important liberatory power in human history. If that is so, then it is critically important to fuel, encourage and above all laicize it in the emerging world of informational capitalism, with its insatiable appetite for profits and resources, its ability to bypass national political restraints, its relentless output of gross inequality among people, and of environmental degradation.

I believe that a highly significant emancipatory moral dynamic of this kind has been gathering momentum in recent centuries and especially in the past half century, targeting the mostly male and white-skinned controllers of political, economic, cultural and spiritual power, with important though still very limited humanizing results. To this I now turn.

Inclusive well-being

In our time, the specific moral axiom that is proving most powerful in the criticism and transformation of faith and politics and their associated praxis is the demand for what I shall call inclusive well-being, the conviction that no religious, political or economic structure can be tolerated if it does not intentionally espouse and practically foster the well-being of all life and its natural environment.[5]

As far as I can see, inclusive well-being chiefly involves six constituent values: equality, inclusiveness, freedom, difference, the flourishing of life, and education for maximum learner empowerment. Of these, the main one historically, in my view, has been and still is human equality, for I see an egalitarian ethic connecting all the main social transformations of recent times, involving a profound sense that it is simply wrong for one human being to have more power than another and thus be able to control him or her, or for one group to control others. In many Western countries things like the vote have long been subject to this norm. But in the world as a whole, even this ballot-box form of egalitarian liberation is far from a reality. In much religion and in nearly all of the economic life of the planet, its impact is still minimal.

Next, equality as a moral value implies inclusiveness. That is what it means to believe that all must have equal opportunities and must stand on an equal footing before laws and constitutions. On matters like ethnicity, the universal scope of human equality is now very widely acknowledged. But as Bosnia and other centres of bitter ethnic conflict show, wide acceptance does not mean acceptance everywhere. And it is very far from being the case that the economic and religious structures of the world acknowledge, let alone actually treat, all people as equals. But the implication of inclusiveness or universality remains inseparably part of the moral demand for equality, and as such it constitutes a powerful potential source of criticism and change.

Directly involved in the perception of equality and universality or inclusiveness as non-negotiable moral demands is a similar perception about liberty. Hegel may have overstated the point in asserting that history is none other than the progress of the consciousness of freedom, but there is no denying its importance, especially in association with the demand for equality.[6] People not only bitterly dislike being under the thumb (or worse) of others; they have learnt to believe that it is their moral right not to be.

The passion for liberty leads to the next component of inclusive well-being, one that is especially prominent in postmodern thinking, namely, the demand for the acceptance of difference, understood as the right of everybody without exception to be the person he or she wishes to be and to become at any time and to use whatever powers he or she may have or acquire, subject only to the cardinal rule of not harming others.

The fifth component of inclusive well-being is the judgement that suffering, misery and relentless hardship are morally intolerable, giving rise to a demand for human flourishing in a safe and durable environment. What, after all, is the point of an egalitarian liberation that results in no more than equal misery for all?

Education that empowers and liberates people, as opposed to prevailing kinds which replicate élites and sustain gross inequities in the distribution of religious, political, cultural and economic power, is the sixth aspect of inclusive well-being. Given the huge impact globally of the prevailing type and the potential of the alternative implied by inclusive well-being to impact decisively on the course of events, especially in the long term, it follows, of course, that the quest for educational transformation must be a major priority of any ethical critique of power at the present time.

I therefore propose that there is in the modern and postmodern world an ethics of power working in the direction of inclusive well-being as explained in the preceding paragraphs. Its potential is for world transformation, but it will achieve very little so long as it remains no more than a half-conscious, *ad hoc* and very fragmented series of moral insights and demands. To change things it must become an explicit, well-directed, networked, transformative praxis. It must enlist the energy potential of religious faith in order to redirect political, educational and economic power. This in turn will require a far-reaching moral critique and transformation of key aspects of prevailing religion, with inclusive well-being as norm, which brings me to my final section, dealing with practical considerations.

Towards a transformative praxis

My own judgement about religion is limited to Christianity as the force that, along with Western secularity, has done most to shape my beliefs and values. I do not consider it appropriate to attempt a critique of traditions to which I am an outsider, however well informed. As far as Christianity is concerned, my judgement is that it falls seriously short of the demands of inclusive well-being in three key respects. Its beliefs are still either exclusivist or at best elitist in basic character, most notably so in its doctrines of God and of salvation; its praxis is much more concerned with ritual satisfactions and personal assurances of salvation than with healing the wound in creation, much more concerned with sanctuary than slum, with priestly and pietistic power rather than prophetic or political and above all people's power; and its internal power relations seem to me to be generally discriminatory and subordinationist, especially in regard to women and laypersons.

The results are an insufficiently humanizing impact on a world with far too much inhumanity, and, worse, far too much direct dehumanization on the part of religion, especially of those outside its ruling, male, clerical élites. We therefore need a thorough-going ethical critique of religion coupled with measures to promote the vast humanizing and world-protecting potential locked up within its own theoretical prioritizing of compassion, service and self-sacrifice. This would be a truly vast project which I shall not even try to define except for one crucial aspect, which I referred to earlier, namely, optimizing the relationship between faith and politics. And it is here that recent South African experience is so instructive.

Everybody knows that the word apartheid stands for a strongly subordinationist and exploitative structure of oppression with a white, urbanized, Christian male élite at the top and large numbers of black women and children, many of them rural and partly traditionalist in belief, at the bottom. Everybody also knows that the dramatic events of recent years have opened the way for a radical transformation of that country into a non-racial democracy. What is not so widely known is that around three-quarters of the population considers itself to be Christian, with an even higher proportion of South African whites designating themselves as Christian. The achievements of people like Archbishop Desmond Tutu reveal something of the important part played by members of that religion in defeating apartheid; but it also obscures the significant part played by Christianity in creating and maintaining the apartheid state.[7]

We therefore have in South Africa not just a graphic and up-to-the-minute example of religion as both a harmful and a beneficial factor in society, but also a case study of a society seeking new, egalitarian ways of distributing political and economic power and of eliminating the abuses of power, both secular and religious, that characterized apartheid.

The key instrument in this quest for a more morally acceptable distribution of both political and religious power is the new South African constitution, adopted formally by a majority of 421 to 2 (with 10 abstentions) on 8 May 1996 in the Constitutional Assembly in Cape Town and duly certified after some further amendments by the Constitutional Court in December 1996. To my mind, what was needed if South Africa was to become a lastingly just and sustainable democracy was a constitutional arrangement whereby the moral potential of religion could be fostered through the greatest possible religious liberty and through the role of the religions as a social conscience targeting politics and the economy; next, we needed an arrangement whereby the harmful potential of religion would be curbed by placing constitutional and legal restrictions on the exercise of religious power; and, third, by a constitutional block on the state allying itself with any religion or group of religions, or with any secular philosophy.

My own term for such an arrangement is facilitative, even-handed neutrality by the state towards all faiths and philosophies. In my judgement, the new South African constitution can be accurately depicted in these terms so far as religion and politics are concerned, notwithstanding an anomaly in the Preamble to this historic document in the form of the words 'May God protect our people' – an anomaly because not all South Africans are theists – which appears to me to owe its presence to conservative Christians in the body that drew up the constitution with sufficient voting strength to threaten the two-thirds majority needed to pass it.

In any event, the relationship of religion and politics in the new South African constitution differs significantly from both the English and the American models and others like them, which provide, respectively, for a state church plus liberty (but not equality) for all other forms of belief, and for a radical separation between state and religion. The South African arrangement is like the American model in that the state is prevented by the equality and non-discrimination clauses in the new Bill of Rights from having any religious affiliation or character, and is thus completely unlike the English model in rejecting any favoured status for a particular church or religion. But it is a bit like the English model and very unlike the American one in nonetheless making the various aspects of the state available for the facilitation of the activities of believers and secularists. Thus, religious activities may, in certain defined circumstances, be conducted in state schools provided that attendance is voluntary; state universities may have Schools of Theology, and state broadcasters may carry religious programmes, as distinct from educational programmes about religion. I think it is very desirable that the independent moral potential of the various religions should in this way be able to make a difference to the state, but without their ever having preferential constitutional and legal status. How this will turn out in practice in a country with a generally conservative religious ethos remains to be seen, but the underlying constitutional arrangement seems to me to have the potential to achieve a near-optimal distribution of both political and religious power.

Much will, of course, depend on how the new system is put into effect. Conservative Christians who grew accustomed to their erstwhile legal and constitutional hegemony are unlikely to become overnight pluralists with a passion for creating space for atheists or Buddhists, or even for progressive Christians. There are also signs of a new Christian élite itching to take over the favoured role played under apartheid by the old, white Dutch Reformed Churches at the elbows of power.

My own hope is therefore that we will now see in South Africa, especially from its Christian majority, a very radical reappraisal of the kind of part it can appropriately play in a constitutional democracy where religious affiliation is irrelevant in the so-called public sphere, and where majority domination is a very real danger, especially in connection with belief.

My point, then, is that the South African experiment, which I certainly interpret as an outcome of the ethics of power in the form of a conviction that inclusive well-being is a non-negotiable moral imperative, offers other parts of the world a model for the regulating of religion and politics in public matters that could optimize the beneficial potential of both spheres of activity and minimize their potential for harm to society and nature.

A device like a constitution provides a binding framework of norms. It does not itself mean that people will focus their energies on the quest for inclusive well-being. I therefore also hope that in the prevailing climate of making new beginnings South Africa will experience a flowering of theological creativity, starting with three key matters: the critique of the kind of traditional theism that co-existed so happily with apartheid, asking, above all, to what extent a world of liberated subjects, every one of whom has the moral right to be different, can continue to give assent to the concept of a deity who expects submission and controls everything, including the amount of freedom we have, for the concept of God is surely even more subject to the ethical critique of power than anything else; next, the critique of the very concept of orthodoxy, which I for one regard as inherently oppressive; and third, the critique of the Christian doctrine of salvation in the light of religious pluralism. A country where liberation from a Christian-sanctioned apartheid was the work of Muslims, Hindus, Africanists, Jews, atheists, agnostics and others as well as being the work of progressive Christians, makes an ideal, and urgent, context in which to address this third theological issue.

Who knows, out of South Africa's political liberation may yet come spiritual liberation. Maybe we will yet see inclusive well-being in the religious life of that country. Most of South Africa's Christians are certainly politically progressive these days, but there is precious little sign that they recognize in their religion similar ethical problems to those that disfigured the political life of the old South Africa: problems of elitism, exclusion and domination which strike me as exactly parallel to the same things in the social and political life of the country under apartheid, to the extent that I have elsewhere argued that the rise of apartheid cannot be understood without reference to what I regard as deeply harmful aspects of the practice of so-called orthodox, mainline Christianity there.[8]

In that country, as in other parts of the world, what is needed if religious praxis is to be a vanguard factor in the world-protecting and humanizing process is thus a thoroughgoing decolonization of religious consciousness, identifying and changing everything in our faiths that is there because of imposition, exclusiveness, ignorance, lack of self-criticality and inability on the part of ordinary people to use to the full their power to create religious meaning. In postmodern idiom, we need a centring of religious marginality and a celebration of religious particularity, which is why I earlier said that I regard the very notion of orthodoxy – as distinct from truth – as oppressive. Its effect is to cage personal and spiritual growth and prevent people from understanding the liberatory power of seeing the history of religions as the ceaseless enthroning and dethroning of false gods to which everybody has an equal right to contribute.

More than anybody else because of their heritage of religious support for apartheid, South African believers need to understand that all faith in anything less than the unsurpassably good corrupts and that nobody ever achieves a perfect or final understanding of that highest good, so that faith needs the redeeming power of regular criticism and growth into ever richer, ever more inclusive experiences of and conceptual approximations to that unsurpassable goodness. If this were to be accepted, religious regeneration could follow, building on the favourable constitutional structure now in place in South Africa, and becoming a potent force in the struggle for inclusive well-being.

What of the wider world? One country, no matter how well its new measures may turn out in practice, does not make a world, particularly when it is as globally marginal as South Africa. But it does seem to me to provide a hopeful instance of a deliberate rearranging of power, religious as well as political, in the direction of inclusive well-being and the empowering of every single citizen on an equal footing, and as such, maybe it is not immodest to believe that it could be a swallow in the early summer skies of the wider world.

Notes

1.   W. Cantwell Smith, *Faith and Belief* (Princeton: Princeton University Press, 1979), p. 12.
2.   John Hick, *Faith and Knowledge* (Glasgow: Collins Fontana, 1974), pp. 120ff.
3.   Martin Prozesky, 'Proposals for a criteriology of religion', *Journal for the Study of Religion*, 5.1 (1992), pp. 67–77.
4.   John B. Cobb Jr, *Sustaining the Common Good: A Christian Perspective on the Global Economy* (Cleveland, OH: The Pilgrim Press, 1994).
5.   Martin Prozesky, *Religion and Ultimate Well-Being: An Explanatory Theory* (London: Macmillan/New York: St Martin's Press, 1984). Cf. Marjorie Hewitt Suchocki, 'In search of justice' in John Hick and Paul Knitter (eds), *The Myth of Christian Uniqueness: Towards a Pluralistic Theology of Religions* (Maryknoll, NY: Orbis Books, 1987), pp. 149ff.
6.   Quoted in Peter Singer, *Hegel* (Oxford and New York: Oxford University Press, 1983), p. 11.
7.   Martin Prozesky, *Christian Amidst Apartheid: Selected Perspectives on the Church in South Africa* (London: Macmillan, 1990).
8.   Prozesky, *Christianity Amidst Apartheid*, pp. 122ff., where my own diagnosis of these problems is given.

11

Christian futures, postmodernity and the state of Britain

Michael S. Northcott

In a recent article on the problems of the Middle East, Edward Said percipiently observed that the problem of the Arabs is essentially one of powerlessness.[1] They have oil, money and national sovereignty but are unable to participate constructively in the just resolution of the Palestinian problem because, fundamentally, Arab governments lack political legitimacy. Arab nations are mostly ruled by oligarchies or monarchies with 'no real civil society, or democracy, or social dynamism'.[2] Sovereignty without participation leads to powerlessness, for real political power is 'the social power that comes from democracy, the cultural power that comes from freedom of expression and research, the personal power that entitles every Arab citizen to feel that he or she is in fact a citizen'.[3] The lack of political participation produces powerless governments, unable to enforce decent terms for the long-term and just resolution of the Palestinian problem, or to resist the growing legitimacy of fundamentalist Muslim groups, and, in some cases, their terrorist outriders.

Britain is also a state which has benefited from oil revenues and yet experiences a continuing decline in its fortunes and influence, both among its chosen political and economic partners in the European Union and in the wider world. A number of observers and political theorists believe that the fundamental cause of Britain's post-imperial decline is the centralized and undemocratic character of the British state and of British capitalism, and the absence of effective public participation in political and economic institutions. Britain suffers from a democratic deficit, and so lacks the collective power and social dynamism to positively respond to social change, and such challenges as environmental crises, globalization, and the technological restructuring of the labour market.[4] Government ministers and corporate directors often argue that this powerlessness is primarily a function of the global market, or the growing power of the European Union over British affairs, or both. However, others believe that the centralized and secretive character of political and economic institutions in Britain sets the corporate sector, and the government, against the interests of consumers and voters, undermines the effectiveness of civil society, and is in danger of destroying the legitimacy of government itself.[5]

In a detailed examination of British politics since 1914, the historian Bruce Lenman argues that the fundamental problem with the British state is the absolute power of the effective monarch, the British Prime Minister, and the inability of alternative centres of power, including local or regional government, and even back-bench MPs in the House of Commons, to effectively exercise political power to counter the sovereign power of Cabinet government and its head.[6] The story of British politics in this century is one of the advance of the power of a centralized state over the lives of individual citizens, and their local communities and governments. This history climaxed under the Thatcher premiership which saw immense advances in the centralization of political power, at the expense both of the freedoms of individual citizens,[7] and of the capacity of individual citizens or groups of citizens, outside of narrow political, corporate and scientific élites, to influence government.[8] In this crucial respect Thatcher was not radically different from her predecessors for, as Lenman puts it,

> most UK premiers had no concept of politics as an integral part of the administrative and legislative process. The peoples of the UK were their subjects. They ruled them until an infrequent general election transferred the ruling prerogative to another, in what Lord Hailsham has described as an 'elective autocracy'.[9]

Of course this analysis of Britain's decline, and of the malaise in British politics, is countered by an alternative and more politically influential explanation, and one which drove the reforming agenda of the Thatcher government. This is the view that British working people (both working and middle class), through their unionized or professionalized intransigence, had prevented British entrepreneurs, industrialists and financiers from adapting to the new realities of Britain's post-imperial status, and the new competitiveness of the post-colonial global economy.[10] Hence, the fundamental project of the Thatcher government was to diminish the power and influence of all those institutions of civil solidarity – including trade unions, worker co-operatives, professional associations, devolved regional, metropolitan and local government, and even the traditionally independent civil service of central government – which she believed were restraining Britain's capacity, and in particular the capacity of British industry and entrepreneurialism, to respond dynamically to social change.

Influential as this theory has been, if it were correct we would expect Britain to have been transformed by the Thatcher reforms: instead, we see growing cynicism about the central institutions of British society including the monarchy, the churches, the judiciary and Parliament, further declines in political participation locally and nationally, and increasing economic and social insecurity with the temporization of work and the fear of unemployment and crime experienced at almost every level of British society. One of the principal 'achievements' of the Thatcher era was growth in the income of those in full-time work, and especially of higher income groups. However, these enhancements were achieved either by borrowings against the future,[11] or by a shift in the taxation burden from progressive corporate and income taxes to regressive indirect taxes so that the poor now share a larger burden of personal taxation in Britain than in any other country in Europe. And as the personal consumption of middle and especially higher income earners has therefore been unsustainably or unfairly enhanced, at the same time, moneys available for public goods such as public transport, health, education and social security provision, have shrunk relative to private and corporate wealth.

Although the Thatcher reforms were said to be radical and far-reaching it is notable that they left untouched the essential elements of the British establishment. The monarchic tendencies of premier-based central government were enhanced in the 1980s, while the powers of the financiers of the City of London and of corporate directors, property and land owners over private citizens were dramatically extended, through privatization and deregulation, through legislative enhancements to the rights of property and land owners and reductions in corporate and land taxes, and through a legislative onslaught on employee, tenant and citizen rights and securities. Under the guise of a spreading shareholder democracy, the British corporate sector acquired much of the public wealth of the nation – water, energy, forestry, telecommunications and transport infrastructure – at knock-down prices, while retaining its cult of sovereignty, and its culture of unaccountability to workers or share-holders. At the same time the direct contribution of Britain's companies and financiers to the public wealth of the nation through the payment of corporation taxes to the British state, or to the private welfare of its citizens through secure employment, was dramatically reduced.[12]

The British state after the Thatcher era is thus even more unaccountable than it was before, and the people of Britain more powerless than ever they were to exercise the kind of active citizenship and social dynamism through which they might positively and creatively respond to the global and local challenges which currently face us. As Will Hutton argues in his justly lauded analysis of our present predicament, *The State We're In*, it is this combination of unaccountable monarchic government and an unaccountable corporate capitalist sector which explains the unique character of Britain's current social, political and economic condition.[13]

The democratic deficit originates in inherent features of British political and economic institutions, and goes back to the original failure of the English revolution in the seventeenth century which enhanced the role of Parliament while never enacting a written constitution wherein the rights of citizens were fully established and defined independently of their subservient status as subjects of the monarch. This failure left in place an ideology of centralized, unitary and monarchic government, and a structure of monarch, land-owning Lords and Bishops linked to a dominant Tory party representing the associated interests of monarch and Court, 'gentlemen' aristocrats, land owners, and financiers.[14] Since the eighteenth century successive premiers, most notably Peel, Churchill and Thatcher, have gradually abrogated to themselves and their office the substantial powers which Britain's unwritten constitution and 'mother of parliaments' had so unwisely left vested in the monarch.[15]

The failure of the English revolution was followed by a new assertion of the power of land owners over peasants when new impetus was given to the enclosures in the eighteenth century which enabled land owners to extend their land holdings, while at the same time creating a large disenfranchised and economically dependent class of people who no longer had independent access to common land to feed their animals, grow food for their families or forage for fuel and game.[16] The enclosures established a pattern of property ownership without responsibility, and of social control and dependency, which has continued to characterize British society from the Industrial Revolution to the present post-Fordist era. For a time in the mid-twentieth century the bias of power in British society towards property owners was halted by the countervailing power of trade unions, but with the demise of trade unions, and the associated rise of long-term mass unemployment, the opportunities for capital and land owners to opt out of their responsibilities to the wider society have never been greater.

It might have been expected that the Labour Party, with its roots in worker associations and the trade union movement, would have used those albeit occasional opportunities which it has had of single-party government in the twentieth century to bring about constitutional reforms which would have ensured a new level of political participation and of active citizenship by working people who, through their solidarity and votes, had brought Labour to power at significant moments in this century, including the end of the Second World War and the 1960s. But, as Hutton points out, Labour politicians have consistently failed to grasp the essentially monarchic and entrenched character of the British political, property-owning and financial establishments, and Labour's principal social and economic reforms – nationalization of certain key industries, the inauguration of the welfare state and the National Health Service – have therefore left largely untouched the unaccountable powers of central government and the City of London, and the tendency to concentrate wealth in the hands of the privileged few.[17] Labour reforms never tackled the systematic undemocratic and oppositional tendencies in British social and economic structures which gave so much power to shareholders and to company and land owners, and so little to workers, consumers and customers – those Hutton and others describe as stakeholders. Labour mistakenly pursued the reforming path of changing the ownership of parts of British capitalism, through nationalization, while failing to tackle the participation deficit in the running of factories and companies, and in the state itself. Many of the new nationalized industries were as centralized and unresponsive to customers and workers as their privatized forebears had been. Thus, the failure of British capitalism to promote the welfare of British society as a whole was not reversed by the nationalization project. Privatization has, however, tended to enhance this failure as it has permitted larger rewards to the new owners of public monopolies and imposed fewer responsibilities on them to contribute to the wider public good or even to respond adequately to the needs of their customers. Labour's failure to reform British capitalism and the unwritten constitutional arrangements of the British state have allowed royal patronage, corporate capital, and inherited wealth – particularly of the large landed estates – to remain largely free from true democratic accountability and popular control.[18]

Those same arrangements in the hands of the reforming Thatcher government proved an efficient vehicle of absolute power through which to subvert the traditional but unwritten checks and balances against the centralizing powers of the state, the narrow interests of the principal party of government, and the wealth-amassing powers of British land owners and financiers.[19] This brought a new and even more socially divisive element into the democratic and participation deficit in British politics in the last twenty years. The abandonment of the redistribution of wealth from rich to poor as a principal aim of the taxation and social security systems – a situation which New Labour so far shows no signs of reversing – resulted in a growing disequalization of incomes which has contributed significantly to a further reduction in political participation.[20] Increased inequality, and the associated loss of collective solidarity, are a major threat to democracy and democratic participation because it occasions the enclavization of social life such that the poorest are either unable or unwilling to participate in the mainstream culture of civil and political society.[21] This pattern of enclavization is also linked to rising crime which in turn generates reductions in a collective sense of well-being and in personal security, especially among the poorest who are more often victims of unemployment and increasing crime than the comfortable, while the comfortable expend greater resources on personal financial services and security systems.

Some believe that these tendencies in contemporary Britain are part of the inevitable denouement of the modern project. As Zygmunt Bauman observes, one of the essential intimations of a postmodern society is the collapse of the social solidarity on which modern secular civil societies traditionally relied.[22] With the disappearance of what Gillian Rose calls 'the middle' of civil society, a disappearance which she suggests is not unrelated to the collapse of the religious narratives of community on which the middle relied, even in secular form,[23] we see the emergence of mechanisms of coercion so that those who have no access to the good life are excluded from participation or protest by electronic security systems, enlarged police and security forces, larger and more punitive prisons and enhanced immigration controls. Frank Field argues that the failure of growing segments of British society to actively participate in the responsibilities of citizenship, including not only voting behaviour but productive work, effective parenting and disciplining of their children, is linked to a moral and civic collapse which is characterized by extreme individualism and value relativism.[24] According to Charles Handy, the disappearance of the middle is advanced by the fragmentation of the work-place, through sub-contracting, down-sizing and the move to temporary contracts. In a postmodern global order, expressed in a global economic and trading system, traditional professions, work organizations and even forms of civic governance are no longer relevant.[25] Advocates of globalization, deregulation and the free market propose that the modern state was never as rational or as inclusive as its proponents argue, and that its postmodern failures in welfare provision, environmental quality or consumer protection are intricately related to essential limitations in the nature of the ballot box and bureaucratic government.[26] Instead, they propose that the diversity of market choices in a deregulated and privatized society represents a more genuinely participative system for decision-making about wealth distribution, environmental quality, consumer safety, and public morality than the ballot box and centralized bureaucracies.[27]

Against postmodern and free market cynicism about democracy and the failures of the modern nation-state there are those who continue to believe that we are living in a period when the world order is moving consistently in a more democratic direction. Thus Samuel Huntington charts what he calls a third wave of democracy since 1974, much of it in Catholic countries, as evidenced in transitions to democratic practices such as public choice of political leaders and multi-party elections in Southern and Eastern Europe, Latin America, East Asia and Southern Africa.[28] He proposes that the internal *aggiornamento* inspired by Pope John XXIII and the Second Vatican Council reversed the historic opposition and more recent ambivalence of Catholicism towards democracy, and gave significant global impetus to this fresh wave of democratization.

Seymour Lipset argues that this link between Christian reform and political change is a long-established feature of transitions from oligarchy, totalitarianism, communism or feudalism towards democracy, and that in particular it is Protestant versions of Christianity which tend to promote democracy because of their emphasis on the authority of the individual conscience, and of individual readings of the Bible as opposed to Catholicism's emphasis on the authority of the priest and on priest-led rituals as the vehicles of grace.[29] Protestant churches therefore tend to be more democratically organized, the Protestant church polity locates power more at the congregational level, and less with bishops or other supra-congregational entities or leaders. Another factor is the organizational pluralism of Protestant churches, which constitutes precisely the kind of organizational pluralism which multi-party democracies require for the effective operation of elections.

However, while it may be true that Christianity has promoted democracy in transitions from oligarchy or tyranny, it is an open question whether it can provide cultural or moral resources for the renewal of democratic life and civil society in the contemporary British state in the light of the demise of the influence of Christian institutions and beliefs in the public life, and increasingly in the private lives, of the British people. The secularization of the political and economic domains is a process which goes back to the origins of modern Western democracy, and is also nascent in Reformation theology, particularly in Luther's doctrine of the two kingdoms. The secularization of politics involves the substitution of technocratic and economic aims and discourses for theological and moral claims as the guiding public good of modern secular democracies.[30] This secularization of the public domain is not necessarily called into question by the recent involvement of Christian churches in overthrowing tyranny and birthing democracy. As John de Gruchy notes, while the churches often play a significant role in fostering the conditions for the emergence of democracy, in the new context of political pluralism which democratic politics generates, the churches tend to decline in political significance.[31] Only in Poland, and to a lesser extent in Russia and South Africa, have churches retained significant political influence after democratic transition.[32]

In Britain, of course, the established churches continued to play a civic role in an alliance with the state cemented by the contiguity of the sovereign's role as head of state and head of the church, a contiguity whose civil utility was commended by, among others, Thomas Hobbes who, as Andrew Shanks notes, feared the subversive potential of 'un-civil religion' which was not so tied to the civil authority.[33] However, in relation to the democratic deficit in British politics, the contiguity of political sovereignty and religious authority has had the effect of providing ecclesiastical legitimation both to the subject status of the British people and to the monarchic and increasingly centralized exercise of power by successive modern governments. Thus, it may be said that the religious establishment has itself been a kind of un civil religion, for through its partnership with the state it has legitimated the democratic deficit, and hence continues to be implicated in the now widespread cynicism about the political process in late modern Britain.

On the other hand, the ideals of popular governance and democracy find their historical roots among the radical tradition of religious dissent and nonconformity. It was not the ideologies of Erastian establish-mentarians such as Edmund Burke, but the utopian projects of the radical reformers which provided the historical base for the protest and agitation which extended democratic participation, and sustained the democratic ideals of liberty and justice for all to the point where universal suffrage was largely achieved in the early twentieth century.[34] The British socialist tradition, and the British Labour Party, are clearly linked to this ancient tradition of radical religious and political dissent, and for the first half of this century derived their ethical idealism from this source.[35] Some of its current representatives, including the new Prime Minister, Tony Blair, and the Chancellor of the Exchequer, Gordon Brown, continue to claim an association with these religious roots of the project of democratic socialism, and espouse the label Christian socialist.

However, there is some doubt as to whether New Labour is committed to the moral vision of the redistribution of wealth, the eradication of poverty and the democratic regulation of society, including the market, which is its historic inheritance. Part of the reason for doubt relates to the present condition of the working class which remains its most loyal elective constituency despite the turn to New Labour at the 1997 General Election by significant sectors of 'Middle England'. Under the influence of consumerism, and of post-Fordism, the size of the British working class of manual workers has shrunk from three-quarters to under a half of the population.[36] Furthermore, the commitment of substantial proportions of working people to the ethical ideals of solidarity, fraternity and egalitarianism has been corroded by the experience of competition in an increasingly fragmented and particularistic labour market so that workers see their interests less in collective terms and more in terms of monetary competition with other individuals or groups of workers.[37] The subversion of solidaristic ideals may also be linked with the corrosion of religious communities and belief systems.

One of the reasons for the failure of Labour in the past to translate the ideals of equality, justice and participation into a longer-term programme of democratic and social reform relates to the oppositional and majoritarian character of the party political system in Britain which guarantees to the leader of one of the two main political parties the centralized powers of the unwritten British constitution, and effectively subverts the construction of a broader social consensus, either in Parliament or outside it. The Labour Party internally is also not especially participative. It has an unwieldy and centralized power structure focused in the past on trade union and party leadership, and in the present increasingly on the party leadership. Both at local and national level Labour politicians are frequently as resistant to popular participation and community involvement in the determination and execution of policy as their Conservative counterparts. As Arend Lijphart has shown, the Westminster majoritarian model of democracy concentrates executive power in the hands of the majority party, and this concentration, aided by government secrecy, enables a political party to mobilize the resources of the state exclusively around its own political programme, so long as it can muster a majority in the House of Commons. By contrast, consensus political systems which operate in countries with a more diverse party structure require a much broader degree of participation both in the formation of government policy, and in its execution.[38] The urgent need is for a new ideology of democracy in Britain which can challenge the model of unitary party and parliamentary sovereignty and gather to it social and collective support for a transformation of the British political and economic system into a more collective, participative and decentralized form of democracy. But where are the sources in the British democratic tradition for such a transformation?

David Nichols argues that models of political power and leadership are associated with theological models of divine power and action in the world.[39] The model of the divinely representative, unitary and arbitrary rule of the monarch, the 'divine right of kings', which emerged in England in the medieval period after the Norman Conquest, was legitimated by the understanding of the arbitrary and sovereign will of a distant divine patriarch which was fostered by nominalist theologians such as William of Ockham. Similarly, the emergent ideal of popular sovereignty which was enunciated by counter-orthodox groups such as the Lollards and the

Beguines in the Middle Ages, and later by the Radical Reformers, was linked to a model of God as Spirit active in the mind of the believer in mystical prayer, in the reading of the scriptures and in participation in rites of public worship performed in the vernacular by the people of God rather than behind the veil of priestly expertise. Linked to this new spiritual egalitarianism was the principle of popular sovereignty, enunciated in the conservative form by Reformation theologians such as Richard Hooker. This principle formed the philosophical ground for the modern idea of representative democracy.[40] However, the sovereign powers which remained vested in the monarch, and by extension in her liegemen of nobles and land owners, continued to exercise a significant restraint on popular participation in economic and political governance in Britain. As we have seen, the single most dramatic extension of monarchic over popular sovereignty occurred as a consequence of the Acts of Enclosure which gave economic and political force to the continuing subject status of the British people, despite their common membership of the 'Christian nation' of Hooker's vision.

The increasing control of the land by the few was a significant factor in the emergence of the radical English tradition of religious and political dissent – particularly the Levellers and the Diggers – in which the ideals of ethical socialism originated.[41] John de Gruchy identifies the radical reformer Gerrard Winstanley as the paradigmatic embodiment of the 'religious democratic utopian ideal in English history'.[42] Winstanley was the leader of the Digger movement, also known as the True Levellers, and he identified the origin of the political repression of the English people with the gradual enclosure of the people's lands into the fiefdoms and private estates of nobles and landlords.[43] The first principle of his utopian movement was the common ownership of land and the right of the common people to dig for their own sustenance and livelihood, a principle he linked with the origination of the land in the divine action of creation.[44] The Levellers believed that the Bible's unambiguous teaching was that no person should ever be subject to the domination of another, whether through land, title or political power.[45] In the new utopian society which Winstanley sought temporarily to establish on common land in Surrey, the people were once again to share the land in common and so provide for themselves from the bounty of God's creation, while through spiritual renewal Christ would rule in the hearts of the new people of God, and thus neither land owners, nor priest and king, would oppress them any longer.

John de Gruchy argues that the fundamental political insight of the radical reformers, that divine guidance and grace are available to each individual and are not reliant on the external mediation of kings or priests, was linked to the Old Testament idea that each individual is made in the image of God.[46] But more crucially it was linked to the early Christian teaching of the agency of God as Spirit in every believer and every group of believers, and to the participative, non-hierarchical forms of social life in early Christianity which this doctrine legitimated.

The early Christians eschewed priestly and hierarchical leadership and encouraged a high level of participation and diversity in ministry and community governance. The form of sovereignty expressed in these communities was, of course, in one sense Messianic – the stories and traditions of the Son of God formed a locus of authority, and in particular those who had known Christ, and witnessed his Resurrection. But the authority of the exclusively Jewish followers of Christ is over-ridden by the authority given to experiences of the Spirit of the Risen Christ, the Holy Spirit. Peter admits Gentiles into the Jewish church in the house of Cornelius because of a dream and the direct command of the Spirit (Acts 10). The Apostle Paul authenticates his own ministry by reference to a spiritual vision on the Damascus Road, and to other significant spiritual experiences (2 Corinthians 12:1–5). The worship of the New Testament communities was characterized by a range of spontaneous spiritual phenomena and there is little evidence of any controlling rite or of ritual leaders within the New Testament itself. The form of leadership exercised in these spiritual communities was charismatic rather than clerical, and involved women as well as men.[47] The authenticating marks of ministry were charismatic gifts such as prophecy, healing, teaching and evangelism which were seen as gifts to the people of God collectively, and not as the skills of one or two individual leaders or representatives (Ephesians 4:1–16). Participation in the life of the Spirit is the form and guarantee of the new life in Christ, and this new life brings extraordinary spiritual liberty so that 'everything is possible to one who believes' (Mark 9:23). This spiritual freedom liberates Christians from the control of the fallen powers of the devil and the law, and liberates them for a radical new relationality and mutuality which remove the necessity for legal rules of relationship. As Jürgen Moltmann points out, this spiritual understanding of liberty is quite different from modern understandings of individual freedom, for it issues in a new form of community where relations are not fractured or dissolved in favour of individual choice or entitlement, but renewed in a solidarity governed by the law of love, a law not written in stone but on the hearts of the people of God.[48]

These spiritual communities experienced a new freedom which, as we know from Paul's letters to the Corinthians, was open to abuse, but this relational freedom explains the dynamic power of the early Christian mission. It challenged the class and gender barriers of the time, and attracted many women, as well as slaves and servants, into active participation in the early house churches alongside free men and citizens of the Roman social order. This spiritual freedom and sociality produced a radically non-hierarchical style of community governance where the quest for the mind of the Spirit through consensus seems to have been paramount. Leadership, where it is spoken of at all, is seen as spiritual service rather than control or rule. The sayings of Jesus include many references to leadership as service, including the dramatic image of the Lord washing his disciples' feet, and many warnings against patterns of leadership which ape the dominating and oppressive style of leadership in society at large (Mark 10:42–45). Jesus is especially scornful of the elitism and oppression which he identifies in the synagogues and amongst the scribes and Pharisees.

Paul builds on this idea of leadership as service and as sacrifice in various texts on leadership, most notably in the early chapters of the First Letter to the Corinthians where he contrasts the power model of Roman leadership, and the pragmatism of Corinthian leadership, with leadership which is identified with the sacrifice and vulnerability of the crucified Christ.[49] Paul subordinates his own apostolic role, and that of Apollos, in planting the church at Corinth to divine action: 'it is not the gardeners with their planting and watering who count, but God who makes it grow. Whether they plant or water, they work as a team' (1 Corinthians 3:7–8). The Apostles are simply fellow-workers and not leaders around whom parties or factions may form. As that great prophet of twentieth-century mission, Roland Allen, has argued, it was the extraordinary trust which St Paul had in the creativity and power of God as Spirit to prosper the new converts of the churches he founded which explains the rapid growth of the earliest Christian movement.[50] Paul spent only a few months on most of his missionary visits, forming a small group of converts whom he then left under the guidance of the Spirit of God to form and extend their church communities, and it was this reliance on the dynamic of the Spirit and the spiritual creativity of the new communities which was the key to the success of the Gentile mission. Allen contends, on the other hand, that it was the failure of most Catholic and Protestant missions to trust their new converts to similarly follow the inclinations of their new spiritual experiences which explains the much more limited effectiveness of many of these missions in the nineteenth century.[51]

When we look at the changing shape of the church in the twentieth century, and the futures of the Christian movement in the twenty-first century, we see how especially prophetic was Allen's analysis, written as it was in the 1920s. The fastest growing style of Christianity in this century has been Pentecostalism, which began as a tiny radical sect in 1906 in North America, and now encompasses approximately 400 million Christians on every continent. The reliance of this new style of Christianity on the experience of the Spirit as the mark of authentic Christian worship and identity, and of spiritual authority and leadership, issues in forms of community sociality and governance which at their best foster individual participation by every member of the community in worship and community life, and sustain relationships of genuine openness and love between members of the community. The participatory character of this style of Christianity also renders it more open to elements of spiritual and folk belief than traditional Protestantism in missionary form, and this is a feature of its growing appeal to converts of the colonial mission churches which so often stifled indigenous cultural forms and beliefs by the imposition of Western mores and rationalism.[52]

The standard socio-scientific explanations of spiritual sectarianism, whether radical reformers in the sixteenth century or Pentecostal converts in the twentieth, rely on the theory of relative deprivation. People from the lower social classes are said to be attracted to prophetic and ecstatic religion because it offers an escape from the oppression and domination which characterize their material experience of social life.[53] While there are clearly elements of truth in this account, even as applied to the early church, by characterizing ecstatic religion as a function of deprivation, a safety-valve for oppressed groups, it tends to discount the possibility that this kind of religious associationalism can itself bring any influence to bear on the wider society.

However, as we have seen, there is evidence from the seventeenth and eighteenth centuries that the Protestant precursors of this style of religion played a significant role in socio-cultural change. The Protestant conception of spiritual subjectivity, expressed among Anabaptist, Quaker and Methodist groups, played a determinative role in the emergence of modern ideas concerning not only popular sovereignty, but also the dignity and rights of each individual, ideas grounded in the potential of each person to be indwelt by the Spirit. As Moltmann observes, spiritual freedom and the 'free society' are intricately related.[54]

In the twentieth century this radical spiritual vision of human freedom has also played a major role in the transformation of Christianity as a global socio-cultural and political force. The idea of spiritual freedom, and the experience of the Spirit as the determinative mark of the church, have produced radical new forms of ecclesiology, most markedly in the theology of Yves Congar whose recovery of the doctrine of the Holy Spirit as the constitutive and ontological ground for the church issued in a new democratic understanding of the church as the people of God in the late 1950s.[55] Congar's theology of the spiritual constitution of the people of God challenged the Christendom and Tridentine understanding of the church as essentially constituted by the orders of bishops and priests. As the first theologian of the Second Vatican Council, his pneumatological and participative ecclesiology contributed significantly to the emergence of a new anti-hierarchical and democratic polity within the Roman Catholic Church, which is writ large in the documents of Vatican II whose principal architect, other than Pope John XXIII, was of course the Pentecostally inclined Cardinal Suenens.

Vatican II contributed to a global shift of Catholic consciousness in Europe and North America, and most dramatically of all in the *comunidades eclesiales de base* of the Church in Latin America. As Leonardo Boff contends, no longer were the people of God dependent on priests and cardinals, and their control of the rites, for the experience of grace. The church conceived as the people of God becomes a popular church, led by the people who participate fully in the constitution of the redeemed community.[56] Sadly, Pope John Paul II has attempted to draw the Catholic Church back from this more participative and pneumatological ecclesiology, reviving instead the cult of Marianism and the male authority of the monarchic magisterium which that cult so effectively legitimates. But he has been unable to quench the Spirit which the renewal of Catholicism in so many countries has released, any more than mainstream liberal Protestants have been able to prevent the drift of their own followers in a Pentecostal direction.

Of course, the liberal interpretation of the Pentecostal drift of world Christianity is often extremely pessimistic. It is assumed that Pentecostal religiosity is world-denying and authoritarian, and can make little contribution to the transformation of society as a whole. But the example of the pneumatologically inspired base communities of Latin America, and even more so of their Pentecostal successors, indicates that the model of the church as the people of God and as constituted by the Holy Spirit, can be a powerful force for change within the institution of the church, and beyond it in the transformation of a society characterized by domination and class oppression towards more participative and democratic forms. Samuel Huntington's account of the third wave of democratization clearly demonstrates that it was the dramatic shift of Catholic ecclesiology and polity in this more pneumatological and participative direction which enabled the emergence of democratic movements in many Catholic countries, not only in Latin America, but also in Spain and Portugal, in Eastern Europe and in other parts of the non-Western world.[57] David Martin's studies of Pentecostalism in Mexico and Brazil indicate that Pentecostals in Latin America are not only embracing new religious freedoms and spiritual experiences, but are also engaging in struggles for economic and political uplift both individually and collectively.[58]

The connection between the possible Pentecostal futures of Christianity and the renewal of democracy in the state of Britain may be said to be more tenuous. The charismatic congregations of the Church of England or the Roman Catholic Church and the independent house churches make little impact on the national stage. However, in the sponsoring of styles of participative worship, shared ministry and functioning communities of neighbourliness and sharing, as well as in the promotion of direct community service in relation to drug addicts or the homeless, supported by extensive tithing amongst church members, the Pentecostal style of Christianity may be said to present a genuine alternative to the 'uncivil' partnership of established churches with increasingly non-participative state and corporate sectors. In the sponsoring of a pneumatological religiosity which is also apparently enjoyable, it demonstrates to a culture with economic advancement as the determinant of life quality and happiness that abundant life is far more connected with participation in the freedom of the Spirit, and in experiences of community solidarity, than in the illusory freedoms and choices of mass consumerism, and the illusory community of the mass media.

But more than in these changes in Christian religious behaviour in contemporary Britain, it is the pneumatological recasting of Catholic ecclesiology, and of much Protestant ecclesiology under the influence of a more pneumatological doctrine of God, which is of most interest in relation to a new vision of politics and the state in contemporary Britain. As we have seen, the state socialism of the traditional Labour Party placed a considerable emphasis on ownership and control of the means of production by the state as the transforming driving force of progress towards a more just society. However, in practice the change of ownership from private to public did not involve greater participation of workers or local communities in these large nationalized industries, any more than the change of government from Conservative to Labour has produced a more participative style of politics.[59] The dominant ideological representation of sovereignty and monarchic control as the motors of political power was never challenged and consequently socialist economics was no more genuinely democratic and participative in practice than capitalist economics, with the possible exception of Tony Benn's pioneering efforts at establishing worker co-operatives in the late 1960s and early 1970s.

With the failure of state socialism to transform the conditions of working people, and the correlative success of market capitalism in wealth generation and limited wealth sharing, European socialists have realized the weakness of the Marxist obsession with ownership of the means of production and are recasting their political theory in democratic mode. Instead of nationalization of the means of production, socialists now commend the extension of democratic governance as the means for achieving a more just and egalitarian society, through increasing participation by the people in every area of economic and social practice, from housing estate and school management to work-place democracy and financial and environmental regulation.[60] New Labour has promised to deliver key elements in this democratic reform process, including devolved government to the regions, a Bill on Open Government, a Bill of Rights and reform of the House of Lords. However, New Labour also speaks of globalization as the reason it is no longer committed to significant wealth redistribution as the principal aim of economic management, despite the fact that growing wealth inequality remains the biggest obstacle to genuine participatory democracy in Britain, and the biggest threat to civil society and social order. In reality, globalization increases the urgency of the devolution of social control over complex economic and bureaucratic institutions precisely because the move towards a global market threatens to remove political control over wealth creation and natural resources from local communities and even nation-states.[61] The unaccountable power of corporations over the lives of citizens, their working conditions and their environments, can only be enhanced by a situation in which national governments abdicate the social regulation of the market to global economic forces.

The emergent theory and practice of a reformed democratic socialism are much closer in spirit to the original utopian idealism of the radical reformers, and their liberationist and Pentecostal successors, than the statist concerns of traditional socialists. It represents active citizenship as the essential bedrock of socialist political praxis and nationhood, rather than membership of a particular economic class. It represents participation in the production and distribution of wealth – through a fair distribution of work and through popular managerial control and regulation of corporate and financial institutions and markets – as more important than the nationalization of the means of production. And it represents political power and sovereignty as essentially the people's work, and as best located close to where people live and work, rather than as the preserve of besuited and predominantly male élites who behind a shroud of party cabbalism and bureaucratic secrecy exercise non-participative rule over the subjects of the monarchic state.[62]

At the time of writing, a degree of scepticism is justified as to whether such a radically participative vision of political economy informs the policy commitments of New Labour, but there are indicators that the Blair Government will embrace at least some elements of political, if not economic, reform. By publicly enunciating the theological and pneumatological grounds for a more participative vision of politics and community, and by practising this style of participation in their churches, Christians can contribute a measure of hopefulness to the process of political reform and renewal which is so long overdue in the state of Britain. Just as the nominalist theology of patriarchal divinity was influential in the emergence of the political ideology of the divine right of kings, and the unchallenged supremacy of the monarch, so the modern recovery of the doctrine of the Spirit can contribute to new political ideologies of popular participation in political and economic life in a postmodern world order.

And this spiritual understanding of participation and popular governance is not just a utopian dream. Already in Britain and in other parts of the world new forms of popular democracy and participation in economic production and community governance are emerging at local level, many of them sustained by the spiritual vision of different faith communities working for social transformation at the grass roots. One of the most significant examples of these emergent forms of popular governance in Britain is broad-based community organizing which began at an assembly of twenty congregations in Bristol's Roman Catholic Cathedral in September 1990. Communities Organised for Greater Bristol draws on the leadership and community resources of local congregations, and other faith communities including Sikhs and Hindus, to address a range of local issues including drug addiction, homelessness, curbing the car, drinking-water quality, and factory noise.[63] Broad-based community organizing has now spread to a number of other English cities including Merseyside, Wolverhampton, East London, and Sheffield in a movement to mobilize local faith communities in the renewal of local democracy and civil society. The movement is still small but it is an important and symbolic sign that the extension of participative democracy and the collective quest for the common good against untamed individualism, materialism and inequality are linked to spiritual renewal. It gives contemporary expression to the belief, linked in Christian thought to the doctrine of the Spirit, that people in families and communities of faith, place and shared interest are the best agents of economic development, social creativity and governance.[64]

Notes

1. Edward Said, 'A powerless people', *The Guardian* (25 April 1996).
2. Said, 'A powerless people'.
3. Said, 'A powerless people'.
4. Michael Jacobs, *The Politics of the Real World: Meeting the New Century* (London: Earthscan, 1996), pp. 105ff.
5. See, for example, Paul Hirst, *Representative Democracy and Its Limits* (Cambridge: Polity Press, 1990); Will Hutton, *The State We're In* (London: Jonathan Cape, 1995) and Tony Wright, *Citizens and Subjects* (London: Routledge, 1993).
6. Bruce P. Lenman, *The Eclipse of Parliament: Appearance and Reality in British Politics Since 1914* (London: Edward Arnold, 1992).
7. See further the forensic examination of the demise of political freedom and civil liberties under the Thatcher government by K. D. Ewing and C. A. Gearty, *Freedom Under Thatcher: Civil Liberties in Modern Britain* (Oxford: Clarendon Press, 1990).
8. Lenman, *The Eclipse of Parliament*.
9. Lenman, *The Eclipse of Parliament*, p. 255.
10. John A. Hall, *Coercion and Consent: Studies on the Modern State* (Cambridge: Polity Press, 1994), pp. 159–71.
11. Lenman, *The Eclipse of Parliament*, p. 277.
12. Lenman, *The Eclipse of Parliament*; Hutton, *The State We're In*.

13. Hutton, *The State We're In*.
14. Hutton, *The State We're In*, pp. 42–4.
15. Lenman, *The Eclipse of Parliament*.
16. See further Edward P. Thompson, *Customs in Common* (London: Penguin, 1992).
17. Hutton, *The State We're In*, pp. 46–52.
18. Hall, *Coercion and Consent*, p. 170.
19. Hutton, *The State We're In*, pp. 46–8.
20. See further Ruth Lister, *The Exclusive Society: Citizenship and the Poor* (London: Child Poverty Action Group, 1990).
21. Frank Field and Timothy Raison, 'Two Westminster perspectives on welfare politics' in Thomas and Dorothy Wilson (eds), *The State and Social Welfare: The Objectives of Policy* (London: Longman, 1991), pp. 263–81.
22. Zygmunt Bauman, *Intimations of Postmodernity* (London: Routledge, 1992), p. 59.
23. Gillian Rose, *The Dialectic of Nihilism* (Cambridge: Cambridge University Press, 1989).
24. Field, 'Two Westminster perspectives'.
25. Charles Handy, *The Empty Raincoat: Making Sense of the Future* (London: Arrow Books, 1995).
26. For a particularly clear exposition of this approach see William C. Mitchell and Randy T. Simmons, *Beyond Politics: Markets, Welfare, and the Failure of Bureaucracy* (Boulder, CO: Westview Press, 1994).
27. From a more left-leaning sociological perspective Anthony Giddens also makes considerable claims for the multiplication of choices in modern political economies, arguing that choice is a principal feature of the reflexivity of the modern project: see his *Beyond Left and Right* (Cambridge: Polity Press, 1994).
28. Samuel P. Huntington, *The Third Wave: Democratization in the Late Twentieth Century* (Norman, OK: University of Oklahoma Press, 1991).
29. Seymour Martin Lipset, *Political Man: The Social Bases of Politics* (revised edn; Baltimore: Johns Hopkins University Press, 1981).
30. For an idiosyncratic and trenchant account of this tendency in the French Republic see Jacques Ellul, *The Political Illusion*, trans. K. Kellen (New York: Vintage Books, 1972). Ellul links the secularization of public life with the politicization of public life, and the growth of the state, and its communicative organs, the mass media.
31. John de Gruchy, *Christianity and Democracy: A Theology for a Just World Order* (Cambridge: Cambridge University Press, 1995), esp. ch. 7.
32. On the public role of the church in Poland after the overthrow of communism see José Casanova, *Public Religions in the Modern World* (Chicago: Chicago University Press, 1994), ch. 4.
33. Andrew Shanks, *Civil Society, Civil Religion* (Oxford: Blackwell, 1995), p. 100.
34. On the significance of Christian utopianism in the construction of modern democracy see further Adam B. Seligman, 'Introduction' in Adam B. Seligman (ed.), *Order and Transcendence: The Role of Utopias and the Dynamics of Civilization* (Leiden: E. J. Brill, 1989).

35. See further Norman Dennis and A. H. Halsey, *English Ethical Socialism: Thomas More to R. H. Tawney* (Oxford: Clarendon Press, 1988).
36. Christopher Pierson, *Socialism After Communism: The New Market Socialism* (University Park, PA: Pennsylvania State University Press, 1995), p. 9.
37. Pierson, *Socialism after Communism*, p. 13.
38. Arend Lijphart, *Democracies: Patterns of Majoritarian and Consensus Government in Twenty-One Countries* (New Haven: Yale University Press, 1984), p. 46. See also Robert D. Putnam, *Making Democracy Work: Civic Traditions in Modern Italy* (Princeton, NJ: Princeton University Press, 1993).
39. David Nichols, *Deity and Domination* (London: Routledge, 1992).
40. F. J. Shirley, *Richard Hooker and Contemporary Political Ideas* (London: SPCK, 1949), cited in de Gruchy, *Christianity and Democracy*, p. 82.
41. In an article in 1946 George Orwell traced the origins of the ideals of ethical socialism from the slave revolts of antiquity and early Christian communism through the medieval peasant revolts, to the Diggers and Levellers, and thence to the Utopians of modern times who, he says, were the only true upholders of the socialist tradition: Bernard Crick, *George Orwell: A Life* (London: Penguin, 1982), cited in Dennis and Halsey, *English Ethical Socialism*, p. 119. See also Tony Benn, *Arguments for Socialism*, ed. Chris Mullen (Harmondsworth: Penguin, 1979).
42. de Gruchy, *Christianity and Democracy*, p. 86.
43. Christopher Rowland, *Radical Christianity: A Reading of Recovery* (Cambridge: Polity Press, 1988), pp. 102–14.
44. de Gruchy, *Christianity and Democracy*, p. 86.
45. Christopher Hill, *The World Turned Upside Down* (Harmondsworth: Penguin, 1975), cited in Benn, *Arguments for Socialism*, p. 26.
46. de Gruchy, *Christianity and Democracy*, p. 42.
47. See Rosemary Ruether's fine exposition of the participative and intra-gendered practices of the early Christian communities in her *Sexism and God-Talk* (London: SCM Press, 1983): see also Elisabeth Schüssler Fiorenza, *In Memory of Her* (London: SCM Press, 1991).
48. Jürgen Moltmann, *The Spirit of Life: A Universal Affirmation*, trans. Margaret Kohl (London: SCM Press, 1992), pp. 117–19.
49. Andrew D. Clark, *Secular Christian Leadership in Corinth: A Socio-Historical and Exegetical Study of I Corinthians 1 – 6* (Leiden: Brill, 1993), cited in Anthony Thiselton, *Interpreting God and the Postmodern Self: On Meaning, Manipulation and Promise* (Edinburgh: T. and T. Clark, 1995), p. 142.
50. Roland Allen, *Missionary Methods: Paul's or Ours* (Grand Rapids: Eerdmans, 1973; first pub. 1921).
51. Allen, *Missionary Methods*.
52. See further Michael S. Northcott, 'The rise of the charismatic movement in West Malaysia and Singapore', *Asia Journal of Theology*, 3 (1989), pp. 29–37.
53. Northcott, 'The rise of the charismatic movement'.
54. Moltmann, *The Spirit of Life*, p. 116.
55. Yves Congar, *Lay People in the Church: A Study for a Theology of the Laity*, trans. Donald Attwater (London: Geoffrey Chapman, 1965).

56. Leonardo Boff, *Church, Charisma and Power: Liberation Theology and the Institutional Church*, trans. John W. Diercksmeier (New York: Crossroad Publishing Company, 1985).
57. Huntington, *The Third Wave*.
58. David Martin, *Tongues of Fire: The Explosion of Protestantism in Latin America* (Oxford: Blackwell, 1989) and David Martin, *Forbidden Revolutions* (London: SPCK, 1996).
59. For an insider account of the secretive, manipulative and centralizing style of the Labour government under Harold Wilson in the 1960s see Joe Haines, *The Politics of Power* (London: Jonathan Cape, 1977).
60. See especially Paul Hirst, *Associative Democracy: New Forms of Economic and Social Governance* (Cambridge: Polity Press, 1994) and Pierson, *Socialism After Communism*.
61. See further Michael Jacobs, *The Politics of the Real World*.
62. For analyses and case studies of participative communities and social movements which are already generating new forms of political, economic and social action see Mary Lean, *Bread, Bricks and Belief: Communities in Charge of Their Future* (West Hartford, CT: Kumarian Press, 1995); Russell J. Dalton and Manfred Kucher (eds), *Challenging the Political Order: New Social and Political Movements in Western Democracies* (Cambridge: Polity Press, 1990); Kay Lawson and Peter H. Merkl (eds), *When Parties Fail: Emerging Alternative Organizations* (Princeton, NJ: Princeton University Press, 1988); and J. Craig Jenkins and Bert Klandermans (eds), *The Politics of Social Protest: Comparative Perspectives on States and Social Movements* (London: UCL Press, 1995).
63. Jay MacLeod, *Community Organising: A Practical and Theological Appraisal* (London: Christian Action, 1993). See also Michael S. Northcott, 'A place of our own' in Peter Sedgwick (ed.), *God in the City: Essays and Reflections from the Archbishop of Canterbury's Urban Theology Group* (London: Mowbray, 1995), pp. 119–38.
64. Mary Lean, *Bread, Bricks and Belief*, p. 173.

Index